Analytical Techniques
for
Financial Management

SECOND EDITION

ANALYTICAL TECHNIQUES FOR FINANCIAL MANAGEMENT

Jerome S. Osteryoung
Florida State University

Daniel E. McCarty
Florida Atlantic University

John Wiley & Sons
New York   Chichester   Brisbane   Toronto   Singapore

Library of Congress Cataloging in Publication Data:

Osteryoung, Jerome S.
  Analytical techniques for financial management.

  Includes bibliographies and index.
  1. Business mathematics.   I. McCarty, Daniel E.
II. Title.
HF5691.083   1985   658.1'5'0151   84-20902
ISBN 0-471-81715-5 (pbk.)

Printed in the United States of America

10 9 8 7 6 5 4 3 2

**This Book Is Dedicated
to
Jay Osteryoung
and
Elaine and Danny McCarty**

PREFACE

This book is written for those who are interested in the application of fundamental theory and analytical techniques of financial management. It is specifically designed to meet the needs of the person who must make or participate in financial management decisions. As such, the text does not attempt to present all topics in financial management; rather, it focuses upon those key concepts and their applications relevant to decision making in both academic and business environments.

Analytical Techniques for Financial Management provides the flexibility that permits its use in a variety of settings. It can serve as a handy reference for undergraduate and graduate finance case courses. It can also be used in seminars and executive training programs that emphasize the application of financial theory to problem solving. And it should also serve as a valuable reference to financial managers at all levels of the organization.

Techniques does presuppose that the user is familiar with basic algebra, statistics, economics, and accounting. Thus, the text is written at a somewhat more advanced level than are other books of this type, covering topics normally found in competing books in more depth as well as topics that are not covered elsewhere. This increased coverage is a direct result of our discussions with practitioners and researchers who indicated a desire to have a more complete exposition of quantitative analytical techniques.

In this second edition of *Techniques*, clarification and simplification of topics are the major changes. In Chapter 1, the relationship between net present value and wealth maximization is emphasized. Payment proportion and present value analysis has been applied to receivables in Chapter 6. Capital budgeting has been changed as has the lease chapter (Chapter 10) to reflect the recent tax law modifications. A new chapter, Chapter 11, has been added and includes a discussion of bond refunding.

In writing the second edition of this book, we had the help of a great number of people to whom we owe appreciation and acknowledgment. First, we thank our students of current and past years for their encouragement, patience, and insights. Their comments and suggestions have certainly improved the contents of *Techniques*. Karen Fortin of the University of Miami has made major contributions to the material by her devotion and skill as an editor. In addition, we appreciate and thank her for comments and suggestions that materially improved the text as well as for providing the questions and problems at the end of each chapter. A special thank you goes to Janice Pollard at the University of Louisville for typing and retyping the many drafts of the first edition. Her skill and patience greatly reduced the problems associated with both the first and second editions. George E. Pinches read the entire manuscript of both editions and made many suggestions, some accepted, some not; for his contributions, we express our appreciation and thank him for his help.

We thank all but absolve them from any responsibility as such must be claimed by the authors.

CONTENTS

PART One
INTRODUCTION

CHAPTER 1

An Overview of
Financial Management

Most business firms are similar in that they are economic units concerned with forecasting, planning, directing, and controlling their current and future operations to attain their objectives, which are either explicitly stated or implicitly assumed. Furthermore, business firms generally share a common organizational structure, usually along functional areas, such as personnel, production, marketing, accounting, and finance. This division allows specialization of efforts and implies a more efficient (least cost) means to accomplish firm objectives. Although it is impossible to isolate these functional areas of a firm perfectly because, of necessity, they must all overlap and interact with one another, the benefits of specialization are best obtained when an optimal level of isolation exists. This book, then, is concerned with just one area, the finance function, treated as an isolated area of activity but conscious of its interface with all other areas of business activity.

The finance function is common to all firms, and the objective of this text is to develop, illustrate, and explain analytical techniques that are useful in making decisions in the finance area. These analytical techniques are applicable to all firms, regardless of size, product areas and legal form.

This chapter first defines the functional area of the firm called finance; next, it discusses the activities normally included in this functional area; and, third, it presents several concepts that provide the necessary foundation for all the analytical techniques.

THE CONCERN OF FINANCIAL MANAGEMENT

Prior to the 1950s, the finance function in a firm generally meant only raising money to operate the firm. Today, the raising of funds still constitutes a part of the finance function, but it is only one aspect of the broader area of financial management. Currently, the finance function is concerned with managerial decisions that give rise to cash flows or money movements not only into but also out of the firm. The finance function viewed in this manner suggests activities that are much broader in scope than just the comparison of costs of alternative sources of funds. The cash used to purchase marketable securities, equipment, advertising, and so on is just as much a concern of finance as deciding whether or not funds should be obtained by selling bonds or common stock. When the finance function is viewed in this extended manner, it becomes apparent that it is an integral part of total firm management dealing with production, marketing, and other functional areas of the firm. Consequently, financial management is defined as an organized body of knowledge concerned with choosing alternative sources of funds with different costs and allocating these funds to alternative uses with different returns. The optimal use of funds requires comparisons of the benefits of alternative uses and the costs of alternative sources of funds.

THE FINANCIAL MANAGEMENT FUNCTIONS

If financial management stresses comparisons of the benefits from using cash and the costs of sources of funds, it seems appropriate to consider what is meant by uses and sources of funds. The area concerned with the use of funds is called the investment decision; the selection of alternative sources of funds is the financing decision.

The Investment Decision

In general, the firm can make two types of investment decisions: it can invest in current assets such as cash, marketable securities, accounts receivable, and inventories, or it can invest in long-term assets such as property, plant, and equipment. That is, the firm makes decisions concerning short-term and long-term assets. The decisions taking the form of deciding on the dollar amounts of cash, marketable securities, accounts receivable, and inventories are the short-term asset decisions and are considered in Chapters 5 and 6 as working capital management. The investment decisions that involve long-lived or long-term asset selection are referred to as capital budgeting decisions and are the subject material of Chapters 7 and 8. The capital budgeting decision is concerned with the evaluation of a new plant, competing plant location sites, competing production methods, and equipment evaluations, for example.

The Financing Decision

An investment decision implies an expenditure; and, of course, expenditures require money, cash or funds. The questions then arise as to how this money is to be obtained, at what cost, and under what conditions? Furthermore, should assets be financed with short-term or long-term funds? In addition, what mix or composition of short-term funds, common stock, preferred stock, bonds, long-term loans, and funds provided from operations should the firm use to obtain assets? These and related questions are categorized as financing decisions; Chapters 9 through 14 are concerned with an examination of these questions.

FOUNDATION CONCEPTS IN FINANCIAL MANAGEMENT

Since financial management is concerned with the wise selection of sources and the profitable uses of funds when investment and financing decisions are made, it seems appropriate to discuss, early in the text, concepts that underlie these decisions. Most managerial decisions involve the following factors: (1) profitability, (2) marginal analysis, (3) cash flows, (4) time value of money, and (5) risk. The remaining pages of this chapter explain and investigate these key concepts. These concepts permeate the entire text and are central to the decision making of both the financial manager and the nonfinancial manager.

The Profitability Concept

A key component of the decision-making process is the resulting impact on income, earnings or profits implied by the decision. In the usually understood sense, earnings are residual dollar values, covering a period of time (month, quarter or year), and result from subtracting a cost from sales or from some other profit measure. For example, Table 1-1 contains a firm's income statement for 1985 and indicates several definitions of earnings.

The following definitions, illustrated in Table 1-1, are encountered and used frequently throughout this book:

1. Gross profit = sales less cost of goods sold.
2. Net operating income = gross profit less selling and administrative expenses.
3. Earnings before taxes (EBT) = net operating income plus other revenue received (e.g., dividends, interest, rentals and sale of assets) less other expenses paid (e.g., interest on debt and amortization of bond discount and expense).
4. Earnings after taxes (EAT) or net income = earnings before taxes less taxes.

Table 1-1   SQUARE CONTAINER CORPORATION Income Statement Actual for the Year Ending December 31, 1985 and Estimated for the Year Ending December 31, 1986

	Actual	Estimated
Sales	$100,000	$130,000
Cost of goods sold	80,000	104,000
Gross profit ·	20,000	26,000
Operating expenses (selling and and administrative)	10,000	14,000
Net operating income	10,000	12,000
Other expenses	2,000	2,000
Earnings before taxes	8,000	10,000
Taxes @ 40%	3,200	4,000
Earnings after taxes (or net income)	$ 4,800	$ 6,000

Although these definitions are provided as illustrative, they are not all inclusive. Other variations or definitions of earnings are developed in the text to examine specific results of the decision-making process.

One variation requires expressing one or more of these definitions of earnings as a percentage of some other item on the income statement, such as sales, or as a percentage of a balance sheet item (e.g., total assets). If gross profits ($20,000) are divided by sales ($100,000), a gross profit margin of 20% results. Likewise, dividing earnings after taxes ($4,800) by a firm's total assets, assumed for this example to be $65,000, produces a rate of return on assets of 7.4%.

However, the major use of earnings is to provide a criterion for decision making. Earnings after taxes (EAT) is often used as the key definition, since it is the "bottom line" and generally understood by just about everyone. Suppose that cost of goods sold can be reduced by substituting a plastic for a metal part in a firm's manufacturing operation. If sales remain constant, gross profit must rise, as would net operating income and earnings before taxes, as long as operating and other expenses do not change. Taxes will rise but so will earnings after taxes. Since earnings after taxes increase, the profitability criterion suggests substituting the plastic for the metal part.

The concept of profitability is one criterion to determine whether or not the financial manager is using funds wisely and making rational choices in selecting the various combination of sources of funds. Although the most usual operational objective of the firm is profit maximization,[1] maximization of cash available to the firm is also an objective. Cash flow as an objective of the firm and its relationship to

[1]See Chapter 12 for a complete development of the common stockholders' wealth maximization model and the factors that influence the current price of common stock.

profitability will be discussed shortly. Whether profitability or cash flow is used as a decision criterion, the concept of marginal analysis is basic to the decision-making process.

Marginal Analysis

Financial decisions, such as the purchase of a new machine or a new plant, the negotiation of a new loan, and a revision in the company's credit terms, have marginal implications. These decisions all suggest change. "Increment" and "marginal" are words synonymous with change; consequently, decision making must mean incremental or marginal consequences. Decision making is always concerned with assessing marginal consequences.

An example may clarify this concept. The management of the Square Container Corporation is considering a $4,000 expansion of its product advertising budget. As a result, sales and cost of goods sold during the next year are expected to increase from $100,000 to $130,000 and $80,000 to $104,000, respectively, as shown in Table 1-1. It is the change in total revenue and total costs that is important. Cost of goods sold, operating expenses and taxes are estimated to rise by $24,000, $4,000, and $800, respectively, for an overall increase in total costs of $28,800. Estimated revenue will rise by $30,000. Thus, the increased advertising expenditure is expected to add $28,800 to total cost and $30,000 to total revenue. Since the marginal revenue, the addition to total revenue, is greater than marginal cost, the addition to total cost (EAT) must increase by $1,200. In general, a firm will always undertake an action as long as marginal revenue is equal to or greater than the margainl cost resulting from that action, since earnings then must increase.

It is essential to note that marginal analysis is defined in terms of changes. Any revenue or cost variable that does *not* change is not relevant to the decision-making process. Referring to Table 1-1, note that the entry for other expenses does not change if the advertising expenditures are increased. The operating expenses change but only by the amount of the increased advertising outlays. The increase in cost of goods sold is due only to the increase in units of output. However, there are additional expenses in both categories that are fixed; that is, they will not change regardless of whether the advertising expenditures are increased or not. For example, management salaries and depreciation charges will not change and play no part in the decision.

The Cash Flow Concept

A key distinction is made in financial analysis between profitability and cash flow or liquidity. Liquidity is defined in terms of a cash position or an ability to pay maturing obligations. Although the two are related, profitability does not necessarily mean liquidity, nor do earnings after taxes indicate accurately the cash posi-

Table 1-2 SQUARE CONTAINER CORPORATION Annual Depreciation, Earnings, and Net Cash Flow Calculations for a Project

(1) Year	(2) EBDT	(3) Depreciation	(4) = (2) − (3) EBT	(5) Taxes @ 40%	(6) = (4) − (5) EAT	(7) = (2) − (5) NCF
1	$2,897	$2,155	$742	$297	$445	$2,600
2	2,897	2,155	742	297	445	2,600
3	2,897	2,155	742	297	445	2,600
Total	$8,691	$6,465*	$2,226	$891	$1,335	$7,800

*Does not equal $6,466 because of rounding.

tion of the firm. The reasoning behind this distinction can readily be understood by an analysis of Table 1-1. First, sales are not synonymous with cash inflow, since the $100,000 of actual sales may represent only $90,000 of cash received during 1985, with the remaining $10,000 being credit sales that will be collected in and represent cash inflow in 1986. Second, cost of goods sold, operating expenses, and other expenses only approximate cash outflows. Depreciation and other amortization charges included in these expenses are not cash outflows in the year in question but represent an allocation of prior-year cash flows. These allocations, however, do reduce annual cash outflows for taxes since they act as a tax shield; that is, they reduce the amount of taxable earnings and thus reduce taxes. Consequently, the $4,800 net profit in 1985 is an accounting number that may not define the cash position of the firm or its ability to meet maturing obligations.

Cash flow analysis, in addition to its use as a measuring device to determine whether a firm can pay maturing obligations, is also important in a decision-making context. A typical capital budgeting example can illustrate this point. A machine with a 3-year life and an initial cost of $6,466 has $2,897 in annual cash earnings before depreciation and taxes. Should the Square Container Corporation accept or reject this machine? Again, marginal analysis can be applied to an examination of cash flow. Table 1-2 contains computations that provide the foundation for answering this question.

EBDT is defined as annual cash revenue less annual cash costs associated with the machine. Depreciation, an allocation of the current $6,466 cash outflow, is found by dividing $6,466 by the 3-year life. Although annual depreciation is not a cash flow, it is a tax-deductible expense and does reduce cash outflow for taxes. Net cash flows (NCF) are found by deducting the annual cash outflow for taxes from the annual cash revenue before depreciation and taxes. The NCF column is more important than the EAT (earnings after taxes) column, since EAT understates, by $2,155, the annual benefits associated with the $6,466 machine purchase.

However, the NCF analysis must be modified before a complete answer can be given to the question of whether to accept or reject the machine. This modification is required because $6,466 of current available funds are exchanged for three future cash flows of $2,600 and because money has a time value.

The Concept of Time Value of Money

Central to any analysis involving cash flow is the presumption that money has a time value. That is, the value of a dollar today is different from the value of a dollar received or disbursed at any future time as long as an interest rate exists. Since an amount less than a dollar today can be invested and earn interest, it will yield a future sum of money equal to a dollar. A dollar received at some future time period is not worth a dollar today since a present amount of money less than a dollar can be invested and earn interest that when added to that amount will produce a dollar in that future period.

The Present Value and Net Present Value. Since money has a time value, an amount of money received at the end of some future period is worth less than that amount today. To illustrate, $1 to be received at the end of the year is worth slightly less than $.91 today if the interest rate is 10%. If amounts of $1 were to be received at the end of 2, 3, and 4 years, today they are worth $.83, $.75, and $.68, respectively. That is, the present values of receiving amounts of $1 at the end of years 1, 2, 3, and 4 are $.91, $.83, $.75, and $.68 if the interest rate is 10%.

In general, the present value (P) of any future dollar amoung (F) is found by using Equation 1-1:

$$P = F\left[\frac{1}{(1 + i)^n}\right] \quad \text{or} \quad P = F[\text{pvf}] \tag{1-1}$$

where i is the appropriate interest rate[2] and n is the number of periods involved. The bracketed term—[pvf]—is called an interest factor. Because there are several such interest factors, as Chapter 2 will develop, it is convenient to name each one. A single amount present value factor, or "pvf," describes the operation of converting a single future value to its equivalent present value.

The need for a pvf is so frequent that tables have been constructed using various values of i and n. For example, if $i = .10$ and $n = 1$, then the pvf = $[1/(1.1)^1] = .90909$. Such tables are found in Appendix A, and .90909 is obtained by locating i equal to 10%, finding the pvf column and reading across the $n = 1$ row. Note that the present value factors in the table are independent of the value of F in Equation 1-1. Once the appropriate pvf is obtained, the present value, P, is found by multiplying F by the pvf.

For example, the present values of the net cash flows in Table 1-2 can be found by using Equation 1-1; the computations are done in Table 1-3. By multiplying each NCF by its appropriate pvf (for $i = 10\%$), the dollars received at the end of three future time periods have been converted to their equivalent present value. Because these future dollars have been converted to their present equivalence, they can be added, as in Table 1-3, or compared with the present sum that is necessary to generate these future amounts.

With this background, it is possible to introduce the decision criterion that relies on the timing of cash flows. The present value concept is the essence of the net present value (NPV). The NPV is defined as the sum of the present values of the

---

[2]In Equation 1-1, i is used in a very general sense. It might be the percentage cost of debt, or a weighted average percentage reflecting the cost of all sources of funds or even a rate of return. That is, i is defined and its symbol changed depending on the nature of the problem to be solved.

Table 1-3 SQUARE CONTAINER CORPORATION Present Value Computations for the Project

(1) Year	(2) NCF	(3) pvf @ 10%	(4) = (2) × (3) Present Value
1	$2,600	.90909	$2,364
2	2,600	.82645	2,149
3	2,600	.75131	1,953
Summed or total present value			$6,466

net cash flows less the initial cost or initial cash expenditure. Equation 1-2 defines the NPV in symbolic terms,

$$\text{NPV} = \sum_{t=1}^{n} A_t \left[\frac{1}{(1 + i)^t} \right] - I_o \tag{1-2}$$

where A_t is the net cash flow in period t, i is the appropriate cost of financing, and I_o is the initial cash expenditure. The summation term is the present value of the net cash flows, and I_o is the initial cost required to generate the net cash flows. Since the present values have been computed and summed in Table 1-3 and the initial cost amounts to $6,466, NPV = $6,466 − $6,466 = 0.

One of the major advantages of the NPV is its self-contained decision rule once the appropriate financing cost has been determined. The decision rule is to accept the investment proposal if the NPV is equal to or greater than zero and reject it if the NPV is less than zero (or negative). A NPV equal to zero implies that the original investment, $6,466 in this example, is recovered plus the 10% financing cost from the three $2,600 net cash flows.[3] If the NPV is positive, which can occur only when the present value of the NCFs is greater than the initial cost, the NCF provides an excess over the initial cost and financing charges. Conversely, a negative NPV indicates that the initial cost may be recaptured but the NCFs are not large enough to provide funds to cover the financing charges. Consequently, a negative NPV means that an investment should be rejected.

The Wealth of the Common Stockholder. The rationale for this decision criterion needs further exploration; it needs to be related to the wealth of the common stockholder. Profitability is almost a universal decision-making criterion for a prof-

---

[3]Because the NPV analysis assumes that the initial investment is recovered as well as the cost of financing, provided the NPV is equal to or greater than zero, dollar interest financing costs are *excluded* when determining the NCFs. If financing charges were included in the NCFs, the financing charges would be counted twice, in the numerator and in the pvf.

it-motivated firm, but difficulties exists. First, for example, a profit-oriented firm such as Square Container Corporation would increase advertising expenditures as long as the increase in revenue exceeds the rise in costs. If such decisions are based on a one-period analysis, they may not be in the best interest of the common stockholders. The interest of the common stockholders relates to a multiperiod analysis. That is, if a firm increases advertising expenditures, will additional sales be larger enough in future years to increase cash flow available for dividends on common stock? Second, profitability analysis does not always focus on the total benefits of a decision. Total benefits are cash flows, as the discussion of liquidity notes. Common stock dividends are paid with cash, not earnings. Third, profitability analysis does focus on earnings per share of common stock, but because profitability ignores the total benefit, it does not show the impact of a decision on the wealth of the common stockholder.

Liquidity focuses on the maximization of common stockholders' current wealth by examining cash flows available to the shareholders. Stockholders' wealth is generally defined as the current market price of a share of common stock; the higher the price of common stock, the higher the wealth of the stockholders. The current price of common stock is related to two phenomena—the short-run stock market fluctuations, which are not directly related to the firm, and the long-run (or intrinsic) value of the firm, which is directly related to the firm. The intrinsic, or long-run, value of the firm is the value justified by the specific facts related to that firm. One determinant of intrinsic value is the future cash position of the firm as reflected by cash available to the shareholders. Maximization of the current market price of common stock, subject to a given level of risk, is the objective of the financial manager.

The NPV concept does directly link the liquidity decision-making criterion to the wealth maximization objective and minimize the problems associated with the profitability concept. When the NPV of a decision is equal to zero, the net cash flows must recover the initial cash expenditure with a return or finance cost equal to the discount rate used to compute the NPV.

This conclusion can be illustrated by continuing the previous example. The three $2,600 net cash flows must return the $6,466 initial cash expenditure plus 10% (or minimum finance cost) on the declining balance. This is shown in Table 1-4. At the beginning of the first year, $6,466 oust be covered. The first $2,600 is received at the end of the year and can be divided into two parts: one is a return (or financing cost); the other is a recapture of some of the initial investment. The return (or financing cost) is found by multiplying the discount rate of 10 percent by the beginning balance, .1($6,466), or $647. The amount of the initial investment recaptured from the first net cash flow is $2,600 less the financing cost of $647, $2,600 − $647, or $1,953. The values for the remaining years are obtained in a like manner. Note that a zero must always occur in the last row, last column, when the NPV = 0. That is, the period cash flows must always recover the initial cash

Table 1-4   A Capital Recovery Schedule

(1) Year	(2) Beginning Balance	(3) Receipt	(4) = (2) × .06 Return Interest	(5) = (3) − (4) Principal Recaptured	(6) = (2) − (5) Ending Balance
1	$6,466	$2,600	$647	$1,953	$4,513
2	4,513	2,600	451	2,149	2,364
3	2,364	2,600	236	2,364	—

expenditure plus the a minimum return specified by the discount rate used when the NPV = 0.

This analysis, however, does not indicate the impact of the decision on the per share price of common stock. To show this impact, suppose that a firm has one common stockholder and expects to pay a perpetual annual cash dividend per share of common stock equal to $1. Thus, an investor buying a share of common stock pays the per share price and receives a perpetual annual cash dividend of $1. The intrinsic value or price of the share is the present value of the $1 perpetual dividend. The present value of a perpetual dividend can be found by dividing the dividend by the investor's required rate of return (the rate of return the investor must have for him or her to want to purchase the share). If this rate of return is 10%, the per share price is $1/.10, or $10. Conversely, if the investor invested $10 in an account that earned 10%, he or she could receive $10 (.1), or $1 per year, forever.

When a firm accepts a project with an NPV = 0, an initial cash outflow occurs that is just equal in dollar amount to the present value of the future cash inflows; in fact, this is the only way a project can have an NPV = 0. Consequently, $1 is still available to the common stockholders, and there is no reason for the per share price to change from $10.

Suppose that the cash inflows associated with the project were $2,600.25 instead of $2,600. The reader may want to verify that the NPV at 10% is now $.44. This means that the firm could invest $.44 at 10% forever and provide an additional per share cash flow of $.44(.1), or $.04, per year. Therefore, the share of common stock can receive $1 + $.04, or $1.04, as an annual dividend. This higher dividend suggest that the per share price of common stock should have a higher price of $1.04/.1, or $10.40.

This analysis can be continued. Suppose that the cash inflows from the project were $2,600.01. The same procedure suggests that the project should be accepted because the cash flow available for dividends would increase, and, hence, the price of a share of common stock would also rise. As long as a penny can be divided into smaller and smaller amounts, which is possible conceptually, cash available for dividends will rise and so should the per share price. Acceptance of projects must be carried to the point where the NPV is zero to ensure an increase in per share price.

Thus, projects should be accepted as long as the NPV is equal to or greater than 0 and rejected otherwise.

In summary, the NPV concept relates directly to the wealth of the common stockholder. If the NPV is zero and cash flows are known with certainty, the decision should be to accept the project. If the NPV exceeds zero, the firm should also accept the project since the present value of cash flows per share will be higher, and consequently, per share price will be higher. However, a negative NPV indicates that the project should be rejected since the per share cash flow will be lower and, hence, have a detrimental impact on per share price and wealth of the stockholder.

The concepts of present value and net present value are used extensively in financial management. As a result, they are introduced early in this text. Another decision-making concept requiring an early introduction is risk analysis.

The Concept of Risk

In the preceding discussions and examples, an implicit assumption existed. If advertising expenditures were increased or a new machine purchased, specific outcomes were assumed certain to occur. However, the very nature of managerial decisions, in which decisions made currently have consequences in the future, precludes knowing outcomes with certainty. Inability to forecast the future accurately requires the conclusion that managerial decisions are characterized by uncertain results or risk.

The first type of uncertainty inherent in managerial finance decisions is business or operating risk. Business risk can be defined as the uncertainty in the investment process that introduces variability in gross earnings (and variability of cash flows). A second type of uncertainty is financial risk—that is, the variability of earnings after taxes (and after-tax cash flows). Business risk results from erratic sales or costs, or a combination of both. Financial risk is related to the proportion of debt to equity used to finance the firm's assets and the degree to which the firm relies on short-term debt financing.

Management can influence sales by product pricing and promotional policies, but factors such as consumer income and tastes, which also influence sales, are beyond the control of management. For example, a change in consumer income that changes sales implies a change in gross earnings. Like sales, costs are subject to internal and external factors. If raw material prices change with sales remaining constant, a change in gross earnings results. Of course, there are many other factors, very specific in nature, besides those illustrated that influence business risk, and they too will be encountered throughout this text.

Perhaps, management has more discretionary control over the amount of financial risk it will accept than in the amount of business risk it will tolerate. Financing with bonds or long-term loans implies contractual or fixed commitments for the firm to make periodic interest and principal payments for protracted periods of time. The risk in this circumstance is that assets may not generate sufficient funds to meet these fixed obligations and a desired level of EAT will not be maintained. Of course, the larger the dollar amount of such fixed obligations, the higher the degree of financial risk. Likewise, the greater the percentage short-term debt is of total debt used by the firm to finance assets, the greater the degree of financial risk. Since short-term debt implies frequent maturity and renewal, renewal risk is encountered with this type of financing. If extremely tight money markets develop, the firm may not be able to renew its short-term bank financing, requiring cutbacks in operations that would result in lower EAT.

Another type of financial risk that develops with short-term debt is the risk of interest rate changes. Frequent renewal of short-term debt implies that the firm is subjected to frequent changes in interest rates. Although changes in short-term interest rates can be either favorable or unfavorable from the firm's viewpoint, such interest rate activity introduces uncertainty or risk into earnings.

Business and financial risk are examined in more detail in Chapter 12. However, certain quantitative techniques will be developed at this time to facilitate the evaluation of risk in the decision-making process regardless of the source of the risk.

Sensitivity Analysis. Sensitivity analysis uses measured deviations in potential risk sources to recompute the values of a key decision variable, thus highlighting the risk source's impact on the decision variable. Both the deviations in the source of risk and the recomputed values of the decision variable are expressed as percentages of their initial values. If the percentage deviation in the potential risk source causes a larger percentage deviation in the decision variable, a major source of risk has been identified. That is, the value of the key decision variable is highly sensitive to changes in the value of the risk source. Conversely, if a percentage deviation in a risk source results in a smaller percentage deviation in a key decision variable, the

Table 1-5   SQUARE CONTAINER CORPORATION—EAT Sensitivity to Sales Deviations

(1)	(2) Sales	(3)	(4)	(5) EAT	(6)
	Deviations			Deviations	
Levels	Dollars	Percentage	Levels	Dollars	Percentage
$104,000	$−26,000	−20	$2,880	$−3,120	−52
117,000	−13,000	−10	4,440	−1,560	−26
130,000	—	—	6,000	—	—
143,000	+13,000	+10	7,560	+1,560	+26
156,000	+26,000	+20	9,120	+3,120	+52

Table 1-6   SQUARE CONTAINER CORPORATION—EAT for Various Sales Levels

Sales	$104,000	$117,000	$130,000	$143,000	$156,000
Less: Cost of goods sold	83,200	93,600	104,000	114,400	124,800
Equals: Gross profit	20,800	23,400	26,000	28,600	31,200
Less: operating expenses					
and other expenses	16,000	16,000	16,000	16,000	16,000
Equals: EBT	4,800	7,400	10,000	12,600	15,200
Less: Taxes @ 40%	1,920	2,960	4,000	5,040	6,080
Equals: EAT	$ 2,880	$ 4,440	$ 6,000	$ 7,560	$ 9,120

risk source is not significant. An application should clarify the nature and general applicability of sensitivity analysis.

Referring to the example of Square Container Corporation in the discussion of the marginal analysis, the single best estimate for the increase in sales was $130,000 if advertising expenditures were increased by $4,000. Suppose, however, that sales could deviate 10% or 20% above or below this $130,000 estimate. What effect would these deviations have on EAT? Table 1-5 includes these levels of sales, the dollar deviation in sales from $130,000 and the precentage deviations in sales in columns 1, 2, and 3, respectively. Columns 4, 5, and 6 show the levels of EAT, the dollar deviations and the percentage for EAT. The EATs were calculated as shown in Table 1-6 for the various levels of sales following the example in Table 1-1, where cost of goods sold equaled 80% of sales, operating expenses were $10,000, other expenses were $2,000, and the tax rate was 40%. As might be expected, EATs are very sensitive to changes in sales. A 10% or 20% change in sales causes a 26% or 52% change in EAT, respectively; that is a percentage change in sales causes a much larger change in EAT.

Although sensitivity analysis does not provide quantitative measures of risk, it is a useful tool in locating potential sources of risk, as the preceding example illustrates. It will be used in many places in this text and should be part of any decision maker's analytical techniques.

Summary

The objective of this chapter is to provide a framework for the study of managerial finance and, in particular, for this book. To obtain this goal, the chapter is divided into three sections. The first develops the meaning of financial management, the process of obtaining and using funds wisely. The second discusses the financial management functions, making investment and financing decisions. Finally, the third section introduces five basic decision-making concepts: profitability, marginal analysis, cash flow, time value of money, and risk.

The remaining chapters in this text are grouped under four headings. Part II, containing Chapters 2, 3, and 4, is concerned with analytical techniques for evaluating, planning, and control. Part III, containing Chapters 5 and 6, and Part IV, containing Chapters 7 and 8, are concerned with the investment function. Chapters 5 and 6 discuss the techniques useful for making current asset decisions; Chapters 7 and 8 provide the analytical tools for capital budget decisions. Part V of the text, which includes the remaining six chapters, developes analytical techniques that facilitate making optimal financing decisions.

Questions

1. Define the principal activities of the modern financial manager.
2. What types of investment and financing decisions might the financial manager be required to make?
3. What is the primary focus of marginal analysis?
4. How do some of the differences between earnings and cash flow arise?
5. Determine the effect on earnings and/or cash flow for each of the following transactions:
    a. Purchase of merchandise for inventory or credit.
    b. Sale of merchandise on credit.
    c. Declaration of a dividend.
    d. Collection of an account receivable.
    e. Placing a bond issue privately.
    f. Payment of an account payable.
    g. Accruing wages for factory employees from the preceding week.
6. Explain the concepts of present value and future value of money.
7. Distinguish between the concepts of present value of cash flow and net present value (NPV).
8. How could the concept of sensitivity analysis be characterized?

Problems

1. The Summer Sausage Co., a premium sausage manufacturer with local distribution only, wants to expand distribution into three bordering states. The company will have to launch an extensive advertising campaign that will cost $50,000. As a result, sales are expected to triple from $750,000 to $2,250,000 during the coming year; but the increased sales will require additional capital expenditures and personnel. Cost of goods sold will rise from 60% of sales to 75%; selling and distribution expenses will increase from $50,000 to $200,000, and other expenses (excluding taxes) will increase from $100,000 to $225,000. The combined corporate tax rate is 40%. Using marginal analysis, determine whether Summer Sausage should undertake the planned expansion.
2. The Tighe T. Wad Company has had an extremely rigid credit policy. S. Ben Thrift, who recently received his MBA degree, has suggested that a more lenient credit policy would increase profits even though collections and bad debt expense would increase. Thrift has proposed two possible policies, A and B, and estimated the following sales and expenses for each policy:

	Credit Policy		
	Present	A	B
Sales	$900,000	$1,200,000	$1,500,000
CGS (70% of sales)	630,000	840,000	1,050,000
Collections expense	5,000	15,000	35,000
Bad debt expense	900	6,000	60,000
Other expenses	250,000	310,000	360,000

Using marginal analysis, determine if either new credit policy should be adopted.

3. **a.** What is the present value of $2,000 received at the end of 10 years if the interest rate is 6%? At the end of 20 years?

   b. What is the present value of $4,500 received at the end of 8 years if the interest rate is 12%? At the end of 15 years?

4. The Classis Chassis Co. can invest $120,000 in a project that is expected to increase cash flows for the next 5 years by $25,000 per year and the following 5 years by $20,000 per year. If the cost of capital is 10%, should the firm undertake the project?

5. See the following estimated data for the Regal Rags Clothing Company. Determine the sensitivity of earnings after taxes to 10% and 20% increases and decreases in sales.

Sales		$1,200,000
Cost of goods sold		
Fixed	$200,000	
Variable	600,000	800,000
Gross profit		400,000
Variable expenses	$200,000	
Fixed expenses	100,000	300,000
Earnings before taxes		100,000
Taxes (40%)		40,000
Earnings after taxes		$ 60,000

6. If Tighe T. Wad Company (from Problem 2) adopts credit policy A, determine the sensitivity of earnings before taxes to a 15% increase or decrease in the expected sales of $1,200,000. Expenses may be divided into their fixed and variable portions as follows:

Expense	Fixed Portion	Variable Portion
Cost of goods sold	—	70% of sales
Collections expense	$7,000	$8,000
Bad debt expense	—	$6,000
Other expenses	$220,000	$120,000

BIBLIOGRAPHY

Kieso, Donald E., and Jerry J. Weygandt. *Intermediate Accounting,* 2nd ed. New York: John Wiley & Sons, Inc., 1977.

Van Horne, James C., *Financial Management and Policy,* 4th ed. Englewood Cliffs, N.J.: Prentice-Hall, Inc., 1977, Chap. 1.

Weston, J. Fred, and Eugene F. Brigham. *Managerial Finance,* 7th ed. Hinsdale, Ill.: The Dryden Press, 1981.

ANALYSIS FOR INFORMATION, PLANNING, AND CONTROL

2

The Mathematics of Finance: Interest Factor Equations and Their Applications

The time value of money is one of the fundamental decision-making concepts developed in Chapter 1. The essential idea contained in the discussion of the time value of money is that money received (or disbursed) in different time periods cannot be compared without adjusting them to an equivalent time basis, such as their present values. A single present value interest factor (pvf) was developed to adjust cash flows to an equivalent time basis; however, there are other interest factors and other uses. The purpose of this chapter is to develop these interest factors and apply them to solve problems.

To accomplish this objective, the chapter is divided into six sections. The first and second develop single amount interest factors. The third and fourth discuss compound and present value interest factors for annuities. And the fifth and sixth develop capital recovery and sinking fund factors, respectively.

COMPOUNDING SINGLE AMOUNTS OF MONEY

When a sum of money is invested (or borrowed), interest is received (or paid) on both the principal sum and all accumulated interest. For example, if $1 is invested at 10% interest compounded annually for 1 year, the future amount (F) is

$$F_1 = \$1 + .10(\$1) = 1 + .10 = \$1.10$$

If interest is terminated at the end of the year, interest has been paid on the principal only.

However, if the money is invested for another year, interest is paid in the second year on both the principal and the interest earned during the first year:

$$F_2 = \$1 + .10(\$1) + .10[\$1 + .10(\$1)] = 1 + .10 + .11 = \$1.21$$

At the end of the second year, $1.21 is available from the investment: $1 of principal, $.10 in interest earned on the principal during the first year, and $.11 in interest earned during the second year. Of the $.11 in interest earned during the second year, $.10 is from the principal and $.01 is from interest of the first year.

Likewise, at the end of the third year,

$$
\begin{aligned}
F_3 &= \$1 + .10(\$1) + .10[\$1 + .10(\$1)] \\
&\quad + .10\{\$1 + .10(\$1) + .10[\$1 + .10(\$1)]\} \\
&= 1 + .10 + .11 + .121 \\
&= \$1.331
\end{aligned}
$$

That is, the $1.331 available to the investor at the end of the third year consists of $1 in principal, $.10 in interest earned on principal during the first year, $.11 in interest earned on principal and interest during the second year, and $.12 in interest earned on principal and interest during the third year. Of the $.12 in interest earned during the third year, $.10 is from principal [($.10)($1)], $.01 is from interest of the first year [(.10)(.10)($1)], and $.011 is from interest of the second year {(.10)(.10)[1 + .10($1)]}.

This process could be continued for the fourth year or any number of years desired. Each time a year is added, the computations would expand by one term and that last term would become larger as the number of years increases. The last term becomes larger because interest is computed on interest for more years. For example, by adding the fourth year to the series, the investor would have $1.4641: $1.331 from the results already obtained plus $.1331 in interest earned during the fourth year.

However, this process can be greatly simplified, because it can be shown that the future value (F) of any principal or present amount for any interest rate (i) and period (n) can be found by applying Equation 2-1:

$$F = P(1 + i)^n \quad \text{or} \quad F = P[\text{caf}] \tag{2-1}$$

The bracketed term is called the single amount compound factor (caf) and is used so frequently that tables are constructed for various values of i and n. The caf columns in the Appendix were calculated using the bracketed term in the equation.

Single amount compound factors for the example can be found in the caf column of the Appendix by first locating the $i = 10\%$ table. For $n = 1, 2, 3,$ and 4, the cafs are 1.1000, 1.2100, 1,331, and 1,4641, respectively. When each caf is multiplied by \$1, the previously obtained future values result.

Note that single amount factors are independent of the value of P. For example, if \$1.80 today is invested at 10% for 3 years, the future amount is \$1.80(1.331), or \$2.40. Or suppose that \$5,000 were invested at 10% annual compound interest for 10 years; the caf is 2.5937 and the future value is approximately \$12,968.50.

Some Variations and Applications

There are various ways in which single compound amount factors can be used to solve problems. A few examples of variations and applications follow to suggest their uses.

Finding Values of i. There are circumstances when both the beginning and ending dollar amounts are known as well as the number of years involved. What is unknown is the value of i. The value of i can either be a cost of borrowing a single amount and repaying it in some future period[1] or be a rate of return on an investment, purchased in one year and sold several years later.

If an asset purchased 15 years ago for \$1,000 has just been sold for \$11,973, what is the rate of return? In this example, instead of using i to find a caf to find F, F and P must be used to determine a caf to find i. The caf factor can be found by substituting the known values in Equation 2-1 and solving for the unknown:

$$F = P[\text{caf}]$$
$$\$11,973 = \$1,000[\text{caf}]$$
$$\text{caf} = \frac{11,973}{1,000} = 11.973$$

A search of the Appendix is required to find the value of i with a caf = 11.973. Start with any selected value of i and $n = 15$, say, 10%. The caf for $i = 10\%$ and $n = 15$ is too small, so a higher interest rate is examined until $i = 18\%$ and $n = 15$ is found. At 18%, the caf is equal to 11.9737, suggesting that a rate of return of 18% has been earned on the \$1,000. That is, if \$1,000 had been invested 15 years ago at 18% compounded annually, an investor would have \$11,973 today.

FINDING PRESENT VALUES OF FUTURE SINGLE AMOUNTS

A single amount less than a dollar compounded at some rate for some number of periods, as just developed, can produce a dollar at the end of the future period. Thus, it must follow that a dollar received at the end of some future period is not worth a dollar today. To illustrate, an amount slightly over \$.91 must be invested

---

[1]Discussions of i as a cost of borrowing funds are found in Chapters 9, 10, and 11.

today at a 10% rate of return if $1.00 is desired at the end of the year. With a caf of 1.1000, if approximately $.91 is invested today, the product $.91(1.1000) yields approximately $1 at the end of the year.

Conversely, $1 received at the end of a year has a present value of about $.91 if the rate of interest is 10%. By the same reasoning, $1 received at the end of 2, 3, and 4 years would today be worth only $.83, $.75, and $.68, respectively. These values multiplied by their appropriate caf, $.83(1.2100), $.75(1.3310), and $.68(1.4641), are all approximately equal to $1.

Consequently, the opposite of compounding a sum of money is finding its present value. As developed in Chapter 1, the present value (P) of any future dollar amount (F) is found by using Equation 1-1:

$$P = F\left[\frac{1}{(1 + i)^n}\right] \quad \text{or} \quad P = F[\text{pvf}] \tag{1-1}$$

This equation is the reciprocal of Equation 2-1 with the bracketed term called the single amount present value factor (pvf). The pvf column in the Appendix provides present value factors for selected values of i and n.

For example, what is the present value of receiving $400 at the end of each year for the next 3 years if the rate of interest is 10%? The appropriate present value factors are obtained, multiplied by $400 and the three products summed. These calculations are shown in Table 2-1, and the present value of the three future cash flows is approximately $996.

Although single amount compound and present value factors can be used to examine multiple cash flows, it is sometimes easier and faster to use alternative approaches. The present value example just examined indicates when multiple cash flow analysis can be simplified. Whenever multiple cash flows are equal (i.e., when an annuity is being investigated), the computations can be simplified. Compounding an annuity is developed next, and finding the present value of an annuity follows.

Table 2-1   Present Value Computations

(1) Year	(2) Amount	(3) Present Value Factor @ 10%	(4) = (2) × (3) Present Value
1	$400	.90909	$364
2	400	.82645	331
3	400	.75131	301
Total			$996

COMPOUNDING AN ANNUITY

The counterpart of the single compound amount factor is the annuity compound amount factor. An annuity is a series or stream of cash disbursements or receipts. If each cash flow is equal, it is called a fixed annuity. The future value of an annuity can be determined by compounding the series of single amounts; if a fixed annuity is involved, the process can be simplified.

For example, what future sum will be received at the end of two years if $1 is invested at the end of years 1 and 2 and the interest rate is 10%? Since the first dollar is not invested until the end of year 1, interest is earned only in year 2. The second dollar is invested at the end of year 2 and is immediately withdrawn along with the first dollar plus the interest on the first dollar. The second dollar, because it is deposited and immediately withdrawn, does not earn interest. The future sum is equal to

$$F = \$1(1.10) + \$1 = \$2.10$$

Likewise, a 3-year fixed annuity of $1 at 10% interest produces a sum at the end of year 3 equal to

$$F = \$1(1.10)^2 + \$1(1.10) + \$1 = \$3.31$$

That is, the deposit made at the end of year 1 earns compound interest for 2 years as shown by the term $\$1(1.10)^2$; the year 2 deposit earns compound interest for 1 year or $\$1(1.10)$; the last deposit earns no interest at all.

The computations to find the terminal value of an annuity become very cumbersome as the number of years (or periods) increases if the compounded amounts for each period are summed in this fashion. A much simpler approach is to use Equation 2-2:

$$F = A\left[\frac{(1 + i)^n - 1}{i}\right] \quad \text{or} \quad F = A[\text{cafA}] \tag{2-2}$$

where A is the amount of a fixed annuity and the second bracketed term is called the annuity compound amount factor (cafA). The columns labeled cafA in the Appendix are the annuity compound amount factors calculated for various values of i and n. The annuity compound amount factors for 2- and 3-year annuities at 10% interest are 2.10 and 3.31, respectively; when they are multiplied by the $1 annuity, the same results are obtained as in the example.

Consider a second example. A $180 fixed annuity invested at 10% for 23 years will yield a future sum of

$$F = \$180(79.5430) = \$14,318$$

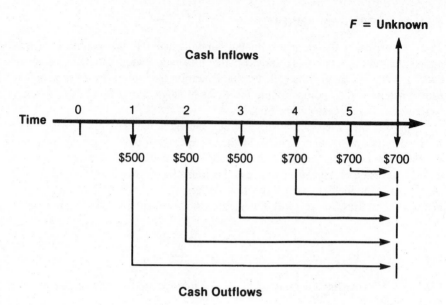

Figure 2-1. A cash flow diagram.

That is, $180 invested at the end of each year for 23 years at 10% interest will accumulate $14,318; this amount can be divided into (23)($180) or $4,140 of deposits and $14,318 less $4,140 or $10,178 of interest earned.

As a further example, somewhat more complicated, suppose that an investor plans to invest $500 for 3 years and then for years 4 through 6 invest $700. What amount of money will there be at the end of year 6 if the fund pays 8% interest? This problem is illustrated in Figure 2-1, a cash flow diagram. The cash flow diagram relates cash outflows, inflows and the time period in which they occur; as such, it can be a useful tool in solving cash flow problems. It indicates several possible ways to solve this problem: compound six annual cash flows; compound three $500 cash flows for 3 years and then compound their future value for 3 years plus compound three $700 cash flows; compound $500 for 6 years plus compound $200 for 3 years. The last alternative indicates

$$F = \$500(7.3359) + \$200(3.2464) = \$4,317$$

The other computational alternatives must also produce a future value of $4,317.

Like the previous interest factors, there are different variations and applications of the annuity compound amount factor. A couple of illustrations are discussed next.

Variations and Applications

In most cases the future value is the unknown value sought, but it is possible to have situations where the contributions are known as well as the future amount to be received. The unknown sought is the interest rate or rate of return involved. Under other conditions, receipts or disbursements occur at the beginning instead of the end of the periods.

Solving for the Value of i. If the value of the annuity and its future value are known, the interest rate involved can be found very easily. For example, if $2,000 is deposited in an account at the end of each year for 10 years that will return $28,973.20, what will be the rate of return over the 10-year period? The steps in solving this problem require finding the cafA for $n = 10$ and then searching for a value i with this cafA. Thus,

$$F = A[\text{cafA}]$$
$$\$28,973.20 = \$2,000[\text{cafA}]$$
$$\text{cafA} = 14.4866$$

The value of i associated with $n = 10$ and cafA $= 14.4866$ is 8%. Consequently, this investment produces a rate of return of 8%.

THE PRESENT VALUE OF AN ANNUITY

In many cases the present value of an annuity is needed rather than the future value. The present value of an annuity can always be determined by using single present value factors and summing the present values as illustrated in Table 2-1. However, if a fixed annuity is being considered, computing its present value can be greatly simplified. Instead of summing the multiple computations as in Table 2-1, the present value can be found in a single calculation using an annuity present value factor (pvfA).

The annuity present value factors for fixed annuities can be found by manipulating Equation 2-2. Instead of finding F, P (the present value or principal) is required. Equation 2-1 states that $F = P[(1 + i)]^n$. Substituting this value for F into Equation 2-2 and rearranging terms produces Equation 2-4:

$$P = A\left[\frac{(1 + i)^n - 1}{i(1 + i)^n}\right] \quad \text{or} \quad P = A[\text{pvfA}] \tag{2-4}$$

Again, the bracketed term is an interest factor, an annuity present value factor (pvfA), and the columns labeled pvfA in the Appendix are computed using this term for various values of n and i.

If the present value of a 3-year, $400 end-of-year annuity at 10% is to be calculated, the computations are simplified by using Equation 2-4. An annuity present value factor for $i = 10\%$ and $n = 3$ is obtained from the Appendix and then is multiplied by $400. The present value is

$$P = \$400(2.4869) = \$995$$

This is the result obtained in Table 2-1 (ignoring errors introduced by rounding).

Likewise, an investment generating three $2,600 end-of-year cash inflows has a present value of $6,466 if the rate of interest is 10%. That is,

$$P = \$2,600(2.4869) = \$6,466$$

Using Equation 2-4 to find the $6,466 is much easier and quicker than is using Equation 1-1 five times and then summing the results.

The annuity present value analysis, as for all the interest factor analyses, has wide applications in decision making. Several illustrations are considered in the following pages.

Annuity Present Value Variations and Applications

To indicate the many uses of annuity present value analysis, two applications are discussed. First, a cost saving problem is examined; second, a bond-pricing problem is solved.

Cost-Saving Analysis. A cost-saving problem is fairly straightforward. A firm must spend an amount of dollars today obtained from some source that requires some cost (i) for supplying these funds. The firm then uses the funds to reduce the costs of an operation, each year for a number of years. The problem is to determine how much must be saved each year to justify spending the initial amount. This is simply a present value problem.

What present investment can be justified today, for example, to save $2,500 a year for 6 years if the interest rate is 12%? The maximum present investment is found by using Equation 2-4, with $i = 12\%$ and $n = 6$:

$$P = \$2,500(4.1114) = \$10,279$$

That is, the current equivalent to six $2,500 cost savings is $10,279 if the interest rate is 12%. The firm should spend today any amount up to $10,279 to reduce annual cost of this operation by $2,500 but should not spend over $10,279. A profit-oriented firm would not spend, say, $11,000 today to save the equivalent of $10,279.

Determining the Price of a Bond. In many situations encountered in financial analysis both the present value of an annuity and of a single amount are needed. For example, it would be necessary to use both the pvf and pvfA to determine efficiently the present value or current price of a bond with a $1,000 face value, a 12% coupon rate (paid annually), and a 10-year life if the market interest rate on similar quality bonds is currently 14%. Three cash flows are involved: the initial cash price of the bond, the 10 $120 yearly interest cash flows, and the $1,000 face value cash flow at the end of the tenth period. A 12% coupon rate means that $120 in interest is paid annually, found by multiplying the coupon rate by the bond's face value. Once a bond is issued, the coupon rate cannot be changed; however, since the current market rate of interest is 14%, if the same bond were to be issued today, it would have to bear a 14% coupon rate instead of 12% to sell at face or par value. Since the 12% coupon rate cannot be changed, the price of the 12% bonds must be lower than like bonds with a 14% coupon rate to compete in the market with 14% coupon bonds. Consequently, the appropriate interest rate to use in determining the interest factors and the price of the 12% bond is 14%. The current bond price computations are as follows:

$$P = \$120(5.2161) + \$1,000(.26974) = \$625.93 + \$269.74 = \$895.67$$

Since the investor will pay only $895.67 instead of $1,000 for the bond, the difference of $104.33 can be invested at 14%. Such an investment means that the investor will receive not only $120 in bond interest from the $895.67 investment but also $20 in earnings on and partial recapture of the $104.33 investment for a total of $140 per year for 10 years. Consequently, the investor will earn an 14% return and be indifferent between paying $895.67 for 10 $120 interest payments and paying $1,000.00 for 10 $140 interest payments.

The $20 in annual earnings from investing $104.33 at 14% can be explained as follows. The annuity present value factor for $n = 10$ and $i = 14\%$ is 5.21612. The present value, then, for 10 end-of-year cash flows of $20 at 14% is equal to $104.33; that is, the pvfA of 5.21612 multiplied by $20 yields $104.33. How this $20 value was calculated, however, is the subject of the following discussion.

CAPITAL RECOVERY OR AMORTIZATION ANALYSIS

The capital recovery factor (crf) or amortization factor, which is the reciprocal of the pvfA, is one of the more important tools of the financial manager when evaluating installment and term loans. In a loan situation, what is known is the principal or amount borrowed and what is unknown is the annuity. Consequently, solving Equation 2-4 for A yields Equation 2-5:

$$A = P\left[\frac{i(1 + i)^n}{(1 + i)^n - 1}\right] \quad \text{or} \quad A = P[\text{crf}] \tag{2-5}$$

Once again, the Appendix contains the crfs for various values of i and n.

Applications of the Capital Recovery Factor

Several examples should clarify the use of the crf. If an investor pays $895.67 for a 12% coupon bond instead of the $1,000 face value because similar quality 10-year bonds currently bear a 14% coupon rate, the difference between $1,000 and $895.67, or $104.33, is available to invest in an asset which will earn 14%. In other words, how much can the investor receive at the end of each year for 10 years on an investment of $104.33 at 14% interest so that at the end of the tenth year the investment has a value of zero? Using the crf obtained from the Appendix for $i = $ 14% and $n = $ 10, which is .19171, yields the value of a 10-year annuity of

$$A = \$104.33(.19171) = \$20.00$$

Thus, if the investor purchases the 12% bond for $895.67 and a second investment of $104.33, his return each year for 10 years would be $140, which is what he would have earned if he had purchased a $1,000 face value bond with a 14% coupon rate.

As a second example, assume that a financial institution loans a company $20,000 for three years at 10% to be repaid in three equal year-end installments. The financial institution would like to know the year-end receipts, and the company would like to know the annual principal and interest payments. The crf for $i = $ 10% and $n = $ 3 is .40211. The annuity is found as follows:

$$A = \$20,000(.40211) = \$8,042.20$$

That is, the principal multiplied by the crf at 10% for three periods yields $8,042.20 in annual receipts from the viewpoint of the lending institution.

It is farily easy to divide the $8,042.20 in annual receipts into the dollar return

Table 2-2   A Capital Recovery or Amortization Schedule

(1) Year	(2) Beginning Balance	(3) Receipt	(4) = .1 × (2) Return (Interest)	(5) = (3) − (4) Principal Recovered	(6) = (1) − (5) Ending Balance
1	$20,000	$8,042.20	$2,000.00	$6,042.20	$13,957.80
2	13,957.80	8,042.20	1,395.78	6,646.42	7,311.38
3	7,311.38[a]	8,042.20	731.14	7,311.06[a]	—

[a]Not equal due to rounding of crf.

and the principal recaptured. When such a division is made for the life of the agreement, it is referred to as a capital recovery schedule (or amortization schedule, from a borrower's viewpoint). Table 2-2 contains the capital recovery schedule for this example.

At the beginning of the first year, $20,000, the amount of the loan, must be recaptured by the financial institution (repaid by the borrowing firm) over the 3-year period. An $8,042.20 receipt is received at the end of the first year; .1($20,000), or $2,000.00, is the return for allowing the firm to use $20,000, during the first year. When $2,000.00 is subtracted from $8.042.20, the remainder, $6,042.42, is the amount of the annual receipt that represents a recapture of principal. The ending balance is that portion of the initial amount lent that must be recaptured over the next 2 years and is found by subtracting $6,042.20 from $20,000, or $13,957.80. The ending balance of $16,724 in year 1 is the beginning balance in year 2.

The borrowing firm has the use of $13,957.80 during the second year. Interest for the year is .1($13,957.80), or $1,395.78. The second receipt, $8,042.20 less the return of $6,646.42, equals $3,604. This amount represents the portion of the second $8,042.20 that is a recapture of principal. The ending balance in year 2 is $13,957.80 less $6,646.42, or $7,311.38. This process continues each year until the full principal, plus a 12% return, is recovered by the financial institution.

SINKING FUND PROBLEMS

Like the crf, the sinking fund factor (sff) is the reciprocal of another interest factor, the cafA. In Equation 2-2, F is an unknown value found by multiplying the value of the known annuity by a cafA. However, if F is known but the value of A is unknown, solving Equation 2-2 for A produces Equation 2-6:

$$A = F\left[\frac{i}{(1 + i)^n - 1}\right] \quad \text{or} \quad A = F[\text{sff}] \tag{2-6}$$

The bracketed term is the sff, the reciprocal of the cafA, and again the Appendix contains sffs for various values of i and n.

Applications of Sinking Fund Factors

To illustrate the use of the sff, assume a firm must retire $500,000 worth of bonds 3 years from now. How much must the firm deposit at the end of each year for 3 years at 10% interest so that these deposits plus the interest earned on them will yield $500,000 at the end of the third year? The sff for $n = 3$ and $i = 10\%$ is .30211, and the annuity is found as follows:

$$A = \$500,000(.30211) = 151,055$$

Table 2-3   A Sinking Fund Schedule

(1) Period	(2) Beginning Balance	(3) = (2) × .1 Interest Earned	(4) Contribution	(5) = (2) + (3) + (4) Ending Balance
1	—	—	$151,055	$151,055
2	$151,055	$15,106	151,055	317,216
3	317,216	31,722	151,055	$500,000[a]

[a]Does not total because of rounding error, sff = .30211.

Stated as an annuity compounding problem, if $151,055 is deposited at the end of each year for three years at 10%, ($151,055)(3.31), or approximately $500,000, will be available to retire the bonds.

The counterpart of a capital recovery schedule is a sinking fund schedule. A sinking fund schedule is often required in governmental finance and is usually associated with bond financing. If in the example a government agency instead of a firm were retiring the $500,000 in bonds, the sinking fund schedule would be computed as shown in Table 2-3. The initial contribution to the sinking fund is made at the end of the first year; consequently, it earns interest of $15,106 in the second year. The sum of the first year's contribution plus its interest during the second year plus the contribution at the end of the second year produces the ending balance at the end of year 2. This process repeats itself until the end of the third year. At that time the agency has the necessary $500,000 in funds to retire the bonds, or $453,165 from contributions plus $46,828 in interest earned on those contributions.

Summary

The purpose of this chapter was to provide an in-depth analysis of the time value of money. This analysis involved developing six interest factor equations and showing how each could be used to analyze cash flows. These interest factors will be used throughout the text to facilitate investment and financing decisions.

Initially, the single compound amount factor was developed. Such an interest factor allows an unknown future dollar amount to be determined when a beginning dollar amount, interest rate, and number of periods are known. Second, the single present value factor was derived to compute the current or present value of a future sum. The first two interest factors deal with single amounts, and the final four involve multiple cash flows. The third interest factor, the annuity compound amount factor, permits determining a future sum that results from equal end-of-period deposits. Fourth, the annuity present value factor was used to find the discounted or present value of a future stream of equal end-of-year receipts or disbursements. The capital recovery factor and sinking fund factor, the fifth and sixth interest factors developed, were shown to be the reciprocal of the annuity present value and compound amount factors, respectively. Both these interest factors were used to find the value of the annuity. The capital recovery factor was used to find the annuity associated with a beginning dollar amount, and the sinking fund factor was used to find tbe annuity when a future dollar amount was known.

Questions

1. How is the single amount compound factor (caf) related to the present value factor (pvf)?
2. Is there a relationship between the present value factor (pvf) and the annuity present value factor (pvfA)?
3. Why are the present value of an annuity factor (pvfA) and the capital recovery factor (crf) considered reciprocals of one another?
4. What are the uses of the sinking fund factor (sff) and what is its relationship to the annuity compound amoung factor (cafA)?

Problems

1. a. What will the future value of $2,500 invested at 6% interest be in 10 years? In 20 years?
   b. What is the present value of $2,500 received at the end of 10 years if the interest rate is 6%? At the end of 20 years?
2. a. What will the future value of $5,000 invested at 8% annual interest be at the end of 5 years with annual, semiannual, and quarterly compounding?
   b. What is the present value of $5,000 received at the end of 5 years at an 8% interest rate with annual, semiannual, and quarterly compounding?
3. a. What is the future value of a 20-year fixed annuity of $2,000 per year invested at 6% interest?
   b. What is the present value of a fixed sum of $7,500 received at the end of each year for 10 years if the interest rate is 7%?
4. What is the present value of the following cash flows if the interest rate is 9%? 15%?

End of Year	Amount Received	End of Year	Amount Received
1	$2,500	4	$5,000
2	2,500	5	4,000
3	5,000	6	2,000

5. Solve Problem 4 of Chapter 1 using the appropriate annuity table rather than the single sum factor table.
6. What is the future value of a deferred 10-year fixed annuity of $5,000 per year invested at 8% interest? Of an annuity due?

7. What is the present value of an annuity of $500 received semiannually for 15 years if the annual interest rate is 4%?

8. What will the required annual installment payments be if a $500,000 loan at 12% interest is to be repaid over 8 years?

9. Ajax Widgets must retire $2,000,000 worth of bonds in 15 years. How much must the firm deposit at the end of each year at 11% interest so that it will have the required $2,000,000 in 15 years?

10. If an investment of $7,500 is expected to yield $13,710 at the end of 7 years, at what interest rate is the money invested?

11. For how many years must a company make annual sinking fund payments of $62,750 if it must retire $1,000,000 in bonds at the end of that time and the interest rate is 10%?

12. If the consumer price index was 100 10 years ago but is currently 283.94, what has the average increase in consumer prices been over the 10-year period?

13. An investor makes 20 $400 contributions at the beginning of each year to a fund that earns 10% interest compounded annually. Will the investor have a $25,000 nest egg for retirement at the end of the 20-year period? If the investor makes the contributions at the end of each year, will the investor have the required $25,000?

14. How much would a firm be willing to pay for a machine that would reduce after-tax labor costs by $1,500 per year for 5 years if the firm's cost of capital is 8%?

15. A four-color printing press will need to be replaced in 7 years at an estimated cost of $200,000. How much must be set aside each year to ensure the availability of the $200,000 at the end of the year 7 if the interest rate is 15%?

16. The Ace Trucking Corporation must accumulate $2,000,000 by the end of 3 years. How much must the firm deposit at the end of each of the 3 years if it can earn 8% on funds deposited? Construct a schedule showing the beginning and ending balances, required contributions, and interest earned for each year.

17. Construct an amortization schedule for the Jet Set Express Company if it borrows $50,000 for 4 years at 11% interest on the declining balance. Assume equal annual end-of-year payments.

BIBLIOGRAPHY

Estes, Jack C. *Compound Interest and Annuity Tables.* New York: McGraw-Hill Book Company, 1976.

Grant, Eugene L., W. Grant Ireson, and Richard S. Leavenworth. *Principles of Engineering Economy,* 6th ed. New York: The Ronald Press Company, 1976.

Kent, Frederick, and Maude E. Kent. *Compound Interest and Annuity Tables.* New York: McGraw-Hill Book Company, 1926.

Simpson, Thomas Marshall, Zareh M. Pirenian, Bolling H. Crenshaw, and John Riner. *Mathemátics of Finance,* 4th ed. Englewood Cliffs, N.J.: Prentice-Hall, Inc., 1969.

CHAPTER 3

The Analysis of Financial Statements

The financial manager must have a variety of analytical tools to make informed decisions designed to achieve the firm's and owners' objectives. This chapter and the next present the tools of financial statement analysis. Financial statements, principally the income statement and balance sheet, are frequently an outsider's major source of information about the operation of the firm. The outsider's analysis of these statements may largely determine the availability of funds to the firm, their cost and other terms.

OUTSIDERS, INSIDERS, AND THEIR CONCERNS

Outsiders interested in analysis of the financial position of the firm would include short-term creditors, long-term creditors, and equity investors. Each of these groups has different specific interests and tends to stress different objectives in financial statement analysis. An individual supplying short-term credit to the firm, a bank or vendor, for example, would be primarily concerned with the firm's ability to pay its maturing short-term obligations. That is, they are interested in liquidity. A bond-holder, on the other hand, who supplies funds to the firm for longer periods of time, would be more interested in the firm's long-run ability to generate earnings, the relative contribution that debt and equity make to the financing of assets, and the major sources and uses of funds. The equity investor, the common stockholder, is primarily interested in the firm's earnings, both current and future.

Insiders are the firm's managers, and they must be interested in all aspects of financial statement analysis. Since it is their responsibility to obtain financing at the least cost and under the best possible terms, they must view the financial condition of the firm through the eyes of both creditors and investors. In addition, management may also find financial statement analysis a useful tool of internal control. For example, comparisons may be made in inventory levels between their firm and other firms in the industry to ensure an optimum level is maintained.

While each of these groups may have a particular interest in different aspects of the financial position of the firm, they have at least one common area of interest. They all need to assess the present financial condition of the firm and to estimate the effect of current decisions on the firm's future financial condition. Consequently, this chapter examines techniques used by creditors, investors, and managers to determine the firm's current and future position by examining its financial statements. Financial ratios used by the various groups of financial statement users are discussed and analyzed. Finally, sources of industry financial ratios are given.

TYPES OF RATIOS: EXAMPLES AND INTERPRETATIONS

Financial statements can provide a great deal of information about the economic well-being of a firm, but certain accounting realities must be considered in the classification and analysis of the data to ensure useful interpretations. It is usually desirable to classify the information on the firm into categories that indicate the firm's liquidity, efficiency, coverage and leverage, and profitability. Ratio analysis is the technique most often employed to analyze and evaluate a firm's performance in these categories.

Liquidity Ratios

The purpose of liquidity ratios is to determine the ability of a firm to meet its maturing obligations. They attempt to determine whether the firm will have sufficient current (or liquid) assets in the form of money or near-money assets that can be converted into money quickly without loss of value, to pay its short-term liabilities. The current and quick (or acid test) ratios are normally used to gain answers to this question. Furthermore, the receivables and inventory turnover ratios provide further insight by measuring how rapidly other current assets are converted into money.

The current ratio is defined as current assets (cash, marketable securities, accounts receivable and inventory) divided by current liabilities (trade accounts payable, notes payable, short-term bank loans, accrued taxes, and accrued wages). Using values from Table 3-1, the current ratio is

$$\text{Current ratio} = \frac{\text{current assets}}{\text{current liabilities}} = \frac{\$580,000}{\$290,000} = 2$$

Table 3-1   THE XYZ COMPANY Balance Sheet December 31, 1985

Assets

Cash	$ 30,000
Marketable securities	40,000
Accounts receivable	190,000
Inventory	320,000
Total current assets	580,000
Property, plant, equipment	1,760,000
Less: Accumulated depreciation	520,000
Net fixed assets	1,240,000
Total Assets	$1,820,000

Liabilities and Equity

Accounts and notes payable	$ 290,000
Total current liabilities	290,000
Bonds payable (8%)	560,000
Total liabilities	850,000
Common stock, $5 par value	300,000
Retained earnings	670,000
Total equity	970,000
Total liabilities and equity	$1,820,000

This current ratio indicates that the firm has sufficient money or near-money assets to pay its maturing liabilities twice, or, alternatively, that the value of the current assets could decrease by 50% and the firm could still pay its bills. This would suggest a fairly strong liquid position, provided that comparisons with industry data, trend analysis and other liquidity ratios confirm this tentative conclusion.

If, the industry current ratio in 1985 were 2.2, or 10% above the firm's ratio, it would indicate that the firm was slightly less liquid than the average firm in the industry. If the industry ratios were 2.3 and 2.1 for the preceding two years, while the firm's ratios were 2.2 and 2.1, then on average the firm is also less liquid (2.1) than the industry (2.2). Furthermore, there is a consistent downward trend in the firm's ratio values: 2.2, 2.1, and 2.0. Thus, both the industry and trend comparisons indicate below-average liquidity, signaling a need for further investigation by checking other liquidity ratios.

The acid test or quick ratio is defined as

$$\text{Acid test} = \frac{\text{current assets} - \text{inventory}}{\text{current liabilities}}$$

The acid test ratio for the firm data in Table 3-1 is

$$\text{Acid test ratio} = \frac{\$580,000 - \$320,000}{\$290,000} = .9$$

In this ratio, the inventory is subtracted from total current assets because it is the most difficult current asset to convert rapidly into cash and its market value may be questionable; for example, the liquidity of an inventory of a fad item like hula hoops or of specialized machinery is very limited. An acid test ratio less than 1 means that the firm could not meet its maturing liabilities with its most liquid current assets. The industry's acid test ratios for the last two years and this year are 1.3, 1.3, and 1.2, respectively, whereas the firm's ratios during the same periods are 1.4, 1.2, and .9, respectively. Analysis of these ratio and industry comparisons confirms the analysis of the current ratio that indicated a liquidity problem. Figure 3-1, which illustrates the deterioration of the firm's ratio relative to the industry average, clearly indicates this conclusion.

The logical place to continue this investigation is to examine inventory practices because, as suggested by the acid test ratio analysis, inventory represents such a large percentage of current assets (55%). An analysis of the inventory turnover ratio may indicate whether part of the firm's liquidity problem is caused by an excessive buildup of inventory. The income statement for the XYZ Company appears in Table 3-2. The inventory turnover ratio is defined and calculated for the firm as follows:

$$\text{Inventory turnover} = \frac{\text{cost of goods sold}}{\text{inventory}} = \frac{\$3,300,000}{\$320,000} = 10$$

If cost of goods sold is not available, sales can be used in the numerator; however, every effort should be made to use cost of goods sold because both cost of goods sold and inventory are valued at cost, whereas sales are valued at selling price, which includes an element of profit. The inventory turnover ratio of 10 indicates that every 36 days inventory is turned into cash or an account receivable, depending on whether it is a cash sale or a credit sale. During the last 2 years, the firm's ratio has decreased from 20 to 13 to the present 10, while the industry average ratio has remained at 18. Thus, the firm has gone from converting inventory into cash or receivables every 18 days to every 36 days, while the industry has maintained a 20-day conversion rate.

While the low inventory turnover could be caused by the firm's carrying too much inventory, there may be other reasons, such as a buildup of obsolete or damaged goods. Whatever the reason, however, the liquidity problem seems to be a direct result of the firm's having too great a proportion of its current assets invested in inventory.

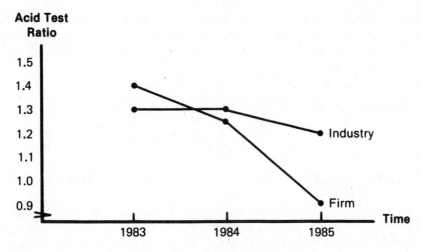

Figure 3-1. Trend analysis of industry and firm acid test ratio.

It has been seen that a decline in the turnover of inventory into cash or accounts receivable can affect a firm's liquidity; it is also important to evaluate how effectively accounts receivable are turned into cash as cash position is also indicative of a firm's liquidity. In the example, accounts receivable constitute 33% of the total current assets, and an examination of their turnover into cash may shed additional light on the firm's liquidity problem.

The receivables turnover ratio is

$$\text{Receivables turnover} = \frac{\text{annual credit sales}}{\text{accounts receivable}} = \frac{\$2,200,000}{\$190,000} = 12$$

If the amount of credit sales is not available, total sales may have to be used, and if beginning and ending receivables are materially different in size, an average should

Table 3-2   THE XYZ COMPANY Income Statement Ending December 31, 1985

Net sales (50% credit sales)	$4,400,000
Cost of goods sold	3,300,000
Gross profit	1,100,000
Operating expenses	500,000
Earnings before taxes	600,000
Income taxes	268,000
Earnings after taxes	$ 332,000

be taken. In the example, credit sales are known and the $190,000 fairly represents the accounts receivable balance during the year. The receivables turnover ratio indicates that receivables are collected 12 times a year. Or, alternatively, the average collection period is

$$\text{Average collection period} = \frac{\text{receivables} \times \text{days in year}}{\text{annual credit sales}}$$
$$= \frac{\$190,000 \times 360}{\$2,200,000} = 31$$

That is, on the average the firm receives the cash from a credit sale 31 days after the sale.

If the industry's receivables turnover ratio is 12, then the average firm in the industry also collects credit sales every 30 days, as does this firm. If the industry's receivables turnover ratios were 11 and 13 during the past 2 years and the firm's ratios were approximately the same, the source of the liquidity problem would not lie with the management of accounts receivable. However, if the industry receivables turnover ratio in this year is 7, then the average firm in the industry collects its credit sales every 51 days as opposed to the firm's 30-day collection period. This would imply that the firm is more liquid than the industry, if the current and acid test ratios were in line with industry averages. Conversely, if the industry turnover ratio is 18, an average collection period of 20 days, then the firm would be less liquid than the industry, other factors being equal.

If the average collection period is 10 days longer than the industry average, further investigation would be necessary to determine whether the firm has a weak collection policy and/or uncollectible receivables. If the company billing or credit terms are 1/10, n 20 (i.e., deduct 1% if the invoice is paid within 10 days or pay in full in 20 days) and this is consistent with industry credit terms, either of these two factors could be the cause of the firm's less liquid condition. However, if the firm's credit terms are 1/10, n 30, while the industry average is 1/10, n 20, then the firm's more liberal credit policy could be the cause of the liquidity problem.

However, a word of caution is required. A number of studies have shown the traditional average collection period analysis to be potentially misleading. The average collection period is calculated by dividing annual accounts receivable by annual credit sales or, alternatively, by dividing average receivables by average daily credit sales. As long as credit sales remain constant, no problems are encountered. Changes in credit sales, however, will cause both the receivables balance and average daily credit sales to change. Thus, the average collection period can change but not necessarily due to a change in the actual collection experience of the firm.

Selling on credit and increasing inventory levels require the firm to use or invest cash in these assets. If an excessive amount of funds is invested in accounts receivable and inventory, the firm may have difficulty in paying its maturing liabilities. The XYZ Company, as evidenced by the current and acid test ratio analysis, has a liquidity problem. Further analysis of the inventory turnover and receivable turnover ratios and industry comparisons helped to pinpoint the causes of the liquidity problem.

Efficiency or Activity Ratios

While inventory and receivables turnover ratios provide information regarding a firm's liquidity position, they also are indicative of how efficiently the firm uses its current assets. Efficient use of fixed assets, however, is measured by the firm's fixed asset turnover ratio. In addition, an overall measure of efficiency is the firm's total asset turnover ratio. Efficient utilization of assets is directly related to the profitable operation of the firm. The more efficiently the firm uses its assets to generate sales, the higher the firm's profitability, whereas an inefficient use of assets implies lower earnings.

The overall indicator of efficiency is the total asset turnover ratio. It is defined and calculated using the example data as follows:

$$\text{Total asset turnover} = \frac{\text{sales}}{\text{total assets}} = \frac{\$4,400,000}{\$1,820,000} = 2.4$$

During the past 2 years, the firm's ratio has declined from 2.6 to 2.5 to the present 2.4. At the same time, the industry's ratios have been 3.0, 3.1, and 3.1. Not only has the firm been less efficient than the industry, the condition has been deteriorating steadily. That is, the average firm in the industry has been generating the same amount of sales with fewer assets; or, with the same amount of assets, the average firm has been producing a larger sales volume than the firm in the example.

A below-average asset turnover ratio, indicating inefficient utilization of assets, implies reduced profitability. That is, with fewer assets, several types of costs could be reduced, and then, if the same level of sales were maintained, earnings would rise. If the firm has invested too heavily in fixed assets, its financing costs, maintenance, and depreciation expenses are too high. Similarly, excessive accounts receivable mean higher financing costs and an abnormal investment in inventory, resulting in excessive carrying costs (storage, insurance, etc.) as well as financing costs. Any cost that is higher than necessary will decrease earnings. A low turnover could be caused by factors other than excessive investment in assets, however. The firm's pricing policy relative to the competition may be causing sales to decline and decrease in the asset utilization ratios. However, above-average asset turnover ratios do not necessarily mean higher profitability.

For example, a low inventory turnover ratio suggests reduced liquidity and lower profitability; however, a higher ratio may mean that the firm is experiencing frequent stockouts and inventory replacement orders because too little inventory is held. A better liquidity position is implied since cash is returned more quickly to the firm for a given receivables turnover. But frequent stockouts mean lost sales, and frequent replacement orders indicate higher ordering costs—both of which lower earnings. Therefore, an apparent contradiction exists since both a higher and a lower inventory turnover can mean lower earnings. Consequently, financial managers must seek a level of inventory that balances or minimizes these costs.

The analysis of the receivables turnover suggested that the company could be in line with the industry (depending on the industry credit terms), indicating no liquidity or profitability problems emerging from this area. However, an unacceptable asset turnover ratio could be caused by a low receivables turnover ratio, with the low receivables ratio suggesting a high level of receivables due to liberal credit terms, weak collection policy, or uncollectible accounts. This condition implies reduced liquidity and profitability levels. Conversely, a high asset turnover ratio may be associated with a high receivables ratio, meaning a better than average liquidity condition but not necessarily better than average profitability. A favorable liquidity position exists because receivables are more quickly converted into cash. But the profitability problem may exist because the firm has too stringent a trade credit policy, which results in lost sales. Thus, another apparent contradiction must be reconciled by the financial manager.

The final efficiency ratio is the fixed asset turnover ratio, defined and calculated for the example as

$$\text{Fixed asset turnover} = \frac{\text{sales}}{\text{net fixed assets}} = \frac{\$4,400,000}{\$1,240,000} = 3.6$$

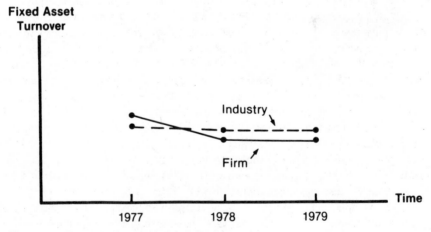

Figure 3-2. Trends in firm and industry fixed asset turnover.

This ratio measures how efficiently the firm is using fixed assets, net of depreciation, to generate sales. A low fixed asset turnover ratio, relative to the industry average, indicates excess production capacity. The excess capacity could be a result of the firm's pricing its products too high relative to other firms in the industry. Conversely, if a fixed asset turnover ratio is high relative to the industry average, the company might be engaged in a competitive price struggle. It is also possible that the high ratio, which implies a high degree of plant utilization, indicates a need for fixed asset expansion, or the high asset turnover could mean that the firm's assets are old and almost fully depreciated, suggesting high production costs and low profits now and problems in the near future because of substantial replacement costs. Figure 3-2, however, suggests that the company is and has been in line with the industry.

Coverage and Leverage Ratios

Coverage ratios are another type of activity measure, similar to efficiency ratios, that are related to the firm's fixed payment obligations and its ability to service them. The leverage ratios examine the relative contributions that the creditors and owners make to the financing of assets, while the interest, debt service, and fixed charge coverage ratios measure long-term liquidity or the firm's ability to meet long-term liabilities.

Interest coverage is computed by dividing EBIT by the dollar amount of interest the firm must pay. The income statement for the XYZ Company does not show the interest payable on the bonds, but the balance sheet indicates there are $560,000 worth of 8% bonds outstanding. Annual interest charges are (.08)($560,000), or $44,800, and when added to EBT, an EBIT of $644,800 results. Thus,

$$\text{Interest coverage} = \frac{\text{EBIT}}{\text{interest}} = \frac{\$644,800}{\$44,800} = 14.4$$

That is, EBIT are 14.4 times greater than are annual interest charges. The EBIT would have to fall by $600,000 or more before the firm would experience financial or legal embarrassment because of its inability to pay interest or debt.

It may be desirable for this firm and the industry in general to maintain such a high interest coverage ratio because of high variability in sales from one year to the next or unusually high fixed charges. If, for example, the industry interest coverage ratio has averaged 20 over the last few years while the firm has averaged only 14, a cyclical decline in firm and industry sales could mean that the firm would not be able to meet its debt interest and/or other fixed charges (e.g., lease payments, rent, sinking fund contributions).

A firm with low interest coverage will find some difficulty in borrowing additional funds. Conversely, a firm with above-average coverage will find borrowing easier, interest rates lower and fewer restrictive conditions (e.g., minimum current ratio, limit on common stock dividends) imposed.

Since most firms have other fixed charges, such as lease payments, which earnings must cover, a fixed charge coverage ratio has been developed as

$$\text{Fixed charge coverage} = \frac{\text{EBT} + \text{interest} + \text{lease payments}}{\text{interest} + \text{lease payments}}$$

For example, if the XYZ Company leases equipment under a long-term contract that requires an annual lease payment of $100,000, the fixed charge coverage is

$$\text{Fixed charge coverage} = \frac{\$600,000 + \$44,800 + \$100,000}{\$44,800 + \$100,000} = 5$$

The comparison, interpretation, and conclusions are similar to those for the interest coverage ratio.

Several additional points must be made in connection with these coverage ratios. First, earnings before taxes are used in the computations because interest and other fixed charges such as lease payments are deducted before determining the tax liability. Consequently, taxes do not influence the firm's ability to cover these payments. However, there are other fixed charges, such as preferred dividends or payments to a bond sinking fund, that would be included in determination of the fixed charge coverage ratio but that are not deductible in determining taxable income. The amount of the nontax-deductible fixed charge would have to be increased by an amount that would permit the payment of taxes. That is, if the bond sinking fund requirement were $100,000 and the tax rate 40%, $166,667 in pretax earnings would have to be available to cover the $100,000 sinking fund payment—$166,667 − (.4)$166,667 = $100,000—or the amount required, $100,000, would be divided by 1 less the tax rate—1 − .4 = .6—to arrive at the pretax required amount—$100,000/.6 = $166,667.

Second, the nature of earnings and fixed charges would be examined. Earnings before interest and other fixed charges are only an approximation of the cash flow available to cover these charges, while interest and fixed charges accurately represent the cash outflow. Not all sales represent cash inflows nor do all costs incurred in arriving at earnings before interest and fixed charges accurately reflect cash outflows. Consequently, an alternative to the fixed charge ratio is the cash flow coverage ratio that solves this problem. The cash flow ratio is

$$\text{Cash flow ratio} = \frac{\text{annual cash flow before interest and lease payments}}{\text{interest} + \text{lease payments}}$$

Annual cash flow is defined as cash revenue minus cash expenses before cash payments for interest, lease payments, and taxes.

The cash flow coverage ratio can be expanded to include any cash charge. The major problem in computing this ratio, at least from an outsider's viewpoint, is that very detailed financial statements are required to obtain the information necessary to make the calculations. In addition, a standard of comparison, in the form of published industry ratios, is generally not available. However, from an insider's or manager's viewpoint (to whom cash flow information is readily available), this can be a very informative ratio.

For example, if annual cash flow after interest and fixed charges is $868,800 and interest and lease payments are $44,800 and $100,000, respectively, then

$$\text{Cash flow ratio} = \frac{\$868,800 + \$44,800 + \$100,000}{\$44,800 + \$100,000} = 7$$

The cash flow ratio indicates that the annual cash flow coverage of 7 is 40% higher than the fixed charge coverage of 5. That is, the fixed charge coverage, based on earnings, understates the firm's cash position. Other things being equal, the earnings measure will always understate the cash position of the firm because annual depreciation charges are a noncash expense deducted in computing earnings.

Closely related to coverage ratios are the leverage ratios that indicate the relative contributions the firm's creditors and owners make to the financing of the firm's assets. Creditors expect owners to provide a fair share of equity funds to operate a firm. If the owners provide only a relatively small percentage of total funds, the creditors bear much more risk than do the owners. The owners are also able to maintain control of the firm with a limited investment when more and more funds are raised by debt. Furthermore, the return to the owners is magnified if the firm is able to earn more on borrowed funds than it pays in interest. For example, if a firm borrows money at 6% interest and invests it in assets that earn 10%, the 4% difference accrues to the common stockholders. However, loss to the owners is magnified, and risk to the common stockholders is increased the more debt the firm has relative to owner-supplied funds. If a firm borrows at 7% interest and assets earn only 5%, the common stockholders must have their return reduced so that the firm can provide the 2% difference to the creditors. This magnification of return to the owners is an example of favorable financial leverage. Leverage can be unfavorable, however; if the assets earn less than the interest cost of debt, the stockholders' share of profits will be reduced. Thus, both creditors and owners must be concerned with the financing of the firm.

Two commonly used ratios used to measure the relative financing contribution of creditors and common stockholders are as follows:

$$\text{Debt to asset} = \frac{\text{total debt}}{\text{total assets}} = \frac{\$850,000}{\$1,820,000} = .48$$

$$\text{Debt to equity} = \frac{\text{total debt}}{\text{total equity}} = \frac{\$850,000}{\$970,000} = .88$$

Total debt, in the debt-asset and debt-equity ratios, includes all current liabilities and long-term debt. The debt-asset (D/A) and the debt-equity (D/E) ratios are transformations of each other (total assets − total debt = equity) and are a broad measure of the relative contributions of creditors and owners.

Since short-term and long-term creditors both expect equity to bear its fair share of risk, they are interested in the D/A and D/E ratios. If the firm's D/A ratio of .48 is above the industry average, creditors are financing a higher proportion than the average firm in the industry or 48%, while the equity owners are financing only 52% of the firm's assets. Consequently, in the event the firm fails, creditors stand to lose more than if the company were in line with the industry. With D/A and D/E ratios above the industry average, the company would also find it difficult to obtain debt funds until additional equity funds were obtained.

Profitability Ratios

The objective of profitability ratios is to measure the overall effectiveness of managerial decisions—that is, to provide a final appraisal of management decisions. Several different ratios are used to evaluate the overall performance of a company.

The gross and net profit margins are two profitability ratios that can provide significant insights into the operation of the firm. The gross margin tells the analyst something about the efficiency of operations and/or the pricing of the firm's products. The gross profit margin is

$$\text{Gross profit margin} = \frac{\text{sales less cost of goods sold}}{\text{sales}} = \frac{\$1,100,000}{\$4,400,000} = .25$$

If the XYZ Company's 25% gross margin is above the industry average, the firm may be more efficient or produce goods at lower cost than other firms in the industry, assuming that the company's pricing policy is in line with industry practice. If the gross profit margin is below the industry average, the firm may have higher production costs or may be pricing its product below other firms.

The net profit margin is

$$\text{Net profit margin} = \frac{\text{earnings after taxes}}{\text{sales}} = \frac{\$332,000}{\$4,400,000} = .07$$

The net profit margin is a measure of the firm's efficiency after operating expenses and taxes are deducted from gross profit. A net profit margin of 7%, if it is below the industry average or is falling, may indicate that selling costs, administrative expenses, or taxes are too high or rising. This is especially true if the firm's gross profit margin has remained unchanged over a period of years.

For example, Figure 3-3 illustrates gross and net profit margins for the firm

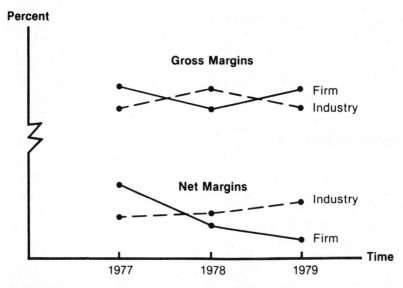

Figure 3-3. Firm and industry gross and net margins.

and industry over the past three years. The gross margins for both the firm and industry have been relatively constant with slight but insignificant deviations from each other. This suggests that the firm's cost of production and pricing policy have been consistent with industry practices. The industry's net profit margin has been fairly constant over the last three years; however, the firm's net margin has been falling continuously over the period of analysis. This implies that selling costs, administrative expenses and/or taxes have risen. Higher federal taxes can be eliminated as a cause since higher taxes would, in general, reduce the net margin for all firms in the industry. Consequently, the company must be incurring higher selling and/or administrative costs than the average firm. If the firm and industry gross profit margins had remained stable while the net profit margins had been rising for both, then lower taxes could be the explanatory variable, or the condition could be due to forces external to the industry that caused selling and/or administrative expenses to fall.

While the gross and net profit margins provide information regarding the firm's profitability relative to sales, another group of ratios has the goal of providing information on profits relative to investment.

The rate of return on equity is

$$\text{Rate of return on equity} = \frac{\text{earnings after taxes}}{\text{equity}} = \frac{\$332,000}{\$970,000} = .34$$

The return on equity indicates the profitability of equity funds. The rate of return for the XYZ Company is 34%. A low return on equity, coupled with a low net profit margin, would suggest that a firm has too large an investment in assets, a product pricing problem, and/or higher costs than do most firms in the industry. The calculation and comparison of the return on investment (ROI) may provide further insight:

$$\text{Return on investment} = \frac{\text{earnings after taxes}}{\text{total assets}} = \frac{\$332,000}{\$1,820,000} = .18$$

If an 18% ROI is lower than the industry average, the company has more assets and/or lower earnings than does the average firm in the industry; that is, the firm's receivables, inventory, and/or fixed assets may be higher than necessary. In any event, the firm should be able to generate the same level of sales with a smaller investment in fixed assets while maintaining the same net profit margin, thus increasing its ROI.

The E. I. du Pont de Nemours & Company originated an analytical technique that has been acclaimed by both practitioners and academicians. The system consists of a rather simple equation and a chart that indicates the underlying factors affecting a firm's profitability as measured by return on investment (ROI). Figure 3-4 charts the various factors affecting the ROI. The top part of the chart measures the efficiency of the firm in using its assets to generate sales; the bottom of the chart indicates how the net profit margin is computed. The total asset turnover ratio is sales divided by the firm's total investment (current assets plus fixed assets). The net profit margin is sales less cost of goods sold, selling and administrative expenses, and taxes (or EAT) divided by sales. The asset turnover ratio multiplied by the net margin yields the ROI.

Symbolically the system is expressed as follows:

$$\text{ROI} = \left(\frac{\text{sales}}{\text{total assets}}\right) \times \left(\frac{\text{EAT}}{\text{sales}}\right)$$

For the XYZ Company, the ROI is

$$\text{ROI} = \frac{\$4,400,000}{\$1,820,000} \times \frac{\$332,000}{\$4,400,000} = (2.4)(.075) = .18$$

as previously calculated. If 18% is below the industry average, reducing the amount invested in assets will increase the asset turnover ratio (with a 7.5% net margin) causing the ROI to rise. There may be an alternative to reducing total assets, however; if the firm's product is price inelastic (i.e., a 1% price increase will cause less than a 1% decrease in units of output sold), a price increase will increase sales

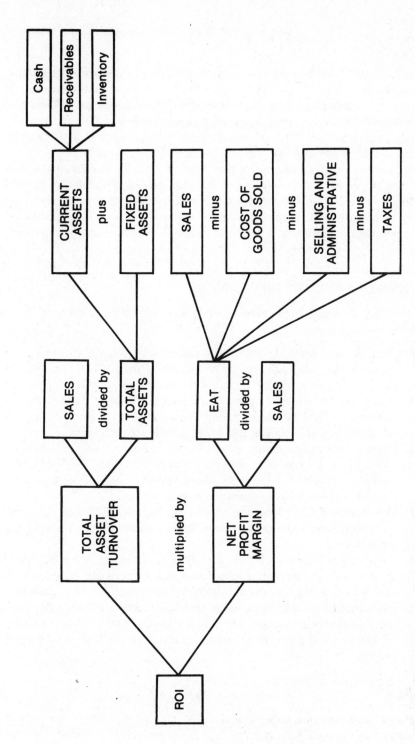

Figure 3-4. Factors affecting return on investment.

49

revenue. The ROI will then increase even though the net margin may remain the same or possibly decrease, depending on how costs behave as sales increase.

However, the basic strategy of the Dupont system is to increase efficiency by improving both the utilization of assets and costs of production. That is, given the company pricing policy, ROI can be increased by reducing total assets and by lowering cost of goods sold and selling and administrative expenses.

Perhaps ratio analysis and use of the Dupont system are matters of skill and experience or an art, but in any event, they can provide valuable information regarding a firm. The firm may not want to look just like the industry, but ratio analysis by comparison is a starting point for the firm or anyone interested in the firm. As emphasized, however, a source of industry ratios for comparison purposes is required.

SOURCES OF INDUSTRY INFORMATION

Standard financial ratios are published for a number of industries. A few of the more important sources are

1. **Dun & Bradstreet.** In financial statement analysis, the standards published by Dun & Bradstreet enjoy widespread use. D & B is a national business credit reporting organization that publishes standards for 14 ratios in 125 industry groups. These groups consist of 24 retailers, 30 wholesalers, and 71 manufacturing and construction areas. D & B gives an upper quartile, median, and lower quartile for each ratio.
2. **Robert Morris Associates.** Robert Morris Associates, a national association of bank loan officers, publishes *Statement Studies*. This publication includes 11 ratios for 156 types of business firms as well as percentage breakdowns for balance sheets and income statements.
3. **The National Cash Expense Norms.** The National Cash Register Company distributes expense percentages based on sales for 63 different lines of business.
4. **Government agencies.** Within the federal government, the Federal Trade Commission and the Securities and Exchange Commission jointly publish quarterly financial data for manufacturing concerns. This joint effort presents balance sheet and income statement information as well as an analysis of industry groupings. The Small Business Administration and the United States Department of Commerce also distribute financial statement studies.

Summary

This chapter was concerned with the analysis of financial statements. One goal of the chapter was to identify the users of financial statements, the reasons for their interest, and the portion of the financial statements they would be most concerned with examining. A second objective of the chapter was to present, illustrate, and interpret the various financial ratios that interested persons have available to gauge the economic performance of a company. The ratios used in this technique of financial statement analysis were divided into four classifications: (1) liquidity, (2) activity, (3) coverage and leverage, and (4) profitability ratios.

Questions

1. Who are the primary users of financial statements? What are their principal areas of concern in the analysis of financial statements?
2. Into what broad classes may the accounting ratios be divided?
3. What operational rules should be consistently applied when using ratio analysis?
4. How does the current ratio differ from the acid test ratio?
5. What financial ratios measure the ability of a firm to meet its maturing short- and long-term obligations?
6. What apparent contradictions exist in the analysis of the inventory turnover and receivables turnover ratios?
7. What is the purpose of coverage and leverage ratios?
8. Why was the cash flow coverage ratio developed? What is the major deterrent to its use?
9. Explain the concept of financial leverage.

Problems

1. Selected financial information for the Pud Corporation is given in the following table. Compute the current ratio, the acid test ratio, the receivables turnover ratio, and the inventory turnover ratio. Evaluate the liquidity of the Pud Corporation:

	1978	1979	1980
Cash	$ 34,000	$ 74,000	$ 90,000
Marketable securities	60,000	48,000	99,000
Accounts receivable	96,000	103,000	111,000
Notes receivable	20,000	16,000	12,000
Inventory	270,000	125,000	155,000
Total current assets	$480,000	$366,000	$467,000
Current liabilities	165,000	210,000	260,000
Annual credit sales	460,000	534,000	585,000
Cost of goods sold	450,000	572,000	600,000

2. Consider the following information for the Gumball Corporation:
a. Balance sheet, December 31, 1980:

Cash	$ 100	Accounts payable	$ 200
Accounts receivable	300	Short-term debt	200
Inventory	300	Long-term debt	300
Net fixed assets	300	Equity	300
Total	$1,000		$1,000

b. Consider the following selected ratios:

	Firm		Industry		
	1979	1978	1980	1979	1978
Current ratio	1.75	1.75	1.50	1.50	1.60
Acid test ratio	1.00	1.10	.90	1.00	.80
Receivables turnover ratio	13	12	12	12	12
Inventory turnover ratio	6	6	5	5	5

If the firm's credit sales and cost of goods sold for 1980 are $3,600 and $1,800, respectively, would you lend this firm $100 for 180 days?

3. The following information was taken from the financial statements of the Whing Ding Company:

	1978	1979	1980
Total sales	$750	$850	$860
Credit sales	420	520	550
Cost of goods sold	450	595	645
Cash	50	60	55
Accounts receivable	150	165	180
Inventory	130	160	170
Net fixed assets	120	260	250
Accounts payable	75	85	100
Short-term debt	125	175	170
Long-term debt	125	185	175
Equity	125	200	210

Calculate those ratios that indicate the efficient use of assets and discuss potential sources of trouble.

4. The Al Falfa Corporation reported the following liabilities and equities for the past year:

Current liabilities	$275,000
Bonds payable (5%)	200,000
Bonds payable (7%)	150,000
Preferred stock (6% cumulative)	100,000
Common stock	100,000
Paid-in capital	50,000
Retained earnings	75,000

In addition, the firm must make a sinking fund payment of $25,000 on the 7% bonds at the end of each year. Al Falfa had earnings after taxes of $22,000 with a combined corporate tax rate of 45%. Compute all coverage and leverage and profitability ratios possible from the data supplied.

5. Given the following information for the B. Low Parr Company at the end of 1980, determine account balances for the income statement and balance sheet as shown:

Net sales	$100,000
Receivables turnover ratio (based on net sales)	2

Inventory turnover ratio	1.25
Fixed asset turnover ratio	.8
Debt-asset ratio	.6
Gross profit margin	25%
Net profit margin	5%
Return on investment	2%

B. LOW PARR COMPANY

Income Statement
for the Year Ending December 31, 1980

Sales	$100,000
Cost of goods sold	_____
Gross profit margin	_____
Other expenses	_____
Earnings before taxes	_____
Taxes @ 50%	_____
Earnings after taxes	_____

Balance Sheet
as of December 31, 1980

Cash	_____	Short-term debt	$50,000
Accounts receivable	_____	Long-term debt	_____
Inventory	_____	Total debt	_____
Net fixed assets	_____	Equity	_____
Total assets	_____	Total liabilities and equity	_____

6. Selected financial data for the Big Sail Boat Company are presented, along with selected ratios for the firm and the industry for several years. If you were the loan officer for the Second River Bank, would you lend Big Sail Boat Company $30,000 for 90 days?

BIG SAIL BOAT COMPANY

Balance Sheet
as of December 31, 1981

Cash	$ 10,000	Accounts payable	$ 10,000
Accounts receivable	30,000	Bank loans (short term)	40,000
Inventory	90,000	Bonds	250,000
Fixed assets	300,000	Equity	130,000
Total	$430,000	Total	$430,000

Income Statement
for the Year Ending December 31, 1981

Sales	$600,000
Cost of goods sold	400,000
Gross profit	200,000
Operating expenses	150,000
Earnings before taxes	50,000
Taxes (40%)	20,000
Net income	$ 30,000

Selected Ratios:	1981 Ind.	1980 Firm	1980 Ind.	1979 Firm	1979 Ind.
Return on investment	7.00%	7.00%	7.00%	7.00%	7.00%
Gross profit margin	30%	30%	30%	30%	30%
Current	2	2.5	2	2.8	2
Acid test	1	1.2	1	1.3	1
Receivables turnover	12	15	12	10	12
Inventory turnover	6	5	6	4	6

7. The following are data from the comparative income statements and balance sheets for 1978, 1979, and 1980 for Sonwil Sporting Goods Company. Calculate all ratios within the four classes of ratios, except the cash flow coverage ratio.

SONWIL SPORTING GOODS COMPANY

Income Statements for Years Ending December 31, 1978, 1979 and 1980
(in thousands of dollars)

	1978	1979	1980
Net sales	$2,000	$2,500	$2,600
Cost of goods sold	1,320	1,700	1,820
Gross profit	680	800	780
Operating expenses:			
Selling, general, and administrative expenses	420	590	570
Depreciation expense (not included in CGS)	110	80	60
Total	530	670	630
Operating income	150	130	150
Other revenue	20	15	25
Other expense	100	85	95
Net income before taxes	70	60	80
Income tax expense (40%)	28	24	32
Income after taxes	$ 42	$ 36	$ 48

Balance Sheets at December 31, 1978, 1979, and 1980
(in thousands of dollars)*

	1978	1979	1980
Current assets			
Cash	$ 20	100	$ 60
Accounts receivable	300	325	340
Inventory	250	300	300
Notes receivable	60 .	81	70
Total current assets	630	806	770
Fixed assets			
Land	125	125	125
Plant and equipment	900	900	1,500
Less: Accumulated depreciation	(575)	715	(890)
Patents	40	35	30
Total fixed assets	490	345	765
Total assets	$1,120	$1,151	$1,535

Current liabilities			
Accounts payable	$ 225	$ 240	$ 265
Notes payable	75	109	92
Current portion of long-term debt	50	50	70
Income taxes payable	28	24	32
Total current liabilities	378	423	459
Long-term debt			
Bonds payable (8%)	100	100	100
Mortgages payable	300	250	400
Total long-term debt	400	350	500
Total liabilities	778	773	959
Stockholders' equity			
Common stock (20,000 shares of $1 par value outstanding)	20	20	30
Paid-in capital in excess of par	100	100	240
Retained earnings	222	258	306
Total stockholders' equity	342	378	576
Total liabilities and stockholders' equity	$1,120	$1,151	$1,535

The bonds are 8%, 10-year bonds. The mortgages carry a 10% interest rate on the unpaid balance; the current portion of long-term debt is paid on January 2 of the succeeding year. Annual lease payments are $25.

8. a. Balance sheet and income statement information for 1980 follow for PepSee Soda Company. Mr. Scrooge of the Last State Bank is considering the company's short-term loan application. He must base his decision on the information provided by the company and the industry averages. If you were Mr. Scrooge, would you approve the loan? Explain.

Assets

Cash	$ 32,000
Accounts receivable	240,000
Inventory	480,000
Net fixed assets	1,536,000
Total	$2,228,000

Liabilities and Equity

Accounts payable	$ 368,000
Accrued liabilities	320,000
Short-term bank loans	160,000
Long-term debt	480,000
Common stock	160,000
Retained earnings	800,000
Total	$2,288,000

Income Data

Sales	$6,400,000
Cost of goods sold	5,120,000
Earnings after taxes	480,000

Industry Averages

Current ratio	1.8
Acid test ratio	.9
Inventory turnover	15.0
Receivable turnover	21.0
Fixed asset turnover	10.0
Net profit margin	8.0%

b. Comparative balance sheet and income statement information (in thousands of dollars) are as follows for PepSee Soda Company for the years 1978, 1979, and 1980. Industry data are provided in (a). Mr. Peek of the Fifteenth National Bank is considering the company's short-term loan application. Should Mr. Peek approve the loan? Explain.

Assets	1978	1979	1980
Cash	$ 858	$ 531	$ 32
Accounts receivable	195	216	240
Inventory	245	384	480
Net fixed assets	556	929	1,536
Total	$1,854	$2,060	$2,288

Liabilities and Equity			
Accounts payable	$ 298	$ 331	$ 368
Accrued liabilities	260	288	320
Short-term bank loans	130	144	160
Long-term debt	432	432	480
Common stock	160	160	160
Retained earnings	574	705	800
Total	$1,854	$2,060	$2,288

Income Data			
Sales	$5,184	$5,760	$6,400
Cost of goods sold	4,147	4,608	5,120
Earnings after taxes	415	461	480

BIBLIOGRAPHY

Bernstein, Leopold A. *Financial Statement Analysis*. Homewood, Ill.: Richard D. Irwin, Inc., 1974.

Chen, Kung H., and Thomas A. Shimerda. "An Empirical Analysis of Useful Financial Ratios." *Financial Management*, Vol. 10, No. 1 (Spring 1981), pp. 51–60.

Kieso, Donald E., and Jerry J. Weygandt. *Intermediate Accounting*. New York: John Wiley & Sons, Inc., 1974, Chaps. 2 and 8.

Lagay, James A. III, and Clyde P. Stickney. Cash Flows, Ratio Analysis, and the W. T. Grant Company Bankruptcy." *Financial Analysts Journal*, July–August 1980, pp. 51–54.

CHAPTER 4

Pro Forma Financial Statements and Cash Budgets

Three of the most important management activities of a firm, regardless of its size, are controlling current operations, planning for future operations, and forecasting events on which plans for future operations can be based. The objective of this chapter is to describe, illustrate, and apply analytical tools that facilitate forecasting, which in turn provides the foundation for planning and controlling the operation of the firm. First, this chapter discusses forecasting, planning, and control. Then the pro forma income statement is developed and the cash budget is considered. The last section formulates the pro forma balance sheet and illustrates how risk can be incorporated into the planning process.

FORECASTING, PLANNING, AND CONTROL

The essential ingredient of planning is the sales forecast. Sales forecasting techniques run the gamut from the very simple to the highly complex. Perhaps the most fundamental, if not the most widely used technique, is the subjective forecast made by a key decision maker in the firm. Such a forecast relies on the decision maker's knowledge of firm, industry, and general economic conditions. A second forecasting technique is a simple time extrapolation or trend analysis of sales. A third approach requires consolidating the sales estimates of several key people such as the firm's sales managers or salesmen. Fourth, a firm may be large enough to have a marketing research department that uses sophisticated statistical and econometric models to forecast sales. Fifth, the company may use an outside consulting firm that specializes in providing sales forecasts.

Regardless of the technique used (or the accuracy of the forecast), the sales forecast is the basis for all else that follows. These single forecasts are the foundation for production planning, marketing, and financial budgets. The various budgets can then be translated into pro forma income statements, cash budgets, and pro forma balance sheets. The pro forma income statement shows the predicted behavior of revenue, costs, and earnings over the planning period. The cash budget indicates the various sources and uses of cash, their amounts, and the timing of receipts and disbursements. The pro forma balance sheet illustrates the impact of operations on assets and liabilities at the end of the planning period.

Control of the firm, once it enters the time period for which plans were developed, requires monitoring actual performance and comparing it to these plans. If performance and plans match, in general little or no corrective action will be needed. However, if performance is contrary to plans, an investigation into the causes of the deviations should be initiated and steps taken to correct the conditions that caused the performance deviation.

THE PRO FORMA INCOME STATEMENT

Once the sales forecast is made, the pro forma income statement can be constructed. To do so, all other revenue besides sales revenue, cost of goods sold, selling and administrative expenses, and all other expenses must be estimated. The pro forma income statement should reflect management's best estimate of operations during the planning period. Cost of goods sold may be estimated by compiling the various production budgets or by top management decree that a specific gross profit margin be attained for each product line or division within the firm. Other expenses may be estimated by compiling estimates from the various departments concerned or by estimating them as a certain percentage of sales or other amount. However these cost estimates are obtained, it must be recognized that past costs or historical costs are relevant to the pro forma income statement only if they are the costs expected to continue in the future. For example, if raw materials and labor costs are expected to increase in the future, these increased cost figures are the ones that must be used to estimate cost of goods sold for the pro forma income statement.

Gross profit is calculated by subtracting estimated costs of goods sold from sales revenue, and EBT are calculated by subtracting operating expenses from gross profit. Selling expenses could include such items as sales representative's salaries and commissions, transportation costs, sales office salaries, postage and stationery expense, advertising expenditures, and travel costs. Administrative expenses could include administrative officers' salaries, clerical salaries, insurance premiums, depreciation (office equipment, etc.), and supplies. Some of these expenses, such as sales commissions, will vary as sales vary; that is, they are considered variable expenses. Other expenses, such as depreciation on office equipment, are fixed; they do not change as sales or output change. However, both variable and fixed expenses can change from one year to the next, and these new costs must be included in the estimates of operating expenses. For example, if sales commissions are to be increased by 2% of sales and officers' salaries will be raised by 6% of their current levels, then these additional costs must be included in the estimation of operating expenses.

After all revenues and expenses have been estimated to arrive at EBT, EAT must be determined. The various municipal, state and federal taxes must be estimated and subtracted from earnings before taxes to arrive at earnings after taxes.

The procedure as outlined can be combined with the sales forecast to illustrate the construction of monthly pro forma income statements for January, February, and March. The assumptions required to construct these income statements are as follows:

1. The most likely sales levels for each month are $150,000, $210,000, $210,000 and $300,000 in January, February, March, and April, respectively.
2. Cost of goods sold is 80% of sales; material purchases are made one month in advance of sales.
3. Operating expenses are estimated at

	January	February	March
Salaries	$30,000	$40,000	$40,000
Rent	2,000	2,000	2,000
Depreciation	2,500	2,500	2,500
Quarterly interest at 6% on $500,000 (accrued)	2,500	2,500	2,500

4. The corporate tax rate is 40%.

Table 4-1 contains the monthly and quarterly pro forma income statement for the first quarter.

These monthly pro forma income statements are an explicit statement of management's expectations of revenues, costs, and earnings during the planning period. Given the assumptions and/or decisions used to construct these statements, a loss is expected each month during the first quarter. The purpose of the pro forma income statement is to indicate expected profitability and allow management sufficient time to control or influence these results by seeking alternatives that could change revenues and/or costs and ultimately its profitability. While management may or may not be able to change its plans and influence these expected losses, it would also want to have an estimate of the cash or liquidity position of the firm over the same

Table 4-1   Three Months and First Quarter, Pro Forma Income Statements

	January	February	March	Quarter
Net sales	$150,000	$210,000	$210,000	$570,000
Cost of goods sold	120,000	168,000	168,000	456,000
Gross earnings	30,000	42,000	42,000	114,000
Operating expenses				
Salaries	30,000	40,000	40,000	110,000
Rent	2,000	2,000	2,000	6,000
Depreciation	2,500	2,500	2,500	7,500
Interest	2,500	2,500	2,500	7,500
Earnings before taxes (loss)	(7,000)	(5,000)	(5,000)	(17,000)
Taxes (credit)	(2,800)	(2,000)	(2,000)	(6,800)
Earnings after taxes (loss)	$ (4,200)	$ (3,000)	$ (3,000)	$ (10,200)

time period because that is another important facet of the firm's operation. Such an estimate or plan is provided by the cash budget.

THE CASH BUDGET

The cash budget is a pro forma statement that the financial manager uses in planning and controlling daily, weekly, monthly, and quarterly cash flows for a period as long as a year. Financial managers are interested in three related areas to plan for and control the cash position of the firm: the sources and uses of funds, their amounts, and their timing.

First, financial managers must identify the sources and uses of cash. The manager needs to know where all funds will be obtained. Additionally, they need to know how the firm plans to expend these funds.

Second, not only must financial managers identify the sources and uses of cash, but they also need to know the total amount of these planned receipts and disbursements. If they can accurately estimate the total receipts and disbursements over a given time period, they will be able to identify the cash shortages or surpluses expected in that period. Financial managers are interested in both shortages as well as surpluses. If they expect a shortage, they can plan for it and find the best, least cost, source of funds to meet the shortage. Worse yet, if an extremely tight money market exists, they can recognize that sources of funds may dry up and alert other managers to the possible necessity of a cutback in operations.

A surplus of cash will be just as much a concern to the financial manager as a shortage, because this also requires planning and advance notice. Cash, above a minimum operating amount, should not be left idle, since by doing so the firm forgoes interest revenue and thus causes net earnings to be less than they would be otherwise. If the financial manager can accurately estimate the amount of surplus cash, he or she can make plans to invest these idle funds in highly liquid, risk-free, interest-bearing assets such as U.S. government securities.

Third, financial managers must know when to expect surpluses and shortages if they are to invest idle funds or search out sources of funds to meet shortages. Consequently, financial managers are interested in the timing of cash shortages and surpluses. The mechanism of the cash budget aids the financial manager in explicitly recognizing and planning for (1) sources and uses of cash, (2) cash shortages and surpluses, and (3) the timing of cash flows.

Although any one of a number of formats may be adopted for the cash budget, the persons constructing and/or utilizing the cash budget must be fully aware of its tentative nature. In constructing the cash budget, many conditions and operating decisions pertinent to cash flows are assumed. Conditions and decisions may change, however, requiring adjustment in the cash budget. If the cash budget is not carefully monitored for possible changes as new information becomes available, it will fail to provide the up-to-date information required for optimum use of cash.

To construct the cash budget for tbe ABC Company, the assumptions on which the income statement were made must be reviewed. These assumptions were

1. The levels of sales in January, February, and March are estimated at $150,000, $210,000, and $210,000, respectively.
2. Cost of goods sold is 80% of sales, with material purchases made one month in advance of sales.
3. Operating expenses requiring cash are estimated at

	January	February	March
Salaries	$30,000	$40,000	$40,000
Rent	2,000	2,000	2,000
Depreciation	2,500	2,500	2,500
Interest at 6% of $500,000	—	—	7,500

4. The corporate tax rate is 40%.

In addition, the following information pertaining to, and decisions affecting, cash movement is assumed:

5. Sales are 75% credit and 25% cash.
6. Credit sales are collected as follows:
   60% collected within the first month following sale.
   30% collected within the second month following sale.
   10% collected within the third month following sale.

7. Total sales in October, November, and December were $300,000, $350,000, and $400,000, respectively.
8. Raw materials that are purchased one month in advance of sale are paid for in the month purchased. However, starting in March, purchases will be paid for the month following purchase.
9. Wages and rent are paid in the month incurred.
10. Interest on the long-term debt is paid quarterly; a quarterly dividend on common stock of $2,000 is to be paid in March.
11. The minimum cash balance required is $100,000, and this is the cash balance at the beginning of January.
12. The firm expects to sell common stock in March with net proceeds of $500,000.
13. A new piece of equipment is to be purchased for $600,000 and paid for in March.
14. Long-term debt is to be reduced by $100,000 in March.

Since considerable detail is required to construct a cash budget, it may be helpful to use a worksheet to compile certain subsections before constructing the complete cash budget. Table 4-2 contains a worksheet designed to facilitate the determination of collections on accounts receivable.

The first entry in Table 4-2 is sales. Sales for the last three months of the previous year are actual values, whereas sales for January, February, and March are expected sales. Assumption 5 allows actual and expected sales to be divided into credit and cash sales. Assumption 6 provides the necessary information to compute collections on accounts receivable. Computations of collections for the latter part of the year are not really required, since we are interested in developing monthly cash budgets for the first 3 months of the coming year, but are included to facilitate understanding of the computation process. In October, credit sales were $225,000 (75% of $300,000). In November, December, and January, collections of 60%,

Table 4-2 Worksheet: Collections on Accounts Receivable

		Oct.	Nov.	Dec.	Jan.	Feb.	Mar.
Sales		$300,000	$350,000	$400,000	$150,000	$210,000	$210,000
Cash sales		75,000	87,500	100,000	37,500	52,500	52,500
Credit sales		225,000	262,500	300,000	112,500	157,500	157,500
Collections:	60%		135,000	157,500	180,000	67,500	94,500
	30%			67,500	78,750	90,000	33,750
	10%				22,500	26,250	30,000
Collections on accounts receivable					$281,250	$183,750	$158,250

Table 4-3 A Cash Budget

	January	February	March
Beginning cash balance	$100,000	$100,000	$100,000
Receipts: Cash sales	37,500	52,500	52,500
Collections	281,250	183,750	158,250
Other	—	—	500,000
Total cash available	418,750	336,250	810,750
Uses: Purchases	168,000	168,000	—
Salaries	30,000	40,000	40,000
Rent	2,000	2,000	2,000
Interest and dividends	—	—	9,500
Other	—	—	700,000
Total Disbursements	200,000	210,000	751,500
Cash available end of period	218,750	126,250	59,250
Less: Minimum Cash Balance	100,000	100,000	100,000
Surplus (shortage)	$118,750	$ 26,250	($ 40,750)
Investment (borrowing)	$118,750	$ 26,250	($ 40,750)

30%, and 10%, respectively, are made. Reading diagonally down the table, the corresponding dollar amounts of $135,000, $67,500, and $22,500 are collected in these 3 months. The calculations of collections for the remaining months are obtained in the same manner. Collections on accounts receivable in each of the first 3 months of the coming year are obtained by summing the collections on the preceding months' sales.

The cash budget can now be constructed using the other assumptions and operating plans specified as it appears in Table 4-3. Total cash available each month is the summation of the cash balances at the beginning of the month, cash sales, collections on accounts receivable, and other sources. Other sources for March contains the entry of $500,000 from the sale of common stock only. Total monthly disbursements are the summation of all cash uses. The use of cash for purchases in March is zero because management, while still making material purchases a month in advance of sales, decides to buy on 30-day credit terms. Because interest on debt and common stock dividends are paid quarterly, March is the only month in which there is an entry. The other entry in March for cash use reflects the $100,000 reduction of debt principal and the $600,000 asset purchase. After the management requirement of a minimum cash balance of $100,000 is met, there are surpluses of $118,750 and $26,250 in January and February that can be invested in highly liquid, risk-free, interest-bearing U.S. government securities. In March, a deficit of $40,750 exists after meeting the minimum cash requirement. The firm has the option of selling $40,750 of the $118,750 invested in U.S. government securities from its January investment, or it may borrow $40,750 in March. It is also possible that management may choose to abandon its minimum cash balance requirement temporarily. All these options are available, and the construction of the cash budget allows management sufficient time to consider the alternatives.

Because there are various types of cash budgets in practice and the amount of detail also varies considerably, it should be helpful to point out that the overriding concept in the construction of a cash budget, regardless of format and detail, is

$$\text{Beginning cash balance} + \text{cash inflows} = \text{cash outflows}$$
$$-\text{ending cash balance}$$

Keeping this concept in mind will aid understanding the cash budget regardless of the format used.

Cash Summary

This cash equation can be used to construct a cash summary. The cash summary does not contain the detail (itemized cash inflows and outflows) found in a cash budget, but it does stress major changes in the cash account. Most firms start a time period with a beginning cash balance (BCB) that increases as cash inflows (CAI) occur and falls because of cash outflows (CAO). An overview of these amounts is frequently desired by management. Furthermore, management may desire to know the amount of borrowing (B), of cumulative borrowing (CUM B), of loans repaid (R), of investigable funds (IF), and of cumulative investment (CUM I).

A modified cash equation using these symbols is developed as follows (where TECB is the tentative ending cash balance):

$$\text{BCB} + \text{CAI} - \text{CAO} = \text{TECB}$$

That is, the beginning cash balance plus cash inflows less cash outflows equals the tentative ending cash balance (TECB). It is a TECB because adjustments must be made for borrowing or sale of marketable securities, if TECB < BCB, or for repayment of loans or for funds invested, if TECB > BCB. Thus,

$$\text{TECB} + \text{B} - \text{R} - \text{IF} + \text{SOS} = \text{ECB}$$

The ECB for any period becomes the BCB for the next period. Since management may have a desired BCB, it may have to borrow (or sell marketable securities, SOS) to insure that this amount is present to begin the next period. When this occurs, B is added to TECB; R = 0, SOS = 0, and IF = 0. If marketable securities are sold, SOS is added to TECB, and all else have values of zero. At other times, the TECB may be large enough to repay previous borrowings. If this is the case, R is subtracted from TECB, and B and IF are both equal to zero. There are other possible combinations as well.

Perhaps, an example will clarify the cash summary. For the previous cash budget, the BCB was equal to $100,000. The cash receipts for each month for the quarter becomes the CAI; and CAO is just total disbursements. These data and IF, SOS, and B are contained in Table 4-3. Table 4-4 shows the cash summary schedule for the first six months of the year. The values for April, May, and June were obtained from cash budgets for these months. These cash budgets are *not* shown.

In March, the firm begins the month with $100,000, experiences a $710,750 cash inflow from all sources, and expects cash outflows to be $751,500. The TECB is $59,250—$100,000 − $59,250—or $40,750 below the ECB desired. The plans are to borrow this amount as shown in the B row. The ECB will then equal $100,000. For this month, there are no plans to repay previous loans, invest funds, or sell marketable securities. The loan balance at the end of December equals $130,000, and no borrowing is expected until March. Consequently, the cumulative loan balance is shown as $130,000 for January and February. In March, the CUM L balance is expected to increase to $170,750 because of the $40,750 shortage. A similar explanation exists for all months.

The last two rows of the cash summary can be important for determining the maturity structure of short-term loans and marketable security investments. The $40,750 loan might have a 30-day maturity if the firm plans to repay it at the beginning of May. Also, the $130,000 loan may have had a six-month maturity

Table 4-4 A Cash Summary Schedule

Item	Jan.	Feb.	Mar.	Apr.	May	June
BCB	$100,000	$100,000	$100,000	$100,000	$100,000	$100,000
CAI	318,750	236,250	710,750	300,000	220,750	300,000
CAO	200,000	210,000	751,500	325,000	200,000	230,000
TECB	218,750	126,250	59,250	75,000	120,750	170,000
B	-0-	-0-	40,750	-0-	-0-	-0-
R	-0-	-0-	-0-		170,750	-0-
IF	118,750	26,250	-0-	-0-	-0-	70,000
SOS	-0-	-0-	-0-	25,000	150,000	-0-
ECB	100,000	100,000	100,000	100,000	100,000	100,000
CUM L	130,000*	130,000	170,750	170,750	-0-	-0-
CUM I	148,750**	175,000	175,000	150,000	-0-	70,000

*Loan balance from December.
**Includes $30,000 in marketable securities purchased in December.

because management had made these decisions in December based on these pro forma statements. Likewise, the firm began January with $30,000 in invested funds and expects to purchase $118,750 and $26,250 more in January and February, respectively. The cumulative investment in marketable securities (CUM I) is $175,000 by March. Since management plans to repay all short-term borrowing in May, the funds invested in January might have a 90-day maturity while funds invested in February might have a 60-day maturity. (Generally, the cost of borrowing exceeds the yield that nonfinancial firms can earn on invested funds; thus, the firm would most likely pay off the borrowing before investing in marketable securities.)

THE PRO FORMA BALANCE SHEET

Whereas the cash budget indicates liquidity and pro forma income statement profitability, the pro forma balance sheet illustrates the expected overall impact of plans and operations on assets and liabilities. Once the pro forma income statement and

Table 4-5 An Actual and Pro Forma Balance Sheet

Assets	December Actual	March Pro Forma
Cash	$ 100,000	$ 100,000
Marketable securities	30,000	175,000
Prepaid taxes	—	6,800
Accounts receivable	427,500	231,750
Inventory	280,000	400,000
Total current assets	837,500	913,550
Plant, property, and equipment	350,000	950,000
Less: Accumulated depreciation	90,000	97,500
Net fixed assets	260,000	852,500
Total assets	$1,097,500	$1,766,050
Liabilities and Equity		
Accounts payable	—	240,000
Notes payable	130,000	170,750
Total current liabilities	130,000	410,750
Bonds payable	500,000	400,000
Total liabilities	630,000	810,750
Common stock, $5 par value	200,000	700,000
Retained earnings	267,500	255,300
Total liabilities and equity	$1,097,500	$1,766,050

cash budget are completed, the pro forma balance sheet naturally follows. The pro forma balance sheet can be constructed for each month, but its relative importance for planning and operations may not justify such treatment. Consequently, the balance sheet is constructed for the end of the first quarter.

Typically, the construction of a pro forma balance sheet requires information from three sources. First, actual asset and liability levels from the last period of operations are required. Table 4-5 contains the actual December balance sheet and the pro forma balance sheet ending in March. Second, taxes and changes in retained earnings through net income (or loss) and dividend payments must be obtained from the pro forma income statement. Third, data from the cash budget are required.

The minimum cash balance, investments in marketable securities, total borrowing, and value of the new fixed asset can be obtained from the cash budget and added to the respective amounts from the December actual balance sheet to obtain the expected values in March. The $6,800 in prepaid taxes reflects first quarter losses and is carried as an asset because it can be used in later quarters to offset the tax liability of future earnings. Accounts payable is determined by the March purchases for April sales that will not be paid for until April. Debt entries are obtained from the changes in debt that are part of the cash budget. The increase in accumulated depreciation of $7,500 is from the pro forma income statements. The change in the common stock is also available from the cash budget. The accounts receivable, retained earnings and inventory entries are somewhat more involved. The accounts receivable entry is found from the relationship of beginning accounts receivable + credit sales = collections + ending accounts receivable:

December accounts receivable	$427,500
Plus: Credit sales for the quarter	427,500
Total	855,000
Less: Collections for the quarter	623,250
Equals: Accounts receivable in March	$231,750

A similar procedure is used to find the March ending inventory inasmuch as beginning inventory + purchases = cost of goods sold + ending inventory:

December ending inventory	$280,000
Plus: Purchases during the quarter	576,000
Equals: Total available	856,000
Less: Cost of goods sold for the quarter	456,000
Equals: Ending inventory in March	$400,000

In addition, ending retained earnings can be obtained in a similar manner:

December retained earnings	$267,500
Less: Dividend	2,000
Loss for the quarter	10,200
Equals: Retained earnings in March	$255,300

SENSITIVITY ANALYSIS OF PROFITABILITY AND LIQUIDITY

In the initial discussion of sales forecasting, probability distributions of future sales were established and the expected sales for each month were calculated from these distributions. The pro forma income statement, cash budget, and pro forma balance sheets were then constructed using only the expected level of sales for each month.

An integral part of the planning process, however, is preparation for unforeseen events. As such, it is appropriate that some measure of risk be incorporated into the analysis of pro forma statements and cash budgets. The framework of sensitivity analysis can be used to identify those areas within the planning process that are particularly sensitive to risk.

It is possible to perform sensitivity analysis of earnings on a monthly basis. For this example, however, it seems more practical to examine percentage deviations from quarterly earnings after taxes as a result of percentage deviations from expected sales for the quarter. A loss is still forecast for each month of the first quarter even if the expected level of sales is achieved. Thus, any corrective measures taken to improve earnings are most likely to apply to all three months of the first quarter.

Table 4-6 shows how sensitive earnings after taxes are to changes in sales. However, several assumptions were necessary to construct the table. First, sales in each month change by the same percentage as the percentage change in quarterly sales. Second, the gross margin remains at 20%, which means that the cost of goods sold changes by the same percentage as the change in sales. Third, operating expenses are fixed or do not change as sales change. Under these conditions, a 10% decrease in sales from the expected level for the quarter will result in a 67% decrease (a greater loss) in earnings. That is, if sales are only $513,000 rather than the expected $570,000, a 10% decline, the loss increases from $10,200 to $17,040, or 67%: ($17,040 − $10,200)/$10,200. Since small changes in sales cause proportionately larger changes in earnings, it can be concluded that earnings are very sensitive to changes in sales.

Note that any change in the assumptions on which Table 4-6 was constructed must change the influence of sales on earnings. For example, if cost of goods sold contains fixed expenses that do not change as sales change, their impact on earnings will be more pronounced than illustrated in Table 4-6.

A similar analysis can be made for liquidity, but it is much more involved because monthly cash flows are necessary. Table 4-6 summarizes the sensitivity analysis of the cash available at the end of the period to changes in sales for the

Table 4-6 First Quarter Profitability Sensitivity

Percentage Deviations in Sales	Sales	Gross Earnings	EBT*	Taxes	EAT	Change in EAT	Percentage Deviations in EAT
-20%	$456,000	$ 91,200	$(39,800)	$(15,920)	$(23,880)	$-13,680	-134%
-10	513,000	102,600	(28,400)	(11,360)	(17,040)	-6,840	-67
—	570,000	114,000	(17,000)	(6,800)	(10,200)	—	—
+10	627,000	125,400	(5,600)	(2,240)	(3,360)	+6,840	+67
+20	684,000	136,800	5,800	2,320	3,480	+13,680	+134

*Operating expenses for all sales levels are equal to $131,000.

Table 4-7 Cash Flow Sensitivity, January

Percentage Deviation in Sales	Sources		Uses		Cash Available End of Period	Changes in Cash Available End of Period	Percentage Deviation in Cash Available End of Period
	Cash Sales	Total	Purchases	Total			
-20%	$30,000	$411,250	$134,400	$166,400	$244,850	$+26,100	+12%
-10	33,750	415,000	151,200	183,200	231,800	+13,050	+6
—	37,500	418,750	168,000	200,000	218,750	—	—
+10	41,250	422,500	184,800	215,800	205,700	-13,050	-6
+20	45,000	426,250	201,600	233,600	192,650	-26,100	-12

Table 4-8 Cash-Flow Sensitivity, February

Percentage Deviation in Sales	Sources			Uses		Cash Available End of Period	Changes in Cash Available End of Period	Percentage Deviation in Cash Available End of Period
	Cash Sales	Collections	Total	Purchases	Total			
−20%	$42,000	$170,250	$312,250	$134,400	$176,400	$135,850	$+9,600	+8%
−10	47,250	177,000	324,250	151,200	193,200	131,050	+4,800	+4
—	52,500	183,750	336,250	168,000	210,000	126,250	—	—
+10	57,750	190,500	348,250	184,800	226,800	121,450	−4,800	−4
+20	63,000	197,250	360,250	201,600	243,600	116,650	−9,600	−8

Table 4-9 Cash-Flow Sensitivity, March

Percentage Deviation in Sales	Sources			Total Uses	Cash Available End of Period	Changes in Cash Available End of Period	Percentage Deviation in Cash Available End of Period
	Cash Sales	Collections	Total				
−20%	$42,000	$132,600	$774,600	$751,500	$23,100	$−36,150	−61%
−10	47,250	145,425	792,675	751,500	41,175	−18,075	−30
—	52,500	158,250	810,750	751,500	59,250	—	—
+10	57,750	171,075	828,825	751,500	77,325	+18,075	+30
+20	63,000	183,900	846,900	751,500	95,400	+36,150	+61

month of January. In January, only one source of cash will change if there is a change in sales. For example, if sales are 10% above the expected value, cash sales will increase from $37,500 to $41,250. Since no other sources change, total sources increase by the change in cash sales ($3,750) from $418,750 to $422,500. The only change in uses of cash will be for purchases for February sales, which will increase by $16,800 if sales are 10% above the expected level in February. The difference between total sources and uses yields the new level of cash available of $205,700. If sales during the quarter are 10% above the expected level, cash available at the end of January will be $13,050 less than the cash available at the expected sales level. Expressed as percentages, the deviation in cash available is a negative 6% as a result of a 10% rise in sales. In an absolute sense, ignoring signs, a 10% change in sales causes a change in cash available of less than 10%; thus, it can be concluded that cash is relatively insensitive to changes in sales.

The sensitivity table for February, Table 4-8, indicates that a 10% deviation in sales causes a 4% deviation in cash available at the end of the period, whereas a 20% deviation in sales results in only an 8% deviation in cash available at the end of February. The signs are opposite to what they were for January. However, as Table 4-9 indicates, the results change dramatically in the month of March, with a change in sales causing a threefold change in cash available. In March, as in February, both cash sales and collections change whereas only cash sales changed in January. Changes in purchases are the same for both January and February, but there will be no change in purchases for March because purchases are to be made on 30-day credit terms beginning in March and thus cash for this purpose is not influenced by the change in sales. The cumulative impact of changes in sales on collections along with the $100,000 reduction in long-term debt now causes sales and cash available at the end of March to move in the same direction, with cash available becoming very sensitive to changes in sales.

The major point indicated by this profitability and liquidity sensitivity analysis is that an immediate profitability problem will exist if sales fall below the expected level but liquidity does not become a concern until March. The concern over liquidity would be justified only if sales fall below their expected levels consistently through the quarter.

Summary

This chapter began with a discussion of forecasting and its role in planning and controlling the operations of a firm. Once sales forecasts were made, pro forma income statements, cash budgets, and pro forma balance sheets were then developed, which are three useful techniques to aid planning and controlling the operation of the firm. Finally, sensitivity analysis was applied to both earnings and cash flow of the firm as a type of contingency budget system that could measure the impact of variability in sales or business risk on the operation of the firm during the first quarter of the coming year.

Questions

1. Regardless of the type of firm, what is the starting point for planning for future operations? In what ways may this starting point be estimated?
2. On what types of data must the pro forma income statement be based?
3. What is the difference between the pro forma income statement and the cash budget?
4. Why is the cash budget important?
5. What information does the pro forma balance sheet provide?
6. How may sensitivity analysis be applied to pro forma statements?

Problems

1. Develop pro forma income statements for the months of July, August, and September for the Klutz Clutch Company from the following information:
   a. Sales are projected at $225,000, $240,000, and $215,000 for July, August, and September, respectively.
   b. Cost of goods is $50,000 plus 30% of selling price per month.
   c. Selling expenses are 3% of sales.
   d. Rent is $7,500 per month; administrative expenses for July are estimated at $60,000, but are expected to rise 1% per month over the previous month's expenses during the next year.
   e. The company has $300,000 of 8% bonds payable outstanding.
   f. The corporate tax rate is 40%.
2. The manager of Sail Aweigh Charter Boat Service has gathered the following information regarding operations in the coming month of May:
   a. Revenue from May charters is expected to be $400,000.
   b. Twenty percent of the charters are paid in cash at the time the boats are taken out.
   c. The remaining 80% are on credit, with collection the month following the charter.
   d. April charter revenue was $300,000.
   e. Variable expenses, paid in the month of charter, are 60% of revenue.
   f. Fixed expenses, paid in the month of charter, are

Wages	$40,000
Depreciation	50,000
Interest	10,000

   g. Beginning cash balance for May is $30,000.
      If the corporate tax rate is 40% and it is assumed the corporation pays its taxes monthly, will the firm have to borrow money in May? If so, how much?
3. Develop a cash budget for the months of January, February, and March for Sam Flott's Jetty Co. from the following information:
   a.

Actual Sales (000)			Projected Sales (000)				
Oct.	Nov.	Dec.	Jan.	Feb.	Mar.	Apr.	May
248	260	320	110	130	160	200	200

of the total, 5% of sales are cash sales, 10% of credit sales are collected in the month of sale, 60% the month following sale, 28% the following month, and the balance are uncollectible.

b. Cost of goods sold is 40% of sales; raw materials, direct labor, and variable overhead are 30%, 50%, and 20% of cost of goods sold, respectively.

c. Finished goods are manufactured each month equal to the average of the next two months' projected sales.

d. Raw materials are purchased 1 month prior to manufacture and are paid for in the month of manufacture. Direct labor and variable overhead are paid in the month of manufacture.

e. Fixed overhead expenses are $75,000 per month paid as incurred.

f. A $25,000 minimum cash balance is maintained and is the beginning cash balance January 1.

g. A quarterly tax payment of $20,000 is due March 15.

h. A $50,000 divided was declared December 15 payable on February 1.

i. The firm borrows or invests in $1,000 units. It must pay 12% interest on funds borrowed and earns 7% on funds invested. Interest on short-term investments and borrowings is paid quarterly.

4. The treasurer of the Bubbling Spring Waterbed Co., Mr. Lee Key, has assembled the following information for you, his new assistant. From this information you are to prepare pro forma income statements and cash budgets for the months of January, February, and March and a balance sheet for the end of March.

Bubbling Spring Waterbed Co.
Balance Sheet
December 31, 1980

Assets		Liabilities	
Cash	$ 5,000	Accounts payable	$ 23,850
Accounts receivable	51,050	6% Bonds payable	150,000
Inventory	31,950	Interest payable	4,500
Fixed assets	200,000	Equities:	
Less: Accumulated depreciation	30,000	Common stock	50,000
Total assets	$258,000	Retained earnings	29,650
		Total liabilities and equities	$258,000

	Actual Sales	Sales Forecasts	
Sept.	$33,000	Jan.	$36,000
Oct.	37,000	Feb.	35,000
Nov.	41,000	Mar.	32,000
Dec.	44,000	Apr.	34,000
		May	38,000

a. Sales are 25% cash; 40% are collected within 30 days; 25% are collected within 60 days; the balance are collected within 90 days.

b. Inventories sufficient for 2 months' projected sales are maintained.

c. Cost of goods sold is 45% of selling price.

d. 50% of purchases for inventory are paid for within 30 days and the balance within 60 days.

e. Selling expenses, paid in the month of sale, are 10% of sales.

f. Rent is $2,500 per month.

g. Other operating expenses, paid in the month incurred, are projected at

Jan.	$15,500
Feb.	12,000
Mar.	11,500

h. A semiannual bond interest payment is due January 1, 1981.

i. Store remodeling in February and March at a total cost of $20,000 will require a cash outlay in March of $10,000.

j. Fixed assets are depreciated at a rate of 1% per month of original cost.

k. Borrowing or disinvestment takes place at the beginning of the month; repayments or investments are made at the end of the month. Investments earn 6% interest; 8% interest must be paid on borrowings. Interest is paid (received) at the beginning (end) of the month following borrowing (investment). Money is borrowed or invested in $100 units only.

l. A minimum cash balance of $5,000 is maintained.

m. Ignore income taxes.

BIBLIOGRAPHY

Orgler, Yair E. *Cash Management: Methods and Models*. Belmont, Calif.: Wadsworth Publishing Company, Inc., 1970, Chap. 1.

Three

Investment in Current Assets

CHAPTER 5

The Management of Cash and Marketable Securities

Typically, a financial manager spends a great deal of time overseeing the funds a firm has invested in current assets—for example, cash, marketable securities, accounts receivable, and inventories. Like fixed assets, current assets tend to have a permanent level in proportion to long-term sales; however, unlike fixed assets, they also tend to have cyclical or seasonal fluctuations proportional to seasonal changes in sales. That is, firms usually maintain a constant ratio of fixed assets to long-term sales, but the level of current assets can be separated into two parts: a permanent portion in which a constant ratio of current assets to the long-term trend in sales is maintained and a cylical portion that rises and falls about this permanent level of current assets as short-term sales change.

Figure 5-1 illustrates this point. The straight lines, from the top of the figure to the bottom, indicate long-term or trend behavior in sales, permanent current assets and fixed assets, respectively. As long as the long-term growth in sales persists, current and fixed assets will also increase to provide the means necessary to satisfy increasing sales. However, seasonal and cyclical changes in sales cause the levels of current assets to rise and fall above their long-term path as indicated by the wavy lines. Note that because of their relatively permanent nature, fixed assets are not subject to change due to seasonal and cyclical changes in sales.

The objective of this and the following chapter is to develop the analytical techniques that make it possible to determine the most profitable levels of cash, marketable securities, accounts receivable, and inventories that a firm should hold

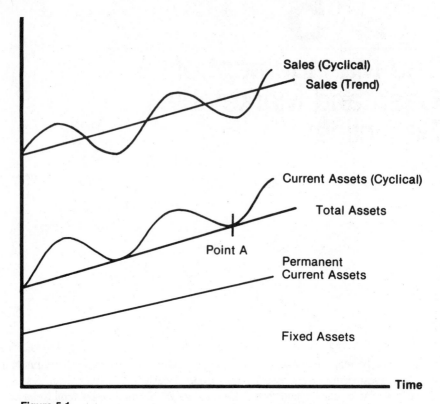

Figure 5-1.

subject to a level of risk acceptable to the firm. Techniques will be developed that
will determine, for a given sales and fixed asset level, the most profitable level of
each of the above current assets which, when added together, will yield a point on a
firm's long-term asset trend line such as Point A in Figure 5-1. Techniques will also
be developed to adjust the levels of each current asset to reflect the risk associated
with seasonal and cyclical changes in sales. This chapter considers the management
of cash and marketable securities; Chapter 6 considers the management of accounts
receivable and inventory.

CASH MANAGEMENT

Individuals hold money (currency and demand deposits) for transaction, precautionary, and speculative reasons. Money held for transaction purposes facilitates economic activity by simplifying the exchange of goods and services. Cash is held for
precautionary reasons because the actual receipt and disbursement of money is
frequently difficult to predict and unforeseen events requiring cash arise often

enough to warrant holding cash to satisfy them (i.e., cash is held to minimize risk). Money is also held for speculative reasons, so that one is able to purchase assets when their prices fall.

The financial manager must be concerned with two specific objectives of cash management: determining the minimum cash balance a firm should hold and determining the amount of funds available to invest in marketable securities. In Chapter 4, the cash budget was summarized by an identity that stated that the beginning cash balance (BCB) plus the cash inflows (CAI) minus cash outflows (CAO) must equal the ending cash balance (ECB). This identity is represented by Equation 5-1:

$$BCB + CAI - CAO = ECB \qquad\qquad (5\text{-}1)$$

The beginning and ending cash balances (BCB and ECB) are decision variables that are under the control of management because they are the levels of cash that management feels will maximize the earnings of the firm and minimize the risk of a cash shortage.

The following example is indicative of how marginal analysis and profitability concepts can be applied to a situation involving cash management.

The management of Speed Manufacturing studied monthly bank statements to determine the pattern of cash receipts and disbursements. A summary of the examination is contained in Table 5-1. The pattern of receipts and disbursements seems to prevail month after month.

A person can be hired to administer cash flows for an annual salary estimated at $10,800, plus $1,500 of support funds. Fringe benefits, over and above the annual salary, are expected to require an additional $3,000 annually.

The bank requires the company to maintain a minimum balance of $50,000, which is the beginning balance for the analysis that follows. If the current interest rate on U.S.

Table 5-1   SPEED MANUFACTURING COMPANY Bank Statement of Cash Receipts and Disbursements

Day of the Month	Amount	Receipts/ Disbursements
2	$500,000	Receipt
5	200,000	Disbursement
11	100,000	Receipt
16	100,000	Receipt
20	200,000	Disbursement
30	300,000	Disbursement

Table 5-2   SPEED MANUFACTURING COMPANY Computations of Interest Earnings and Costs of Investing Cash

Amounts	Free Days	Monthly Interest Earnings	Annual Interest Earnings	Monthly Brokerage Costs	Annual Brokerage Costs
$300,000	28	$1,865	$22,380	$150	$1,800
200,000	3	133	1,596	100	1,200
100,000	9	200	2,400	50	600
100,000	4	89	1,068	50	600
Total		$2,287	$27,444	$350	$4,200

government securities is 8% (a .000222 daily rate based on a 360-day finance year) and the brokerage fee is .05% of a security purchase, should a person administer the cash flows?

Table 5-2 provides data on the amount of temporarily idle cash, the approximate number of days it is idle, the monthly and annual interest earnings, and brokerage fees. For example, of the $500,000 available on the second day of the month, $200,000 is available for investment in securities with a 3-day maturity while $300,000 can be invested in securities with 28-day maturities. The monthly interest earnings are computed by multiplying the idle funds by the daily interest rate and then multiplying this product by the number of free days. The brokerage costs are found by multiplying the brokerage fee by the amounts invested. The marginal contribution to the company's earnings is presented in Table 5-3. Since the addition to revenue ($27,444) is greater than the addition to costs ($19,500) to obtain this revenue, net earnings rise. Consequently, the firm should hire a person to manage the company's cash flow.

The analysis could be extended to consider the implications of variations in the

Table 5-3   SPEED MANUFACTURING COMPANY Revenue, Costs, and Earnings from Cash Management

Annual interest revenue		$27,444
Less: Annual brokerage fees	$ 4,200	
Annual salary	10,800	
Fringe benefits	3,000	
Support funds	1,500	19,500
Equals: Annual addition to earnings before taxes		7,944
Less: Corporate taxes @ 40%		3,178
Equals: Net addition to earnings		$ 4,766

interest rate, receipt and disbursement of cash and the days cash is idle. Again, sensitivity analysis can provide insights into the decision-making process by determining how sensitive net earnings are to changes in these variables. The approach implemented here can also be used to examine other potential cash management technologies and whether or not they should be adopted.

MARKETABLE SECURITIES MANAGEMENT

If cash receipts and disbursements could be forecast with certainty, the firm would hold only enough cash to meet disbursements. All excess cash would be invested in accounts receivable, inventory, or fixed assets. The firm would never invest in marketable securities unless the interest rate on them were to exceed the firm's overall cost of obtaining funds (the cost of capital). Since the interest rate on marketable securities almost never, if ever, exceeds a firm's cost of capital, the firm simply would never hold marketable securities. The point is moot, however, since forecasts of cash receipts and disbursements with pinpoint accuracy are not possible. To compensate for this lack of accuracy and to maximize profits, firms must hold marketable securities because cash and demand deposits do not earn an explicit interest return. Thus, the types of marketable securities and investment evaluation techniques must be examined.

Types of Marketable Securities

Marketable securities are highly liquid, interest-earning, risk-free paper assets. Common stock, preferred stock, and corporate bonds provide earnings in the form of dividends or interest, but they are not highly liquid without risk of price declines. Marketable securities are money market or short term market instruments that are highly salable and are risk free of default on principal and interest payments and on major changes in their value. Included in this definition of marketable securities are several instruments.

Treasury Bills. Treasury bills and certificates are short-term debt of the U.S. government. T-bills, as they are often called, are initially offered in $10,000 denominations with 91- and 182-day maturities and, infrequently, certificates are issued with 9- and 12-month maturities. Treasury bills are noninterest-bearing notes; that is, they are sold at a discount, at less than their face value of $10,000. Their yield or interest return is computed on the difference between the purchasing and selling (or maturity) price.

A very large secondary market exists that allows buying and selling to take place any time between issuing and maturity dates. Since this makes the Treasury bill highly liquid and because the government cannot default on principal repayment, they are a very attractive investment for idle cash. These factors result in the yield on these securities being, in general, the lowest of all money market instruments.

Government Agency Securities. Several agencies of the U.S. government—Federal Intermediate Credit Banks, Banks for Cooperatives, Federal Land Banks, Federal Home Loan Banks, and Federal National Mortgage Associations—offer instruments with higher yields normally than Treasury bills. The secondary market for these securities is large, but their liquidity is not quite as good as that of Treasury bills, which accounts for the yield spread between T-bills and these securities.

Certificates of Deposit. Certificates of deposit (CDs) are time deposits of commercial banks. The largest commercial banks provide the most liquid CDs, which are actively traded in the secondary market. The bulk of the transactions in the secondary market are in round lots of $1 million or multiples thereof; odd lots are transactions in multiples of $100,000 and $250,000. Again, the secondary market for CDs is not as large as that for Treasury bills, but it is sufficient in size to make CDs bear an interest rate just slightly higher than the yield on Treasury bills.

Commercial Paper. Commercial paper is perhaps the oldest of all money market instruments. Commercial paper is negotiable, short-term promissory notes issued by well-known corporations in such fields as manufacturing, retailing, finance, transportation, and mining for a period of 270 days or less. These notes are available in face amounts of $100,000, $250,000, $500,000, and $1,000,000 and in combinations of these amounts. The National Credit Office (a subsidiary of Dun & Bradstreet) rates commercial paper as prime, desirable, and satisfactory. Most commercial paper is rated as prime. The secondary market is not as large as the market for Treasury bills, CDs, and government securities but is adequate enough to provide a fair amount of liquidity. Yields are generally higher than the interest rate on Treasury bills and are compatible with other money market instruments.

Bankers' Acceptances. Bankers' acceptances are one type of a broad class of credit instruments known as bills of exchange. Bills of exchange are drafts or orders to pay specified amounts at a specified time (e.g., in exchange for goods). The draft is drawn by an individual, business firm, or financial institution (the drawer) against another individual, firm, or financial institution (the drawee). The drawee acknowledges or accepts his or her obligation to the drawer by writing "Accept" or "I Accept" and signing his or her name across the face of the draft. At this point an "acceptance" or promissory note has been created; it can be sold and purchased in what is called the acceptance market.

While the acceptance market is relatively small, it is of sufficient size to provide acceptable liquidity if the investor decides to sell prior to maturity. Furthermore, the investors assume very little risk from principal loss; no records exist indicating such a loss has occurred from 1913 to the present.

Objectives of Marketable Securities Management

Absolute maximization of the yield or interest return is not the objective of the management of marketable securities. If it were, idle cash would be invested in common stock or bonds. Rather, the objective is the maintenance of liquidity first and yield improvement second. The various types of money market instruments and variations in their yields allow a great deal of investment discretion while company requirements necessitate that flexibility in cash flows be maintained. However, the necessary cash budgets and desired cash balance requirements must be obtained prior to any decision regarding the type of marketable securities in which the firm is going to invest.

Cash Budgets and Cash Management Models Revisited. As developed in Chapter 4, the cash budget is a plan that attempts to determine sources and uses of funds, cash shortages and surpluses, and the timing of these shortages and uses. In the event of a shortage, the firm must plan to borrow funds; if there is a surplus, the firm should invest the temporarily idle funds. A shortage or surplus cannot, however, be determined until the desired cash balance is known.

An abbreviated cash budget is presented in Table 5-4. The BCB and ECB are the desired cash balances. At best, the determination of future cash receipts and disbursements and, thus, of investible funds is uncertain. The use of the desired cash balance reflects this condition. The receipts and disbursements are obtained by constructing a cash budget. Investible funds (IF) can be computed by Equation 5-2

$$IF = BCB + (CAI - CAO) - ECB \qquad (5\text{-}2)$$

or as illustrated in Table 5-4. Equation 5-2 states that investible funds are equal to the beginning cash balance plus the difference between the cash inflows (CAI) and the cash outflows (CAO) less the ending cash balance. It should be noted that IF could be a negative amount, depending on the values of CAO and ECB. When this

Table 5-4 THE PHARMACEUTICAL COMPANY Cash Budget, Friday, January 24

Beginning cash balance	$ 43,089
Plus: Receipts	477,117
Equals: Total cash available	520,206
Less: Disbursements	277,117
Equals: Cash available	243,089
Less: Required ECB	43,089
Equals: Investible funds	$200,000

is the case, the firm would have to borrow instead of invest funds. However, in this illustration the firm has $200,000 to invest.

Selecting the Money Market Investment. In selecting the investment instrument for idle cash, the primary consideration is liquidity, and only after that should the highest return be sought. An appropriate amount of cash might be invested in the most liquid of money market instruments—Treasury bills. The appropriate amount can only be determined by the financial manager's considering the unique features of the firm. An appropriate amount might be that portion of the available $200,000 not specifically earmarked for future use. If, for example, $30,000, $50,000, and $20,000 will be required in 30 days for taxes, bond interest, and equipment purchases, respectively, the $100,000 tagged for these uses should be invested for 30 days in CDs at a higher interest return but with less liquidity than Treasury bills. The uncommitted $100,00 can be invested until needed in more liquid Treasury bills at a lower return, as a ready reserve.

Buying and Selling Treasury Bills. Treasury bills are traded on a discount basis at bid and ask yields. When a T-bill is purchased, the buyer pays less than its face value. If it is held to maturity, the bill will be redeemed by the Treasury at face value; when it is sold prior to maturity, it is sold for less than its face value. The yield to the holder is the difference between the purchase price and the selling price or face value if held to maturity. A bill that matures in 30 days earns one-thirtieth of the discount each day. For this reason, it is too complicated to quote dollar prices, so trading is done in terms of yields or rates of return. However, the bid and ask yields can be converted into bid and ask prices.

Table 5-5 shows selected bill maturities, their bid and ask yields, and their bid and ask prices. A bid yield is the annualized rate of return that the bill dealer will realize if he or she purchases a bill and holds it to maturity. The ask yield is the rate of return that the buyer will receive if he or she purchases a bill from the bill dealer and holds it to maturity. The difference between the bid and ask yield is the dealer's spread or gross profit; thus, bid and ask yields are net of the bill dealer's transaction costs. However, a firm buying or selling bills incurs incidental transaction costs

Table 5-5   Selected Maturities, Bid and Ask Yields, and Bid and Ask Prices on Treasury Bills

Days to Maturity	Yields		Prices	
	Bid	Ask	Bid	Ask
15	5.4%	5.0%	$99.7750	$99.7917
30	5.7	5.3	99.5250	99.5583
60	6.1	5.7	98.9833	99.0500
90	6.6	6.2	98.3500	98.4500

such as salaries, phone calls, and paperwork associated with trading in marketable securities.

Equation 5-3 can be used to calculate the bid and ask prices (P) per hundred dollars of face value

$$P = \$100\left(1 - \frac{M \cdot D}{360}\right) \qquad\qquad (5\text{-}3)$$

where M = the maturity 30, 60, etc.
       D = the bid or ask yield
       360 = the number of days in a finance year.

For example, the 30-day bid price, which is the amount the bill dealer will pay for a 30-day maturity, is

$$P = \$100\left[1 - \frac{(30)(.057)}{360}\right] = \$99.5250$$

and the ask price, which is the amount a firm must pay to buy a 30-day maturity from the dealer, is

$$P = \$100\left[1 - \frac{(30)(.053)}{360}\right] = \$99.5583$$

If the dealer pays $99.5250 per $100 for a bill and holds it to maturity, he or she receives a 5.7% return for the 30 days. If the the investment is repeated 12 times during the 360-day finance year, the dealer can earn an annual return of 5.7%. Similarly, a firm purchasing a 30-day bill for $99.5583 per $100 of face value realizes a 5.3% rate of return. The remaining bid and ask prices were computed in the same manner, using Equation 5-3.

Since the firm expects to have $200,000 available for 30 days, $100,000 of which will be invested in 30-day CDs and the other $100,000 in T-bills, the financial manager must decide on which maturity of bills to purchase. The financial manager may match maturity and holding period; that is, since the cash is expected to be idle for 30 days, he or she may purchase a 30-day bill and hold it to maturity. Or, he or she might purchase a bill with less than a 30-day maturity, for example, a 15-day maturity bill, hold it until maturity, and purchase a second 15-day maturity bill, holding it until maturity. Furthermore, the financial manager might purchase a 60-, 90-, or 180-day maturity bill and sell it at the end of the 30-day holding period. Since the bill market allows the financial manager to sell a bill at any time, any of these or other possible strategies ensure liquidity. Since it is assured that the funds can be obtained earlier than 30 days if a sudden need arises, the financial manager can then become interested in increasing his or her yield or rate of return.

Risk-Return Investment Strategies. One approach to increasing the yield on invested funds is to purchase a Treasury bill with a maturity longer than the planned holding period, where the holding is the length of time the firm expects to have funds invested in marketable securities. By buying a longer maturity, a lower price would be paid but a higher yield earned. Between the purchase and sale dates, the yield would fall and the price of the instrument would rise as the maturity date approaches. Consequently, by purchasing a longer-maturity instrument and selling it at the end of the holding period, the financial manager hopes to take advantage of the difference between the purchase and selling price, increasing the holding-period return.

For example, consider the information in Table 5-6. If a financial manager purchases the 30-day bill and holds it to maturity, he or she will earn a 5.3% yield over the holding period. Suppose, however, that she elects to purchase the 60-day maturity, paying $99.0500 for the $100 face value bill. If the interest rates do not change over the 30-day holding period (i.e., assuming no shift in the yield curve), she can sell the bill for $99.5250. The question is whether or not the financial manager has improved the yield over the 30-day holding period using this type of strategy.

If the selling price (SP) is sufficiently greater than the purchase price (PP), then yield improvement should have occurred. Equation 5-4 can be used to calculate the 365-day annualized holding-period yield (Y):

$$Y = \frac{SP - PP}{PP} \cdot \frac{365}{H} \qquad\qquad (5\text{-}4)$$

The term $(SP - PP)/PP$ is the holding-period yield; H is the number of days in the holding period; and $365/H$ is the number of holding periods in a 365-day year containing H days. Their product is the annualized yield over the holding period, (i.e., it is the annual return, provided that the investment is repeated under the same conditions $365/H$ times per year).

Table 5-6 Selected Maturities, Bid and Ask Yields, and Bid and Ask Prices on Treasury Bills

Days to Maturity	Yields		Prices	
	Bid	Ask	Bid	Ask
15	5.4%	5.0%	$99.7750	$99.7917
30	5.7	5.3	99.5250	99.5583
60	6.1	5.7	98.9833	99.0500
90	6.6	6.2	98.3500	98.4500

Since the financial manager pays $99.0500 for the T-bill and sells it 30 days later for $99.5250, the difference is $.475. The holding-period yield is

$$Y = \frac{\$99.5250 - \$99.0500}{\$99.0500} \cdot \frac{365}{30} = 5.8\%$$

Consequently, with an annualized holding-period return of 5.8%, a 60-day maturity bill purchased, held for 30 days, and sold would earn 5.8% instead of the 5.3% that would be earned if a 30-day bill were purchased and held until maturity.

Likewise, yield improvement can be made if a 90-day bill is purchased and sold 30 days later. The annualized holding-period yield is

$$Y = \frac{\$98.9833 - \$98.4500}{\$98.4500} \cdot \frac{365}{30} = 6.5\%$$

This is an improvement over the strategy of purchasing the 60-day maturity and selling after 30 days.

This approach to yield improvement increases the yield by taking advantage of the price differential that exists on different maturities; however, it increases the firm's exposure to risk. The risk is due to interest rate variations. If the firm purchases and holds the 30-day maturity, the yield to the firm will be lower, 5.3% as illustrated, but it is completely free of any concern over interest rate variations during the 30 days. If the firm purchases a 90-day maturity with intentions of selling 30 days later, the holding-period yield increases if interest rates fall during the 30-day period because bill prices will rise. However, purchasing a 90-day maturity with intentions of selling 30 days later could produce a smaller holding-period yield if interest rates rise during the 30-day holding period because bill prices will fall.

For example, if the firm purchases a 90-day T-bill with a 6.2% ask yield for $98.4500 and the interest rates fall so that the bid yield on 60-day bills falls to 5.8%, the selling price becomes

$$P = \$100\left[1 - \frac{(60)(.058)}{360}\right] = \$99.0333$$

and the 30-day annualized holding-period yield is then

$$Y = \frac{\$99.0333 - \$98.4500}{\$98.4500} \cdot \frac{365}{30} = 7.1\%$$

Thus, if interest rates fall during the holding period, the holding-period yield increases from 6.5 to 7.1%—both of which are higher than the 5.3% yield on a buy and hold 30-day strategy.

However, if the interest rates rise during the 30-day holding period so that a 60-day bill sells at a 6.8% bid yield for

$$P = \$100\left[1 - \frac{(60)(.068)}{360}\right] = \$98.8667$$

then the annualized holding-period yield is

$$Y = \frac{\$98.8667 - \$98.4500}{\$98.4500} \cdot \frac{365}{30} = 5.1\%$$

The yield is now less than the yield on buying and holding a 30-day bill until maturity. Since short-term interest rates tend to change frequently and rapidly, the strategy of purchasing a longer maturity than the planned holding period and selling it prior to maturity may improve yields, but it also increases risk.

Various other strategies are also possible to achieve yield improvement. For example, a 182-day T-bill may be purchased with the intention of rolling it over weekly. If a purchase is made and a week later the yield spreads are such that the initial bill can be sold profitably, it is sold and another 182-day bill purchased, and so on throughout the year. Regardless of the strategy undertaken, if the holding period is not rigidly fixed (i.e., if the 30-day period is flexible), the financial manager can wait until conditions improve instead of selling under unfavorable conditions, or she can hold the investment until maturity. If this is possible, risk from interest rate variation can be minimized.

Portfolio Strategies. As suggested earlier, the yields on other money market instruments are usually higher than are those on Treasury bills. If the financial manager divides the investible funds, investing part in bills and the rest in other instruments such as CDs, a higher combined yield may result.

For example, the firm may invest $100,000 in both CDs and Treasury bills for 30 days at yields of 5.5% and 5.3%, respectively. The combined annualized holding-period yield is then .5(5.5) + .5(5.3), or 5.4%; this is a higher yield than would have been possible with the purchase of 30-day bills and holding to maturity. In addition, liquidity is maintained and risk minimized.

Summary

This chapter has discussed cash and marketable security management. Initially, cash management was discussed. The second part of the chapter developed a strategy for marketable securities management. To invest in marketable securities, a firm must first know its desired cash balance, its cash inflows, cash outflows, and the timing of the cash flows (provided by the cash budget). Once these items are known, the amount of funds that can be invested in marketable securities can be determined. Types of marketable securities were then discussed along with the term structure of interest rates or yield curves to indicate how they could be used to improve yield. But it was pointed out that yield curve strategies would increase risk from interest rate variations. Finally, a brief discussion of portfolio strategies noted that the purchase of several types of securities could improve holding-period yields while minimizing risk.

Questions

1. Why is cash management an important part of the management of current assets?
2. What are the risk-return characteristics of Treasury bills, certificates of deposit, and commercial paper? How "marketable" is each of these marketable securities?
3. Why must marketable securities be managed?
4. Explain the significance of the bid and ask yields quoted for Treasury bills. What is the spread?
5. What is "riding the yield curve"?
6. Why would a financial manager want to "ride the yield curve"? What trade-off is the result of riding the yield curve?

Problems

1. Rick Rack, accounts receivable/payable manager for Weaver Fabrics for the past year, has instituted a program of cash management in addition to his regular duties. He feels that he has earned a substantial raise of 50% of the annual cash savings due to his cash management. Determine the amount of the raise he desires if the interest rate on U.S. government securities is 6%, brokerage fees are $10 plus .01% of securities purchased, the bank requires a $20,000 minimum cash balance, and the pattern of monthly receipts and disbursements is as follows:

Day of the Month	Amount	Receipt/ Disbursement
1	$ 20,000	Beginning balance
5	50,000	Receipt
8	90,000	Receipt
10	100,000	Disbursement
12	80,000	Receipt
25	60,000	Disbursement
25	100,000	Receipt
30	160,000	Disbursement

2. **a.** What is the asking price for a $10,000 security that has a 180-day maturity and an ask yield of 9.8705%?
   b. How much will a bill dealer pay for a $1,000 T-bill with a 45-day maturity and a bid yield of 7.85%?

    c. What is the ask yield of a $100 face value T-bill if the asking price is $99.25 and it has a 30-day maturity?

3. T. William Buyer believes in "riding the yield curve." For each of the following cases, compare the yield earned by buying a security and selling prior to maturity with the yield earned if the same security were held to maturity:

    a. Purchases a 90-day maturity T-bill at $98.55; sells at $99.40 60 days later.

    b. Purchases a 180-day maturity T-bill at $98.05; sells 30 days later at $98.45.

    c. Purchases a 30-day maturity T-bill at $99.65; sells 15 days later at $99.90.

BIBLIOGRAPHY

Gitman, Lawrence J., Edward A. Moses, and I. Thomas White. "An Assessment of Corporate Cash Management Practices." *Financial Management,* Spring 1979, pp. 32–41.

Orgler, Yair E. *Cash Management Methods and Models.* Belmont, Calif.: Wadsworth Publishing Company, Inc. 1970.

Osteryoung, Jerome S., Gordon S. Roberts, and Daniel E. McCarty. "Ride the Yield Curve When Investing Idle Funds in Treasury Bills?" *Financial Executive,* April 1979, pp. 10–18.

———, Daniel E. McCarty, and Gordon S. Roberts. "Riding the Yield Curve with Treasury Bills." *The Financial Review,* Fall 1981, pp. 57–66.

———, Daniel E. McCarty, and Gordon S. Roberts. "Riding the Yield Curve: A Further Investigation of Investing Idle Funds in Treasury Bills." *The Financial Planner,* February 1982, pp. 64–68.

Stigum, Marcia. *Money Market Calculations: Myth, Reality, and Practice.* Homewood, Ill.: Dow Jones-Irwin, 1977.

———. *Money Market Calculations: Yields, Break-Evens, and Arbitrage.* Homewood, Ill.: Dow Jones-Irwin, 1981.

CHAPTER 6

Accounts Receivable and Inventory Management

Although firms could sell their products for cash only, most firms' sales are largely on credit. Similarly, firms could produce goods on an order basis only, but they generally produce a standard product in advance of sales. Credit sales and goods produced in anticipation of sales give rise to accounts receivable and inventories. It is up to the firm to decide the dollar amount that should be invested in each of these two current assets. Analytical techniques are developed in this chapter to assist in determining the optimal level of accounts receivable and inventory.

MANAGEMENT OF ACCOUNTS RECEIVABLE

The management of a firm must be concerned with accounts receivable and the amount of funds committed to them. Accounts receivable are influenced by the credit standards and terms of sale established by the firm. Credit standards refer to the amount of default risk the firm is willing to accept, whereas terms of sale are concerned with the amount of the cash discount for early payment, the length of time the credit customer has in which to take the cash discount, and the total length of time credit is extended. In addition, the management of accounts receivable includes establishing a collection policy.

Determining Credit Standards

The level of accounts receivable is first influenced by the number of entities to which a firm extends credit. Just which individuals or firms should be extended credit is a practical problem faced by most firms on a continuing basis. However, before a credit analysis and decision can be made, information on the credit applicant must be obtained.

Sources of Credit Information

Several sources of information are available to a firm evaluating a credit request from another firm. While this discussion assumes that the credit applicant is a firm, similar sources exist for credit information on individuals.

The initial information source is the firm's own experience with the credit applicant. A check of the firm's records should indicate the amount of credit extended in the past, the promptness of payment, and the existence of any prior default. This is perhaps the fastest and cheapest information source. It is, however, limited to historical data and, in the case of an old credit customer, past history may not accurately reflect the current behavior of the applicant. In the case of a new customer, there is no past history on which to rely; consequently, other information sources must be found.

The second source of information is the credit application and/or financial statements provided by the applicant. They include a variety of information that can be analyzed to determine the three C's of the applicant's credit: character, collateral, and capacity. Character is concerned with the applicant's attitude toward obligations; collateral refers to the security that can be offered for the amount of credit granted; and capacity measures the applicant's financial strength to pay maturing obligations. Financial statements can be analyzed using the financial ratios considered in Chapter 3. Note that when using financial statements for credit analysis, audited statements are preferred to unaudited statements.

Third, information can be sought from companies that currently extend credit to the applicant. The National Association of Credit Managers acts as a clearinghouse for credit information. Information on the maximum credit extended, the length of time the credit relationship has existed, and the applicant's payment habits can be obtained to help the firm evaluate the applicant.

Fourth, commercial banks often maintain credit departments, and the firm's bank may be able to obtain valuable information from the applicant's bank. Although banks are reluctant to respond to direct credit inquiries by one firm about another, they usually have reciprocal agreements between themselves. This source can provide information on the applicant's average cash balance, outstanding loans, and line of credit.

Finally, the firm can seek credit ratings and reports from credit rating organizations such as Dun & Bradstreet. D & B's credit rating system appraises the credit of firms of a particular size as measured by their net worth. Furthermore, a D & B credit report contains a history of the company, its officers, the nature of the business, and financial data and a check of trade suppliers' experiences with the firm.

Credit Analysis

Even though a large amount and variety of credit data are frequently available, it may not be possible in some cases for a firm to take advantage of all of it. The amount of credit sought may be too small to justify the cost of a complete search and analysis. In other situations, time is of the essence, and a firm must provide credit fairly quickly or lose the credit sale.

Many approaches have been developed to minimize both the cost and time involved in processing credit applications while simultaneously attempting to either minimize bad-debt losses or limit them to a predetermined percentage of sales. Another approach to credit analysis considers both liquidity and default risk. As a firm extends credit to higher default risk classes, sales rise.

For example, a firm is considering extending $50 credit to 85 individual firms. Column 1 of Table 6-1 shows the account numbers for 12 firms from the 85 seeking credit. Columns 2, 3, and 4 indicate the scores for credit characteristics that the evaluating firm considers most indicative of the creditworthiness of a credit customer. These characteristics are selected by the evaluating firm from an examination of its records to determine which of the many possible characteristics best indicate whether or not a credit applicant will default. To do this the evaluating firm divides its records into good and bad risk accounts, looking for characteristics such as the current ratio, fixed charge coverage, age of the firm seeking credit, etc., that are the most predictive of an applicant's creditworthiness.[1]

Once these characteristics are selected, each account receives a score between 4 and 0, depending on the quality of its performance on that characteristic. For example, the first firm in Table 6-1, Account 10, has a high current ratio; few suppliers, if any, report refusing it credit, and it is an old and established firm. Consequently, the evaluating firm assigns the highest possible score of 4 to each characteristic. The higher the individual characteristic scores, the higher their summed values or credit score (column 5) and the lower the probability that the account will default.

The firm could conclude its credit analysis at this point using a default risk decision criterion solely and, for example, extend credit to those accounts that have a default probability of 2% or less. However, a decision at this stage of the analysis neglects liquidity. It would be more appropriate to combine risk, liquidity, and

[1]See David C. Ewert, *Trade Credit Management: Selection of Accounts Receivables Using a Statistical Model,* A Research Monograph, No. 79, Georgia State University, Spring 1978, for a description of how stepwise regression can be used to find characteristics associated with good and bad credit risks.

Table 6-1   Example of Information Required for Credit Risk Evaluation

(1) Account No.	(2) Current Ratio	(3) Percentage of Suppliers Reporting Refusing Credit	(4) Age of the Firm	(5) Credit Score	(6) Probability of Default	(7) Default Class
10	4	4%	4	12	.1%	A
14	4	4	4	12	.1	A
20	4	3	4	11	.1	A
3	3	4	3	10	.5	B
8	3	3	3	9	.5	B
31	3	2	3	8	.5	B
17	2	2	3	7	2.0	C
60	2	2	2	6	3.0	D
85	2	4	3	9	.5	B
44	4	2	1	7	2.0	C
53	1	4	2	7	2.0	C
76	3	1	4	8	.5	B

shareholder wealth into the credit decision. Equation 6-1 defines the NPV as the basic credit model that links risk and liquidity to the common stockholders' wealth.

$$\text{NPV}_j = \frac{S_j(1 - p_j)}{(1 + k)^1} - V_j \tag{6-1}$$

where NPV_j = the NPV of extending credit to the jth risk class
S_j = sales to the jth risk class
P_j = the probability of the jth risk class defaulting
$(1 - p_j)$ = probability of the jth risk class not defaulting
k = the period discount rate
V_j = the cash investment necessary to produce sales

To illustrate, if a firm extends an account $50 in goods for 1 month when the discount rate is 1%, the cash investment is 80% of sales, and the probability of the account defaulting is zero, then Equation 6-1 produces

$$\text{NPV}_d = \frac{\$50(1 - 0)}{(1.01)^1} - \$40 = \$9.51$$

Because this risk-free NPV is larger than zero, this account should be extended credit.

The opposite example is the case in which the default probability is at a maximum, at 1 instead of 0. When an account defaults, the firm loses the variable cash investment, $40 in this example. In general, the probability of an account defaulting is a number between 0 and 1, for example, as those shown in Table 6-1, column 6.

Table 6-2 merges this concept with the information and analysis previously discussed. Columns 1 and 2 show the risk classes and default probabilities, respectively, as suggested by the analysis of Table 6-1. Columns 3 and 4 denote the number of firms in each risk class and the total sales to that risk class. Column 5 is sales net of bad debts determined by the numerator of Equation 6-1. For example, risk class A would provide $250(1 − .001), or $249.75, in sales net of bad debts. The present value of collections on this sale, 1 month later, is $227.05, as shown in column 6. When the cash investment, shown in column 7, is subtracted, an NPV of $27.05 results from extending credit to this risk class. The values for the remaining risk classes are calculated the same way.

If the firm had terminated its analysis as indicated earlier and had used the default risk decision criterion solely, risk classes A through C would have been accepted. However, if the firm uses the risk-adjusted NPV criterion, risk classes A through F are acceptable.

There are, however, several subjective considerations in the application of this criterion. First, the numerical example assumed equal $50 sales to each customer. If a firm sells to many small firms but only a few very large firms, the expected bad-debt ratio is not a good measure of risk. In this situation the firm must be concerned with the maximum loss because default by a large customer could bankrupt the selling firm; thus the firm might not make the credit sale at all. Second, firms that fall into the unacceptable risk classes should be considered conditional instead of absolute rejections. If a firm would be willing to pay cash for 50% of its purchases,

Table 6-2 An Example of Esablishing Credit Standards

(1) Risk Class	(2) Default Probability	(3) No. of Sales	(4) Credit Sales	(5) Net Sales	(6) PV Sales	(7) V	(8) NPV
A	.1%	5	$ 250	$ 249.75	$ 227.05	$ 200	$ 27.05
B	.5	3	1,500	1,492.50	1,356.82	1,200	156.82
C	2.0	20	1,000	980.00	890.91	800	90.91
D	3.0	15	750	727.50	661.36	600	61.36
E	5.0	5	250	237.50	215.91	200	15.91
F	10.0	4	200	180.00	163.64	160	3.64
G	15.0	3	150	127.50	115.91	120	−4.09
H	30.0	2	100	70.00	63.64	80	−16.36
I	50.0	1	50	25.00	22.72	40	−17.27

the credit manager should consider the possibility of extending credit for the balance. Third, introducing a new product or idle plant capacity might require management to lower its credit standards.

Terms of Sale

Terms of sale or trade credit terms vary from industry to industry and may even vary from firm to firm within a single industry. For example, credit terms may be stated as 1/10, n 30; that is, deduct 1% from the face amount of the invoice if payment is made within 10 days or pay the face amount in 30 days. The term 1/10 is the cash discount or, more realistically, the penalty for not paying promptly, whereas n 30 specifies the length of time credit is extended. Deciding to offer or changing the cash discount can be used to stimulate early payment, whereas changing the length of time credit is extended can be used to increase sales.

When determining or changing credit terms, the concepts of marginal analysis and NPV provide the decision criterion. The basic NPV model, for example, Equation 6-1, must be modified to allow collections on receivables to occur over several time periods and to allow for the early discount (essentially, an "early" collection). Instead of finding collections at the end of a single period, the model must allow credit sales to be collected over several time periods. Thus, a summation term must be used. Because credit sales in a given time period will be collected over several time periods, payment proportions must also be used. A payment proportion is the cash collected (actual or estimated) in a future time period divided by the initial credit sale in a previous time period. For example, credit sales for January are expected to be $100,000, with collections of $70,000, $20,000, and $10,000 expected in February, March, and April, respectively. The payment proportions are $70,000/$100,000, $20,000/$100,000, and $10,000/$100,000, or 70%, 20%, and 10%, respectively.

Equation 6-2 summarizes these ideas as follows:

$$NPV = \frac{p_1' S_0}{(1 + k)^{t_1}} + \frac{p_2' S_0}{(1 + k)^{t_2}} + \cdots - V \qquad (6\text{-}2)$$

where S_0 = daily credit sales in the current period
p' = payment proportions
k = daily discount rate
V = daily cash investment to produce credit sales
$\cdots$ = continue until $p_1 + p_2 + \cdots + = 1$
t_s = number of days from the present until a collection is made

The subscripts on the payment proportions refer to the first collection (1), the second collection (2), and so on. Because 100% of credit sales must be collected (assuming no bad debts), an addition of all the payment proportions must sum to 100% (or, in decimal form, the payment proportions must sum to 1).

For example, consider the following information labeled "Existing":

	Existing $1,000	Proposed $1,000
Credit Sales per Day (Collections)	Payment Proportions	
10 days	0	40%
30 days	20%	0
40 days	70	50
50 days	10	10
Terms of sale	n 40	1/10, n 40
Daily discount rate	.05%	.05%
Daily investment (% of sales), V	80%	80%
$V = vS =$	$800	$800

The payment proportions indicate that the firm expects to collect 20% of credit sales 30 days after the sale date, 70% 40 days after, and so on. If all credit sales are collected in 50 days, the payment proportions sum to 100%.

The existing terms of sale for the firm, n 30, are associated with an NPV that can be found by application of Equation 6-2. These calculations are shown in Table 6-3. For example, the first payment proportion is 20%; thus, the firm expects to collect 30 days after the credit sale of $1,000, namely, .20($1,000) or $200. When the discount rate is .0005 per day, this amount has a present value (PV) of

$$\frac{\$200}{(1.0005)^{20}} = \$197.02$$

Table 6-3 Calculations for a Change in Terms of Sale

(1)	(2)	(3)	(4)	(5)	(6)	(7)
	Amounts		Net Discount		Present Value	
Item	Exist	New	Exist	New	Exist	New
Collections						
10 days	—	$400	—	$396	—	$394.03
20 days	$200	0	$200	—	$197.02	—
30 days	700	500	700	500	686.14	490.10
40 days	100	100	100	100	97.53	97.53
Total PV					980.69	981.66
Less: V					800.00	800.00
Equals: NPV					$180.69	$181.66

The remaining PV calculations were done in a like manner and are shown in column 6. Once the collections have been discounted to the present, they can be added to find a total present value. The cash investment is then subtracted to yield an NPV for the existing terms of sale, $180.69.

A weighted average collection period can be found by multiplication of the payment proportions and days and then adding; that is, .2(30) + .7(40) + .1(50) = 39 days. This 39-day weighted average collection period is with the 40-day terms of sale. However, the firm might consider a discount for customers that desire to pay early. From the firm's viewpoint, such a discount may reduce the level of accounts receivable and weighted average collection period and, consequently, financing costs. The firm is also reducing the cash collected. If the financing costs decrease by more than the lost cash inflow, the NPV of the new policy should increase.

The incorporation of the early payment discount requires a slight modification of Equation 6-2. This modification is shown in Equation 6-3:

$$\text{NPV} = \frac{p_1'S_0 - dp_1'S_0}{(1 + k)^{t_1}} + \frac{p_2'S_0}{(1 + k)^{t_2}} + \cdots - V \tag{6-3}$$

where p' = payment proportions
S_0 = daily credit sales
k = daily discount rate
d = discount for early payment
t_s = number of days from the present in which collections are made
$dp_1'S_0$ = the discount amount

Tbe discount amount is found by multiplication of the discount, the payment proportion, and credit sales, that is, .01(.4)($1,000), or $4.00. This amount is subtracted from the first collection amount, $400 − $4, to find the net collection in 10 days of $396. The present value of this amount is found as illustrated in Table 6-3, column 7, $394.03.

The remaining calculations are identical to those for the existing terms of sale. The decision criterion is to change terms of sale if the "NPV, New" is equal to or greater than "NPV, Existing" or, otherwise, reject the affirmative decision. Since the "NPV, New" is $181.66 and the "NPV-Existing" is $180.69, the firm should change its terms of sale. The reason for the higher NPV with the new terms of sale is the lower financing cost due to a reduction in the weighted average collection period: .4(10) + .5(40) + .1(50) = 29 days. Alternatively, a reduction in the level of accounts receivable reduces financing costs more than does the lost cash flow due to the early payment discount.

This decision criterion assumes accuracy in the forecast of payment proportions, credit sales, and discount rate. If there is uncertainty of these values, risk adjustment can be built into the model.

Furthermore, if the change in credit terms will result in an increase in bad-debt losses, these losses should be treated as a cost and be deducted from the present value of cash collections. However, liberalization of credit terms does not necessarily mean that higher risk classes are extended credit; rather, the more favorable terms are designed to attract customers falling into risk classes already acceptable. For example, Equation 6-3 has default risk built in, and if the firm is currently accepting default-risk classes that result in a 1% bad-debt loss, then no adjustments to the analysis in Table 6-3 need be made.

Collection Policy

Most firms selling on credit have credit customers who are late in paying their accounts as well as customers who default on their obligations entirely. The firm, as part of its management of accounts receivable, must establish a plan to cope with these events.

Ideally, the collection policy should be considered along with the credit standards because the potential bad-debt loss is directly related to the degree of default risk allowed by the credit standards. The lower the credit standard, the greater the potential bad-debt loss. The stronger the collection policy, however, given the credit standard, the lower the bad-debt loss; but the stronger collection policy results in a higher cost per dollar of bad debts recovered. There are many different combinations of credit standards and collection policies, with each combination being associated with different earnings levels. But, to this time, no analytical technique has been developed that can combine these relationships.

INVENTORY MANAGEMENT

Inventory management is concerned with the amount of funds the firm invests in inventories of raw material, semifinished goods, and finished goods. The objective or goal is to hold enough inventory so that profits are not reduced by lost sales resulting from inventory shortages, higher ordering costs from too frequent orders, and/or higher carrying costs from holding excessive inventory. To hold such an optimal average inventory, a firm must order (or produce) an appropriate quantity of goods each time an order is placed (or a production run is scheduled).

The Economic Order Quantity

Such an appropriate order quantity is called the economic order quantity, or EOQ, and is defined as the quantity to order that minimizes inventory costs. Figure 6-1 summarizes the basic EOQ inventory model, which assumes that sales are known with certainty and occur at a constant rate during the period, reducing inventory at a

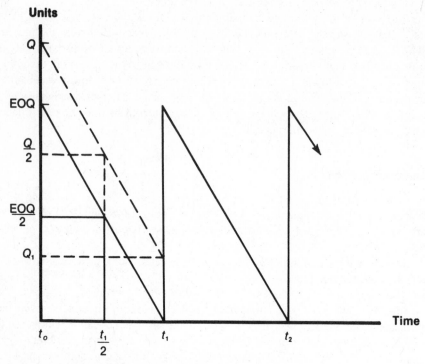

Figure 6-1. Graphical presentation of the EOQ model.

constant rate. According to the model, the firm initially (t_0) orders the EOQ quantity of goods; at t, the inventory has been reduced to zero and an immediate reorder and delivery are made so that the firm has the EOQ to start the next period. This selling, ordering, and delivery pattern continues throughout the year.

Under the model assumptions, the average inventory is EOQ/2 halfway through a period if the EOQ is ordered. If an order is for more or less units than the EOQ, then $Q/2$, the average inventory, will be either greater or less than EOQ/2. For example, if Q (Figure 6-1) is ordered instead of the EOQ, the average inventory ($Q/2$) at the midpoint in the period is larger than the optimal average inventory (EOQ/2), and the end-of-period inventory is not zero but Q, an excess. A firm can order any value of Q, but it desires to find a unique Q, the EOQ, that minimizes inventory is EOQ/2. To determine the EOQ, the firm must first determine its total inventory costs, which are made up of the ordering costs plus carrying costs.

Ordering costs include the cost of placing orders (salaries, paper, clerical, productionsetup expenses, etc.), shipping, receiving, and handling costs. Total ordering costs depend upon the number of orders (n) placed during the year and the dollar cost of placing an order (O). Given the cost of placing an order, ordering costs will fall if fewer orders are placed each year. However, if fewer orders are placed, the number of units carried in inventory must be greater.

Inventory carrying costs include the financing costs of the funds devoted to inventory as well as the costs of storage, insurance, taxes, obsolescence and damage. Given a per unit carrying cost (C), the total carrying costs will increase as the number of units in inventory rises. The total cost of holding a particular level of inventory is the sum of these two components at that level. The interrelationship among ordering, carrying, and total costs is shown in Figure 6-2.

The total inventory cost (K), for any inventory level, is found by Equation 6-4:

$$K = C\left(\frac{Q}{2}\right) + O\left(\frac{S}{Q}\right) \tag{6-4}$$

where　　Q = units purchased (or produced)
　　　　　$Q/2$ = the average inventory
　　　　　S = unit sales or usage
　　　　　$S/Q = n$ = the number of orders placed or the number of production runs during the year
　　　　　O = costs per order placed

This equation can be solved for the values of EOQ and EOQ/2 that appear in Figures 6-1 and 6-2, respectively,[2] resulting in Equations 6-5 and 6-6:

$$\text{EOQ} = \sqrt{\frac{2 \cdot S \cdot O}{C}} \tag{6-5}$$

$$\frac{\text{EOQ}}{2} = \frac{1}{2}\sqrt{\frac{2 \cdot S \cdot O}{C}} = \sqrt{\frac{S \cdot O}{2C}} \tag{6-6}$$

For example, if annual usage, ordering costs, and carrying costs are 10,000, $20, and $.10, respectively, then

$$\text{EOQ} = \sqrt{\frac{(2)(10,000)(\$20)}{\$.10}} = 2,000 \text{ units}$$

[2]To find the value of Q, the EOQ that minimizes K, Equation 6-4 is differentiated with respect to Q. The derivative is set equal to zero and solved for Q as follows:

a.　$\dfrac{\partial K}{\partial Q} = \dfrac{C}{2} - \dfrac{SO}{Q^2} = 0$　　　　c.　$Q^2 = \dfrac{2SO}{C}$

b.　$\dfrac{C}{2} = \dfrac{SO}{Q^2}$　　　　d.　$\text{EOQ} = Q^* = \sqrt{\dfrac{2SO}{C}}$

Q.E.D.

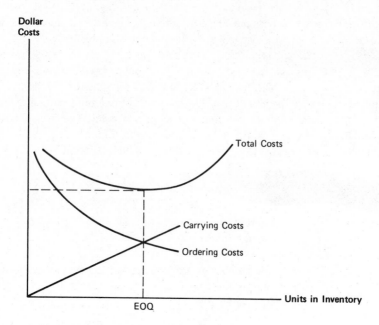

Figure 6-2. Ordering, carrying, and total costs of inventory.

and

$$\frac{EOQ}{2} = \frac{2,000}{2} = 1,000 \text{ units}$$

Thus, the optimal order quantity and average inventory are 2,000 and 1,000 units, respectively.

If the firm orders 2,000 units each time an order is placed, then the number of orders placed during the year is found as follows:

$$n = \frac{S}{EOQ} = \frac{10,000}{2,000} = 5$$

The ordering costs for five orders, one placed every 365/5 or 73 days, is found by multiplying the cost of placing one order ($20) by the number of orders placed (5); the carrying costs are found by multiplying per unit carrying cost ($.10) by the average inventory (1,000). Substituting these values in Equation 5-4, total annual inventory costs are

$$K = \$.10(1,000) + \$20(5) = \$200$$

If other than 2,000 units are ordered each time, meaning more or less than five orders are placed during the year, inventory costs will rise and earnings will be lower. Inventory carrying costs increase more than the reduction in ordering costs if more than 2,000 units are ordered less than five times a year. Conversely, if less than 2,000 units are ordered, total ordering costs from more frequent orders increase more than the reduction in carrying costs from carrying a reduced amount of inventory.

In many cases a vendor allows a firm a quantity discount on large orders. If, for example, a vendor allows a $.01 per unit quantity discount (d) on orders of 2,500 or more, should the firm order this larger quantity instead of the EOQ of 2,000 units? The factors involved in this decision are the savings on the per unit purchase price, the savings on ordering costs, and the additional carrying costs of the larger inventory. Thus,

$$\text{Savings on purchase price} = d \cdot S$$
$$= (\$.01)(10,000)$$
$$= \$100$$

$$\text{Savings on ordering costs} = O\left(\frac{S}{Q_2}\right) - O\left(\frac{S}{Q_1}\right)$$
$$= \$20\left(\frac{10,000}{2,000}\right) - \$20\left(\frac{10,000}{2,500}\right)$$
$$= \$20$$

$$\text{Additional carrying cost} = C\left(\frac{Q_1}{2}\right) - C\left(\frac{Q_2}{2}\right)$$
$$= \$.10\left(\frac{2,500}{2}\right) - \$.10\left(\frac{2,000}{2}\right)$$
$$= \$25$$

If the savings on the purchase price and ordering costs are equal to or greater than the additional carrying costs, the larger order should be placed. That is, if

$$d \cdot S + O\left(\frac{S}{Q_2} - \frac{S}{Q_1}\right) \geq C\left(\frac{Q_2}{2} - \frac{Q_1}{2}\right) \tag{6-7}$$

then the larger order should be placed. In this case, the savings on purchases and ordering costs, $120, exceed the higher carrying costs, $25, by $95. Consequently, the firm should place the larger orders because earnings would increase by $95.

Summary

This chapter focused on two current assets: accounts receivable and inventory. The objective of accounts receivable management involved determining the amount of funds that should be invested in receivables. Credit standards and terms of sale were analyzed using NPV and risk as guides to decision making because these three factors influence the amount of funds committed to accounts receivable.

To determine the amount of funds invested in inventory, profitability and risk were also used to analyze inventory decisions. The basic EOQ inventory model, which minimizes inventory costs, was developed.

Questions

1. What sources of credit information are available to a firm that must assess the creditworthiness of a prospective customer?
2. What trade-off exists for the firm when it extends credit to customers who may default?
3. Explain the terms 1/10, n 30; 2/10, n 60; and 1/20, n 45.
4. What factors must be considered when a firm is deciding upon its terms of sale?
5. Explain completely the significance of the economic order quantity for inventory management.
6. What effect may quantity discounts have on the determination of the economic order quantity?

Problems

1. Eve R. Glade is a Florida land developer who has experienced a drastic decline in sales recently due to unfavorable publicity on land sales. Ms. Glade plans to alter her stringent credit policy to increase sales on her three types of lots: lakefront lots, which sell for $15,000 each; lots bordering the golf course, which sell for $12,500 each; and inside lots selling for $8,000. Given the default classes and probabilities shown, to which classes should Ms. Glade extend credit if she desires to limit default risk to less than 10%? Less than 20%?

Risk Classes	Probability of Default
A	1%
B	5
C	10
D	20
E	30
F	60

2. Using the information provided in Problem 1, which default classes should be extended credit if the basic NPV credit model is used? The cash investment on each of the lots is

approximately 50% of its selling price. Credit will be extended for 6 months at a discount rate of ½% per month, at which time buyers must pay for the lots in full.

Default Class	Lakefront Lots	Golf Course Lots	Inside Lots
A	10	20	5
B	10	20	10
C	10	15	10
D	5	10	15
E	5	10	20
F	0	5	20

3. What is the economic order quantity if annual usage, ordering, and carrying costs are (a) 2,000,000, $40, and $.15, respectively; (b) 750,000, $30, and $.50?

4. The Can Can Canning Company uses 5 million cans annually. If order costs are $25 per order and carrying costs are $.001 per can, what is the economic order quantity? The average inventory? Total number of orders placed and annual order costs? Annual inventory costs?

5. Intercontinental Container Corporation will offer Can Can Canning Company (Problem 4) a 5% discount on its price of $.025 per can if it will purchase in 1 million can units. Should the company purchase in this quantity or in the economic order quantity determined in Problem 4?

Bibliography

Atkins, Joseph C., and Yong H. Kim. "Comment and Correction: Opportunity Cost in the Evaluation of Investment in Accounts Receivable." *Financial Management*, Winter 1977, pp. 71–79.

Boggess, William P. "Screen-Test Your Credit Risk." *Harvard Business Review*, November–December 1967, pp. 113–122.

Carpenter, Michael D., and Jack E. Miller. "A Reliable Framework for Monitoring Accounts Receivable." *Financial Management*, Winter 1979, pp. 37–40.

Frantz, E. F., and J. A. Viscione. "What Should You Do About Cash Discounts." *Credit and Financial Management*, May 1976, pp. 30–36.

Hill, Ned C., and Kenneth D. Riener. "Determining the Cash Discount in the Firm's Credit Policy." *Financial Management*, Spring 1979, pp. 68–73.

Kim, Y., and J. Atkins. "Evaluating Investments in Accounts Receivable: A Maximizing Framework." *Journal of Finance*, May 1978, pp. 403–412.

Lewellen, Wilbur G., and Robert Johnson. "Better Way to Monitor Accounts Receivable." *Harvard Business Review*, May–June 1972, pp. 101–107.

Sartoris, William L., and Ned C. Hill. "Evaluating Credit Policy Alternatives: A Present Value Framework." *The Journal of Financial Research*, Spring 1981, pp. 81–89.

Stone, Bernell K. "The Payment-Pattern Approach to the Forecasting and Control of Accounts Receivable." *Financial Management*, Autumn 1976, pp. 65–82.

Four

ANALYTICAL TECHNIQUES FOR LONG-TERM ASSET SELECTION

CHAPTER 7

Capital Budgeting: An Introduction

One of the most important features of an expanding American economy is the growth in capital expenditures for new plant and equipment. Growth of capital expenditures and changing patterns of production and consumption have definite effects on the finance functions. Perhaps the major effect has been to heighten the importance of investment decisions, both to the firm and the economy. Increased emphasis has been placed on the development of new methodologies and practical tools to aid the decision maker in the area of capital budgeting or capital asset selection.

A capital investment can be defined as a current outlay or series of outlays of cash resources that will provide in return an anticipated flow of future benefits. Any investment decision has three distinguishing elements: anticipated benefits, a time or temporal dimension, and an element of risk involved in the realization of these benefits. The magnitude of these elements distinguishes the capital budgeting decision from other types of investment decisions. In other words, capital investments are characterized by potentially large anticipated benefits, a relatively high degree of risk, and a relatively long time between the initial outlay and the anticipated return.

The unique characteristics of capital investment decisions have brought about the development of special decision-making tools for use in their resolution. The desirability and necessity for such tools lie in the relative importance of capital budgeting decisions as compared with other types of investments. To understand the importance of capital budgeting decisions, it is necessary to examine the context in which these decisions are made.

First, capital investments demand a commitment of relatively large amounts of the firm's resources at some given point, or points, in time. As a consequence, a firm's ill-advised capital investment decision can pose a real threat to its existence. The Ford Motor Company is one of the few firms large and rich enough to afford a mistake like the Edsel. On the other hand, a particularly astute or opportune investment decision can yield spectacular returns to a small or moderate-sized company. For example, The Haloid Corporation (now Xerox) was a small producer of photographic copying paper that committed a relatively large amount of its resources to the development of xerography over a period of many years.

Second, the consequences of a firm's selection of capital assets extend well into the future. Once the producer of a synthetic fiber has invested in the plant, equipment, and technology necessary to manufacture his or her product, many of the costs (power, maintenance, labor) are fixed by the decision to invest in that particular manufacturing process. Depending on the demand for his or her product, the level of competition, and so on, the producer may or may not make a profit. Even if the return on investment is less than anticipated or considered desirable, these fixed costs will have to be met unless the investment is written off completely. In short, a firm's future costs, break-even points, sales, and profits will all be determined to some extent by the firm's selection of assets. Furthermore, a large firm's capital expenditures may affect a whole industry and even the adjacent society. A major firm may set high standards of technology and efficiency that competitors must meet to enter or stay in the industry. The firm's choice of location can have pronounced effects on area employment patterns, residential patterns, and the existence and location of suppliers.

Third, in addition to determining future conditions, capital investment decisions, once made, are not easily reversible. There may be little market for secondhand plant and equipment, and their conversion to other uses may not be financially feasible. The fiber producer in the foregoing example would probably find a very limited market for a used polyester plant, particularly in an area of manufacture where production methods are rapidly outmoded by increasingly higher levels of technology. As a result, the firm that miscalculates its selection of assets must take a total loss on its investment or learn to live with the level of technology it has selected, although the return provided is less than expected. These three factors impinge to varying degrees on the capital budgeting decision. Their overall effect is to heighten its importance and to emphasize the element of risk to the firm.

A discussion of the initial costs and the anticipated benefits relevant to the capital budgeting decision is included in this chapter. Investment evaluation techniques, investment risk, and capital rationing are discussed in the following chapter.

ESTIMATING COSTS AND BENEFITS: SOURCES AND INFLUENCES

The collection and organization of data in support of specific projects, proposals, or investments are perhaps the most tedious aspect of capital budgeting. The problem of what and how much data to collect can become very complicated for several reasons. First, the technological requirements of the project may be beyond the engineering capability of the firm. A wholesaler investing in a computer to handle billing, inventory, and payroll may need to hire an independent consultant to determine which line of equipment and software is most suitable. Often, the vendor of such specialized equipment can be helpful in making the determination, but he or she can also be self-serving. Second, when new products and manufacturing processes are involved, little information may be available beyond that which the firm can obtain through its own research. Third, since each project proposal has its own distinct data base, the guidelines for data collection are often vague. Much depends on the nature of the particular project the firm has in mind, the type and amount of resources at the disposal of the firm, and even the firm's position in relation to other firms in the industry.

The information sought when developing project proposals generally falls into one of two broad categories. The first category of data collection deals with the size of the outlays necessary to produce future benefits—the cost of accepting the project. Depending on the nature of the project, the firm may or may not require specialized outside help to determine these costs. If the equipment required for a capital project is available in standard units from a number of manufacturers (e.g., stainless steel pipe, copper tubing, and electric motors) the problem is merely one of competitive shopping, taking into account the user's needs and the quality of the various lines offered by the manufacturers. If more sophisticated equipment is required (e.g., high-temperature industrial furnaces or sophisticated electronic controls) the purchaser needs greater knowledge to analyze his or her own requirements and the relative merits of alternative equipment. The pricing of such specialized equipment also presents difficulties, particularly where items must be custom built to the firm's specifications. Sometimes it is possible for the firm to make an estimate by considering the known prices of similar equipment. At other times, competitive bidding may be used as a way of determining costs. It may be possible to get a rough idea about the costs of a proposed plant by comparing different plants and facilities possessing similar equipment. Since even a good-sized firm might not have the scientific and engineering expertise needed to conduct this kind of evaluation, consultants are often employed to help collect and evaluate this type of data.

Sometimes an investment project requires the construction of a new plant that will be one of only a few facilities of its kind and which differs in many respects from those already in existence. A very large, specialized firm might be able to undertake such a project itself with a minimum of assistance from outside consultants and vendors. More often, however, the firm will contract with an engineering firm specializing in the construction of such facilities under one of several rather complicated contractual arrangements. Cost-plus contracts or guaranteed-maximum-price contracts are two popular forms. Such projects often require a demonstration or series of demonstrations of the facility by the contractor before acceptance by the firm. Oil refineries are often built under such arrangements. Although the examples in this discussion deal largely with equipment, all other costs associated with the project—variable material, labor, and administrative costs—must also be included when considering the total outlays involved in the proposal.

The second category is concerned with the measurement of future benefits. For example, a firm considering the introduction of a new project could commission extensive market research on which to base estimates of future revenues through sale of its new product. For some other capital projects, however, the benefits would be measured in terms of cost savings. A firm considering automating a portion of its assembly line would receive its benefits in the form of lower unit costs rather than increased sales.

THE INITIAL OR ORIGINAL COSTS

The data on the initial or original costs of the proposed project must be compiled from the various sources and analyzed. The compilation of the data may come under headings such as material or equipment purchases, shipping and transportation expenses, labor and administrative costs, working capital requirements, installation expenses, salvage value of old equipment, and tax implications.

Regardless of the headings used to compile data on the proposed initial cost of the project, two points must be considered in analyzing the information. The analysis must first determine which items of data are relevant and which are not relevant to the asset selection decision. Marginal analysis is a useful technique for determining the relevancy of information. In marginal analysis, only information that is altered or changed by the acceptance of the project is considered pertinent to the decision. Other information, such as overhead costs, that remains the same whether or not the project is accepted or rejected, is not considered. If a clothing manufacturer requires additional labor to extend a firm's line of apparel to include children's sizes, she would consider the labor costs relevant. The fixed overhead costs would not be a relevant consideration, however, because rent, electricity, and property taxes would not be affected by the introduction of this new product line.

Second, only cash outflows are relevant in determining the initial cost of a proposed project. For example, a machine the firm already owns has some remaining economic life if it is transferred to a new project from a project that is being terminated. No remaining value for this machinery would be included as part of the initial cost of the project because no cash outflow is required by the firm. (However, future depreciation of this equipment would influence the annual benefits, along

Table 7-1   Project Initial Cost Computations

Equipment purchase price	$226,400
Plus: Shipping and transportation charges	11,320
Labor installation expenses	13,100
Material installation costs	9,850
Equals: Basis and total cash outlay or initial cost	$260,670

with any forgone salvage value, and would have to be considered.) The cost of all new machinery, including its purchase price, shipping and transportation charges, installation costs, and tax effects, would have to be included in the calculations to determine the initial cost of the project.

For example, a company is evaluating a new piece of equipment as an addition to its factory and finds that the purchase price will be $226,400. Shipping and transportation costs are projected at 5% of the purchase price. Management further estimates that once the equipment is on the plant site, the cost for electrical wiring and plumbing to put it into operation will be $13,100 and $9,850 for labor and materials, respectively. The initial cost of procuring any future benefits is computed in Table 7-1.

Net Working Capital

A major element in asset selection is the amount of net working capital necessary to support a project. Net working capital is defined as current assets minus current liabilities. If a firm purchases some new equipment that adds a new product to its existing line, there will be an increase in current assets in the form of a larger inventory and a greater number of accounts receivable. However, part of this buildup of current assets will be offset by an increase in current liabilities in the form of increased accounts and notes payable. The difference between the increases in current assets and current liabilities is the amount of working capital that will be needed to support this new investment. For example, assume that the equipment purchased in the preceding example is for a product line addition requiring a $35,000 and $65,000 increase in inventories and accounts receivable (current assets). Of this increase in current assets, $40,000 is offset by increases in current liabilities to trade creditors (accounts and notes payable). The remaining $60,000 difference is the net working capital requirement for the project and would be included as part of the initial cost of accepting the project. Table 7-1 reconstructed as Table 7-2 illustrates the influence of net working capital on the initial cost of the equipment.

Almost all capital projects will require an increase in working capital. This would not be the case, however, if tbe project increased the firm's efficiency in such a way that the amount of inventory on hand or accounts receivable could be re-

Table 7-2 Book Value and Initial Cost Calculations for a Project

Equipment purchase price	$226,400
Plus: Shipping or transportation charges	11,320
labor installation expenses	13,100
material installation costs	9,850
Equals: Basis	260,670
Plus: Increase in accounts receivable	65,000
Increase in inventory	35,000
Less: Increase in trade and notes payable	40,000
Equals: Cash outlay or initial cost	$320,670

duced. Examples of the latter would be improved inventory control systems or improved billing and collection systems.

It is important to remember that all or a portion of the increased net working capital would be returned to the firm at the end of the project's life. When this happens, the working capital returned in the last period should be treated as a cash inflow in the same manner as other cash flows in evaluating the project.

The Investment Tax Credit

The investment tax credit has been used off and on since 1962 to spur capital investment in machinery and equipment. Generally, the credit has been suspended during inflationary periods and restored during periods of lagging domestic economic growth. The investment tax credit (ITC) currently allows a credit of 6% or 10% of the cost of qualified investments against the federal income tax liability in the year in which such property is put into service.[1]

Section 38 of the Internal Revenue Code describes the qualified investment property eligible for the ITC. It generally includes 3 and 5 year cost recovery property.

The percentage of the basis of the assets that can be taken as an ITC depends on the tax life of the property. For tax purposes, all depreciable property is placed into four life classes: 3-, 5-, 10-, and 15-year property. The total qualified investment in a given year is equal to the allowed value of new Section 38 property plus up to $125,000 ($150,000 after 1988) of the cost of used Section 38 property. The tax life property and ITC credits are summarized in Table 7-3.

[1]An alternative ITC provision exists in the ACRS. If a firm elects not to reduce the recovery basis by 50% of the ITC, it must reduce the ITC from 6% to 4% for a 3-year tax life and from 10% to 8% in the other ACRS tax lives.

Table 7-3 Tax Life and the ITC

Type of Property	ITC
3-Year property	6%
5-Year property	10
10-Year property	10
15-Year property[a]	10

[a]Most 15-year property is real property however, which is ineligible for the ITC.

The maximum credit allowed is limited by the tax liability of the firm before considering the ITC. A firm may take the full ITC in the year it is put into service if its tax liability is $25,000 or less and the ITC does not exceed its tax liability. If, however, a firm's qualified investments for the tax year are $100,000 but its tax liability is only $6,000, the ITC of $10,000 is limited to the $6,000 tax liability in the year of the investment acquisitions. In addition, if the firm's tax liability exceeds $25,000, the credit may not exceed $25,000 plus 85% of the tax liability over that amount in the year of acquisition. If a firm has an annual tax liability of $40,000 and has qualifying investments of $500,000, 10% of its qualified investments would be $50,000. The firm's ITC, however, is now limited to $37,750—that is, $25,000 plus 85% of the $15,000 of the tax liability over $25,000. However, the tax code permits the $4,000 and the $2,250 unused portions of the ITC from the two preceding examples to be carried back 3 years and forward 15 years.

Table 7-4 illustrates the initial cost computations for four projects that qualify for the credit as well as the amount of taxes the firm must pay after adjustments are made for the ITC.

Table 7-4 ITC, Initial Cost, and Tax Computations

Project	Basis Prior to ITC	Life	ITC	Cost Net of ITC
A	$ 20,000	3	$ 1,800	$ 18,200
B	90,000	5	9,000	81,000
C	50,000	10	5,000	45,000
D	10,000	15	1,000	9,000
Total	$170,000		$16,800	$153,200

Federal tax liability	$100,000
Less: ITC	16,800
Equals: Adjusted federal tax liability	$ 83,200

Book Gains and Losses

A gain or loss arises on the sale of an asset whenever the asset's adjusted basis differs from the selling price. The adjusted basis of an asset is its initial acquisition price less cost recovery (or depreciation) allowances taken up to the date of the sale. Cost recovery (or depreciation) is an allocation of the initial cost of an asset—such as buildings, machinery, or equipment—whose life extends beyond 1 year, over an actual or assumed useful life for that asset. (Note that land is not a depreciable asset.) Under the current Accelerated Cost Recovery System, assets are assigned to classes of 3, 5, 10, or 15 years. Costs are recovered over these assigned periods or over an allowable longer period. The cost recovery life, however, is now totally unrelated to the asset's actual useful life to the user. Under prior systems of depreciation for tax purposes, the useful life of the asset was related to the tax life. Thus, if a piece of equipment had an initial cost of $10,000 and a useful life of 5 years, the $10,000 could be allocated equally over the 5-year life by recognizing $2,000 of depreciation expense each year. This allocation was in recognition of the fact that one-fifth of the value of the asset was used up each year. While we no longer have to deal with the actual useful life of the asset as a factor in determining cost recovery amounts (annual cost recovery percentages are specified for the assets by their class), the adjusted basis is still the initial cost less cost recovery to date. Gain or loss on the sale of an asset is determined by the difference between the selling price of the asset and its adjusted basis.

Frequently, a book gain or loss will occur and influence the replacement decision by affecting the initial cost of the new asset being purchased to replace the old asset. Since the annual recovery charge is a tax deductible item, it is necessary to make an adjustment in federal taxes when the sale of an asset results in a book gain or loss. If the sale results in a $1,000 book gain when the corporate tax rate is 40%, the firm's taxes will be $400 higher in the year the asset is sold. The $400 in additional taxes now is in recognition of the fact that the firm was permitted to deduct too much through cost recovery charges in prior years. The reduction in prior year's taxes is now "recovered" through a tax on the gain on the sale of the asset. Conversely, if the sale of an asset results in a $1,000 book loss, too little was permitted in prior years for cost recovery charges. Since taxes paid in prior years were too high, the firm is now allowed to deduct the loss on the sale and lower taxes in the current year. If the firm's corporate tax rate is 40%, the $1,000 book loss would result in a $400 reduction in taxes for the year of sale.

The sale of an old asset can influence the new asset's initial cost both by the cash flow from its sale and by the tax impact of a book gain or loss. Table 7-5 contains computations to determine the sale price and tax impact of a book loss on the initial cost of a new machine.

Under prior tax depreciation systems, the annual depreciation charges should have reflected the loss in economic value or wearing out of an asset. Theoretically,

Table 7-5 Sale Price and Book Loss Impacts on the Initial Cost of a New Asset

Adj. Basis, old asset	$30,000
Less: Sale price, old asset	25,000
Equals: Book loss	5,000
Times: Corporate tax rate	.40
Equals: Positive cash flow from tax loss	2,000
Plus: Sale price, old asset	25,000
Equals: Total cash flow from sale, old asset	$27,000
Purchase price, new asset	$64,000
Plus: Shipping and transportation charges	3,400
Installation costs	1,600
Basis, new asset	69,000
Less: 10% ITC	6,900
Cash flow from the old asset	27,000
Equals: Initial cost of the new asset	$35,100

then the asset's book value, the initial cost less cumulative annual depreciation charges, should have equalled the salvage value or the sale price of the asset in any year. From a practical standpoint, however, this hardly ever occurred. Under ACRS no such correspondence is intended. Cost recovery deductions are simply artificial in nature and it is now highly unlikely that the sale price or salvage value would equal the adjusted basis of the asset at the time of the sale. A book loss on the sale of an asset gives rise to a current deduction and a reduction in taxes because of the cost recovery amounts which were too little in prior years. In the example in Table 7-5, the $30,000 book value exceeds the $25,000 sale price, and there is a $5,000 book loss. The firm is permitted a current $5,000 deduction, reducing the firm's tax liability in the year of sale by $2,000. The sum of the reduction in tax liability due to the book loss, $2,000, and the sale price of the asset, $25,000, is the total cash flow from disposing of the old asset. This $27,000 cash inflow reduces the initial cash outflow required for asset replacement.

Table 7-6 illustrates a book gain that produces the opposite tax effect of a book loss. When a firm sells an asset for more than its adjusted basis, the firm received a tax benefit in prior years. The book gain in the year of sale increases current taxes. In the example, an $84,000 sale price for an asset with a $53,000 adjusted basis yields a book gain of $31,000 and an additional tax liability of $12,400. The tax on the book gain reduces the cash inflow from the old asset from $84,000 to $71,600. This raises the initial cost of the replacement asset from $64,530 to $76,930, due to the additional tax burden of $12,400 resulting from disposal of the old asset at a gain.

Table 7-6   Sale Price and Book Gain Impacts on the Initial Cost of a New Asset

Sale price, old asset	$84,000
Less: Adj. Basis, old asset	53,000
Equals: Book gain	31,000
Times: Corporate tax rate	.40
Equals: Tax on book gain	$12,400
Sale price, old asset	$84,000
Less: Tax on book gain	12,400
Equals: Cash flow from sale, old asset	$71,600
Purchase price, new asset	$113,000
Plus: Shipping and transportation charges	1,950
Installation costs	14,080
Increase in net working capital	19,500
Basis, new asset	148,530
Less: Cash flow from the old asset	71,600
Equals: Initial cost	$ 76,930

Federal Capital Gains Tax

The federal capital gains tax is another major federal tax. Generally, this tax applies only to assets that are sold in other than the normal course of business and that have been owned at least 12 months.[2] Most depreciable assets fall into this category. Examples of transactions subject to the capital gains tax are

1. The sale of a year-old automatic canner by a food processor
2. The sale of a heavy-duty sewing machine no longer used by a shoe manufacturer
3. The sale of stock in another company at a profit
4. The sale of a grading tractor by a building contractor

The capital gains tax is 28% and is levied on the positive difference between the sales price of the asset and its original cost.

THE ANNUAL BENEFITS FROM AN INVESTMENT

The previous section discusses in detail the items that must be considered in computing the initial cost of an investment. The second category of information needed

---

[2]The Economic Recovery Act of 1981 requires recapture at ordinary corporate tax rates if a firm uses the ACRS rates. Firms electing, however, to use the straight-line option on non-residential real estate avoid recapture, and have capital gain instead.

to evaluate a project proposal is the stream of annual benefits resulting from the initial investment cost. The necessary information to make a complete evaluation would include such things as annual revenue, costs, cost savings, salvage values, earnings, taxes, and cash flow.

Why Cash Flows Are Important

Most practitioners agree that there are two types of annual information available for any project: earnings and cash flow. Earnings are defined as revenue minus expenses. Annual revenue from a project is the dollar amount of additional sales produced by the investment during one year; project expenses are the actual costs incurred in the production of goods sold in the same year.

Earnings are relevant because the principal long-term objective of the firm is maximization of owners' wealth. Stock price appreciation is an important element in this maximization. Because many investors evaluate a firm's stock in relation to its prospective earnings, the importance of the earnings contribution realized by new projects is apparent. Another reason why earnings are relevant is found in the way in which executives are compensated. Many firms with decentralized divisions judge each division's performance on its ability to generate accounting income. An executive who is rewarded in terms of his or her unit's overall earnings is going to be very interested in the earning power of each project. The importance of each project's earnings to the asset selection process should not be overlooked.

However, the use of earnings as input to asset selection has some serious shortcomings. First, earnings afford only an accounting view of the project and neglect the project's cash flow position. Under usual accounting practice, revenue is recognized when the product is sold, not when the cash is collected from the sale; revenue may remain a paper figure for months or years before payment of the invoice is received. Expenses, too, are recognized when incurred and not when actually paid. Second, annual depreciation charges for plant and equipment are deducted from gross revenue to arrive at before-tax earnings. While this practice gives an accurate picture of the true benefits of a particular project, it ignores the increased flow of funds potentially available for other uses.

Table 7-7 compares the annual earnings and cash flow of a project. The earnings of $78,000 differ from the cash flow of $178,000 by the depreciation charge of $100,000. Notice that the $178,000 is the actual amount of cash that is available. Because recovery charges are a noncash deduction from revenue, net earnings give only a partial picture of the tangible benefits available. A complete picture of each project's benefits is required to account for the potential reinvestment of these benefits. Consequently, the use of earnings as an input to the asset selection process is excluded in subsequent discussions in favor of cash flows because they represent the total benefits of the project available for reinvestment.

The cash flow of a project may be described as the actual or estimated inflow

Table 7-7 Annual Benefits Accounting Profit and Net Cash Flow

	Earnings	Net Cash Flow
Revenue	$480,000	$480,000
Expenses	250,000	250,000
EBDT	230,000	230,000
Depreciation	100,000	—
EBT	130,000	—
Taxes @ 40%	52,000	52,000
Earnings	$ 78,000	—
Net cash flow		$178,000

and outflow of cash that occurs over a given period of time. If during that time inflow exceeds outflow, the result is net cash proceeds; if outflow exceeds inflow, the result is net cash outlays. The entire series of net proceeds and net outlays associated with an investment constitute the cash flow of the investment.

The Federal Corporate Tax Rate

As the computations in Table 7-7 indicate, the annual benefits associated with an investment are determined on an after-tax base. However, it is not immediately apparent whether before- or after-tax cash flow is more relevant to asset selection. Table 7-8 is a comparison of two projects, each of which is evaluated on the basis of its before- and after-tax cash flow. Projects A and B are equal in all respects except that project A includes a $25 recovery allowance charge. Both projects have the same cash flow before taxes. However, project A's after-tax cash flow is $10 greater than project B's. The before-tax cash flow excludes the effect of noncash

Table 7-8 Before- and After-Tax Evaluation of Two Projects

	Project A		Project B	
	Earnings	Cash Flow	Earnings	Cash Flow
Revenue	$100	$100	$100	$100
Expenses	50	50	50	50
Recovery allowance	25	—	—	—
EBT	25	—	50	—
Cash flow BT	—	50	—	50
Taxes @ 40%	10	10	20	20
Earnings	$ 15	—	$ 30	—
Net cash flow		$ 40		$ 30

charges, such as the recovery allowance, which reduce taxes, thereby increasing project A's net cash flow. As the impact of taxes between projects becomes more pronounced, it is apparent that after-tax cash flow is more relevant.

The corporate tax rate becomes important when cash flow is measured on an after-tax basis. The present corporate income tax rate is 15%, 18%, 30%, and 40% of the first, second, third, and fourth $25,000 of earnings, respectively. A maximum rate of 46% is applied to all income above $100,000.[3] For given levels of revenue, expenses, and recovery allowance, the lower the corporate tax rate, the higher the after-tax cash flow. The converse is also true. For simplicity, a combined tax rate of 40% will continue to be used in this text. In addition, there are other features of tax law that influence annual cash flows.

Asset Depreciation

Asset depreciation is the allocation of the book value of an asset over its useful life. The federal and most state tax codes allow a firm to deduct annual depreciation or cost recovery charges from earnings to arrive at before-tax earnings. Federal depreciation laws have been changed several times in the past couple of decades. The most recent changes occurred in August 1981, with the introduction of the accelerated cost recovery system (ACRS), and in 1982 by the Tax Equity and Fiscal Responsibility Act (TEFRA). A major purpose of the ACRS was to simplify tax depreciation computations and selection of tax lives for depreciable assets.

Asset Depreciation Requirements. First, to be depreciated, an asset must be used in the business to produce earnings rather than held for sale in the ordinary course of business. A truck used by one firm to haul materials would be a depreciable property, but the same truck awaiting sale on a truck dealer's lot would not be depreciable. Second, the asset must have a limited useful life. Land, for example, is not depreciable, but improvements to the land are depreciable. Third, the firm must have a capital interest in the asset; thus, a leased asset is not normally depreciable. Finally, an asset with a useful life of less than 1 year cannot be depreciated, but it may be deductible as a current operating expense.

The Accelerated Cost Recovery Systems. While ACRS may have simplified depreciation calculations, it may have caused, at least initially, some confusion over terminology. For example, depreciation has been replaced by the term "recovery allowance" or "recovery deduction." The old and new terminology is given in Table 7-9.

Under ACRS, all recovery property is assigned to a 3-year, 5-year, 10-year, or 15-year class. The type of property assigned to the 3-year class includes automobiles, light trucks, and tangible personal property used in research. Five-year property includes most machinery, equipment, and furniture. The 15-year property

---

[3]The Tax Reform Act of 1984 limits the benefit of the lower tax rates for corporations with taxable income in excess of $1,000,000.

Table 7-9   Changes in Depreciation Terminology

Depreciation Term	ACRS Term
Depreciable property	Recovery property
Depreciation deduction	Recovery allowance or deduction
Tax life	Recovery period
Depreciation rates	Recovery rates

Table 7-10   ACRS Periods and Recovery Rates

	Recovery Rate for Recovery Period			
In Year	3-Yr	5-Yr	10-Yr	15-Yr
1	25%	15%	8%	5%
2	38	22	14	10
3	37	21	12	9
4	—	21	10	8
5	—	21	10	7
6	—	—	10	7
7	—	—	9	6
8	—	—	9	6
9	—	—	9	6
10	—	—	9	6
11	—	—	—	6
12	—	—	—	6
13	—	—	—	6
14	—	—	—	6
15	—	—	—	6

Table 7-11   ACRS Recovery Deductions

(1) Year	(2) Basis	(3) ACRS Rates	(4) = (3) × $9,700 Recovery Deduction	(5) = (2) − (4) Ending Basis
1	$9,700	25%	$2,405	$7,275
2	7,275	38	3,686	3,589
3	3,589	37	2,200	—

class contains most real property. The 10-year (and a second 15-year) property class contains public utility and other real property.

The full cost of the property is recovered over the appropriate 3-, 5-, 10-, or 15-year period. Furthermore, no adjustment for salvage value is required and the taxpayer is no longer concerned with straight-line, double-declining-balance or sum-of-the-year's-digits rates. Rather, the taxpayer multiplies a statutory recovery rate by the recovery basis of the property to obtain the recovery deduction. Table 7-10 contaiins the recovery percentage for each of the recovery periods.[4]

The recovery basis is the total dollar amount that can be deducted over the asset's life. Under one tax treatment, the recovery basis is determined by subtracting 50% of the investment tax credit from the book value of the asset. Thus, an asset with a book value of $10,000 and a 3-year ACRS tax life has a recovery basis of $10,000 − (.5)(.06)($10,000), or $9,700. The ACRS rates are applied to the reduced basis of $9,700, not to the $10,000 full basis.[5]

For example, suppose that an asset has a basis of $10,000, a salvage value of $1,000, and a recovery period of 3 years. Table 7-10 indicates recovery percentages of 25%, 38%, and 37% in years 1, 2, 3, respectively. The recovery deduction for year 1 is $9,700(.25), or $2,425; for year 2, it is $9,700(.38), or $3,686; and for year 3, it is $9,700(.37), or $3,589. Thus, the ACRS rates allow the $9,700 to be recovered without consideration or adjustment for the $1,000 estimated salvage value. These computations are summarized in Table 7-11.

A COMPREHENSIVE EXAMPLE

It may seem that determining the initial cash expenditures, annual cash flows, and terminal cash flows (salvage value) is difficult and complex. Perhaps a comprehensive example can suggest how these tasks can be simplified by examining them sequentially as subproblems and review several of the major topics covered in the chapter.

The management of a firm is considering an investment project that promises to have a purchase price of $150,000 and a scrap value of $10,000 at the end of its 5-year life. Transportation charges are expected to be $5,000, with installation charges for labor and material estimated to be $15,000 and $10,000, respectively. If the project is accepted, a spare parts inventory of $10,000 must also be acquired initially and maintained. It is estimated that these spare parts will have an estimated scrap value in 5 years equal to 60% of their initial cost.

Annual revenue from this project is expected to be $170,000, with annual

[4]The ACRS does permit the taxpayer to use the straight-line method as an alternative to these statutory recovery rates.

[5]This is the standard ACRS treatment that allows the firm to claim the full ITC. An alternative treatment allows the full book value to be recovered, but the ITC percentage must be reduced. See footnote 1.

Table 7-12 Initial Cash Expenditure Computations

Purchase price	$150,000
Plus: Transportation charges	5,000
Installation expense	
Labor	15,000
Material	10,000
Equals: Basis	180,000
Less: ITC ($180,000)(.06)	10,800
Plus: Spare parts inventory	10,000
Equals: Initial cost	$179,200

labor, material, and maintenance expenses estimated to be $15,000, $50,000, and $5,000, respectively. While the proposed asset has an expected economic life of 5 years, its ACRS recovery period is 3 years. If the firm uses a 40% corporate tax rate and the ITC, determining the basis, cash expenditure, annual earnings after taxes, annual cash flows, and the salvage value is done as follows.

The initial cash expenditure consists of the sum of the purchase price, transportation charges, installation expenses, and spare parts inventory less the 10% investment tax credit. In addition, the spare parts inventory is not a depreciable asset; consequently, it is not eligible for the 10% investment tax credit, but it is part of the initial cost because a $10,000 cash outflow occurs. The computations of the project's initial cost are shown in Table 7-12.

To calculate the annual earnings after taxes, annual labor, material, maintenance, recovery charges, and taxes must be subtracted from the annual revenue. Labor, material, and maintenance charges are estimated to be the same in each year (as is revenue); their total is $70,000, and this is subtracted from $170,000 to yield annual earnings before depreciation and taxes of $100,000. The recovery deduction in each year for 3 years is found by multiplying the 3-year ACRS rates and $180,000 − (.5)(.06)($180,000), or $174,500. Since the asset has a tax life of 3 years and an economic life of 5 years, there will be no recovery deduction in years 4 and 5. If the recovery charges are subtracted from earnings before depreciation and taxes (EBDT),

Table 7-13 Annual Earnings after Taxes and Cash Flow Calculations

Year	EBDT	Recovery Charges	EBT	Taxes	EAT	NCF
1	$100,000	$43,650	$ 56,350	$22,540	$33,810	$77,460
2	100,000	66,348	33,652	13,461	20,191	86,539
3	100,000	64,602	35,398	14,159	21,239	85,841
4	100,000	—	100,000	40,000	60,000	60,000
5	100,000	—	100,000	40,000	60,000	60,000

Table 7-14 Salvage Computations

Salvage value, project	$10,000
Salvage value, spare parts (60% × $10,000)	6,000
Equals: Total salvage value, end of year 5	$16,000

earnings before taxes (EBT) results. The tax rate times EBT yields taxes that are then subtracted from EBT to produce earnings after taxes. Annual net cash flows (NCF) are found by subtracting the total outflow of cash from the $170,000 of annual cash inflows. These computations are shown in Table 7-13.

Salvage value computations are shown in Table 7-14. The total salvage value consists of the scrap value on the asset plus the expected cash inflow from the disposal of the spare parts.

Summary

This chapter has focused on the development of the information that permits meaningful comparisons among investment alternatives. Data in support of specific projects are concerned with the size of the initial cost and the measurement of future benefits.

Earnings are relevant to the asset selection decision because of their impact on stock price appreciation. However, earnings ignore the flow of funds from noncash charges such as depreciation and, as a result, do not give a complete picture of the firm's cash position. Cash flows then are usually used in place of earnings to analyze investment opportunities. Because of the impact of the federal tax structure and its provisions governing depreciation methods and investment incentives, after-tax cash flow is more relevant to the asset selection decision.

The discussion of taxes and depreciation is meant as a concise picture of the major provisions governing a rather complex topic. The selection of the best method of depreciation for a particular project is discussed in more detail in the next chapter. When considering a particular project, it is necessary, of course, to consult the relevant sections of the Internal Revenue Code for special provisions and eligibility of particular assets.

Questions

1. What are the characteristics of capital investments?
2. When making capital investment decisions, what types of information must be gathered?
3. Define marginal analysis in terms of the capital investment decision.
4. What types of costs must be considered when determining the original cost of a capital investment?
5. What is the investment tax credit?

6. How do book gains and losses on disposal of old assets affect the cost of a new investment?

7. Describe the application of the capital gains tax to a sale of a business property by a firm.

8. Why is cash flow superior to earnings when evaluating the benefits of a proposed capital project?

Problems

1. The Val N. Tine Corporation is considering the purchase of a more efficient machine for the manufacturing of hunting bows. What initial cost would be used for capital budgeting decisions from the following data:

Machine purchase price, f.o.b. factory	$28,000
Installation costs	2,000
Start-up expenses	1,500
Shipping costs	750
Salvage value at end of life	2,250
5-year ACRS property	

2. The X-AM Company has several projects under consideration. Determine the initial cost that would be used for each project from the following data:

	Project A	Project B	Project C	Project D
Purchase price, f.o.b. factory	$43,000	$125,000	$95,000	$180,000
Transportation charges	7,000	5,000	3,000	10,000
Installation costs	500	7,000	4,000	8,000
Employee retraining costs	—	2,000	1,000	4,000
Increase in accounts receivable	—	30,000	10,000	50,000
Increase in inventory	10,000	20,000	20,000	40,000
Increase in accounts payable	—	20,000	20,000	40,000

3. Terry Knot, the financial analyst for Biggs and Smallish Corporation, failed to consider the 10% ITC when determining the total initial outlay for several projects under consideration. Would the initial cost be affected by the ITC in each of the following cases?

	Project L	Project M	Project N	Project O
Purchase price, f.o.b. destination	$75,000	$21,000	$8,000	$28,000
Installation costs	10,000	3,000	500	2,000
Net increase in working capital	20,000	—	—	5,000
ACRS Property Class	10 yr	5 yr	3 yr	5 yr

4. The Eager Beater Company manufactures a revolutionary egg beater for home and commercial uses. It is considering expanding its operations and has two expansion options available. What initial cost would be used for each of the projects, given the following information?

	Project Q	Project R
Purchase price, f.o.b. factory	$240,000	$600,000
Transportation charges	15,000	20,000

	Project Q	Project R
Installation materials cost	8,000	10,000
Installation labor cost	12,000	15,000
Selling price of asset to be replaced	40,000	50,000
Book value of asset to be replaced	30,000	60,000
Net increase in working capital	40,000	50,000

The corporate tax rate is 40%, the current ITC is 10%, and the ACRS property class of both alternatives is 5 years.

5. Compare accounting income (earnings) and cash flow for two projects from the following data if the corporate tax rate is 40%:

	A	B
Revenues	$25,000	$36,000
Expenses	12,000	10,000
Cost recovery	3,750	5,400

6. Chuck Hole, of the Hole Chucker Corporation, must evaluate the purchase of a new grinding machine. To assist in the evaluation, construct a cost recovery schedule and a cash flow schedule under the following conditions:

Initial cost	$100,000
Salvage value	$15,000
ACRS property class	5 years
Corporate tax rate	30%
Investment tax credit	10%
Estimated annual earnings	$12,000

BIBLIOGRAPHY

Commerce Clearing House, Inc. *Explanation of Economic Recovery Tax Act of 1981.* Chicago, Commerce Clearing House, 1981.

Johnson, James M. "Optimal Tax Lives of Depreciable Assets." *Financial Management,* Autumn 1979, pp. 27–31.

Johnson, James M. "Optimal Tax Lives of Depreciable Assets: Reply." *Financial Management,* Autumn 1980, p. 79.

Osteryoung, Jerome S. *Capital Budgeting,* 2nd ed. Columbus: Grid, Inc., 1979.

———, Daniel E. McCarty, and Karen A. Fortin. "A Note on the Optimal Tax Lives for Assets Qualifying for the Investment Tax Credit." *The Accounting Review,* April 1980, pp. 301–306.

———, Daniel E. McCarty, and Karen A. Fortin. "Optimal Tax Lives of Depreciable Assets: Comment." *Financial Management,* Autumn 1980, pp. 77–78.

———, Daniel E. McCarty, and Karen A. Fortin. "A Note on Optimal Depreciation Research." *The Accounting Review,* July 1981, pp. 719–721.

———, Karen A. Fortin, and Daniel E. McCarty. "How the New Cost Recovery System Compares with Prior Methods." *Management Accounting,* November 1981, pp. 13–20.

Prentice-Hall, Inc. *1985 Federal Tax Course.* Englewood Cliffs, N.J.: Prentice-Hall, Inc., 1985.

8

Capital Budgeting: Evaluation Techniques

Once data are collected on the characteristics common to all projects—earnings, expenses, tax liabilities, and cash flows—a method is needed to compare and evaluate the different projects under consideration. Many methods have been developed for project evaluation. They range from simple rules of thumb to sophisticated mathematical models. This chapter considers the advantages and disadvantages of the four most commonly used methods. These evaluation techniques are discussed assuming that all costs and benefits from each project are known with absolute certainty, that the firm's investment plans are not limited by any lack of funds, and that the firm has a singular objective of maximizing just one goal when evaluating projects. These assumptions simplify the discussion by excluding for the moment consideration of the concepts of risk, funds limitation, and multiple goals. The assumption regarding risk is relaxed in the second section of this chapter.[1]

EVALUATION TECHNIQUES

The four evaluation techniques most frequently used for project evaluations are (1) average rate of return (ARR); (2) payback (PB); (3) net present value (NPV); and (4) internal rate of return (IRR). Each of these methods will be examined and evaluated in turn.

[1] For a more detailed discussion for some of the topics in this chapter, see Jerome S. Osteryoung, *Capital Budgeting*, 2nd ed. (Columbus: Grid, Inc., 1979).

Average Rate of Return

The average rate of return, known also as the accounting rate of return or simply the rate of return, is defined as the project's average earnings divided by the average investment. In mathematical notation, Equation 8-1 defines the average rate of return as

$$\text{ARR} = \frac{\sum_{t=1}^{n} E_t \big/ n}{[(B - S)/2] + S} \tag{8-1}$$

where E_t = earnings after taxes in the tth period
        n = the life of the project
        B = basis
        S = the salvage value
   $B - S$ = basis − salvage

The numerator of Equation 8-1 is the average earnings for the project and is the sum of the project's total earnings divided by the life of the project. The denominator, the average investment, is one-half the project's basis less salvage plus any anticipated salvage value.

Table 8-1 presents the schedule of annual earnings for a project with an initial cost of $1,800 and a salvage value of $200. The basis base for this equipment is $1,600 (the initial cost minus the salvage value). The average investment is $1,000, one-half the basis less salvage ($800) plus the salvage value ($200). This $1,000 is a proxy for the average amount of funds invested in the project over its life-time. The average earnings are $900/3, or $300, and the average rate of return is $300/1,000, or 30%. A firm that uses this method normally must decide beforehand what is a desirable average rate of return. Projects exceeding this rate are deemed acceptable; projects whose earnings fall below this desired rate are rejected.

Recent empirical studies indicate that this method is widely used by business

Table 8-1   Project Initial Cost, Salvage Value, and Earnings

Initial cost	$1,800
Salvage value (at the end of 3 years)	200
Year	*Earnings after Taxes*
1	$ 200
2	300
3	400

Table 8-2   A Comparison of Two Projects

	Project A	Project B
Initial cost	$3,600	$3,600
Salvage value	400	400
Earnings in year		
1	400	800
2	600	600
3	800	400

firms. The popularity of this technique probably stems from its ease of calculation; more important, it is the only evaluation technique explicitly using project profitability as a decision criterion. Since profitability is the goal of the firm, the continued popularity of the ARR is, no doubt, assured.[2]

Although the ARR offers an evaluation based on profitability, it has several serious deficiencies. Principally, it does not consider the timing of the receipts of a project's benefits. Table 8-2 provides data for a comparison of project A and project B using the ARR method. While the ARRs for both projects are equal to 30%, the benefits are received in different time periods. Most firms would prefer project B because the return is greater in the early years. The earlier a project's benefits are realized, the sooner they can be reinvested. The ARR method of evaluation cannot differentiate with respect to the timing of returns between projects.

Second, this method does not take into account any benefits that might be received from the sale of the old equipment that is replaced. If the initial cost of a new machine is $1,800 but $300 is received from the sale of the old machine, the ARR method does not provide for a reduction in the initial cost of the new machine by $300.

A third problem of the ARR is its singular attention to earnings to the exclusion of cash flow. Earnings calculations do not take into account the total reinvestment potential of a project's benefits; cash flow analysis considers this potential and hence the total benefits of the project.

Finally, the ARR does not differentiate between the size of the investment required for each project. Several proposed projects may have the same ARR but different average investments, as illustrated in Table 8-3. That is, the ARR cannot discriminate between projects with different initial fund requirements.

---

[2]The average rate of return method uses accounting income which, under generally accepted accounting principles (GAAP), must use methods of depreciation that differ from the ACRS recovery amounts used for cash flow determinations. The accounting method for determining straight-line, sum-of-the-years'-digits, or double-declining-balance depreciation methods are used for depreciation. Many firms for convenience will use tax depreciation methods for accounting income, but it is not GAAP.

Table 8-3   A Comparison of Average Earnings, Investments, and Rates of Return

	Project		
	A	B	C
Average annual earnings	$ 3,000	$1,000	$ 2,000
Average investment	15,000	5,000	10,000
Average rate of return	20%	20%	20%

Payback

One of the deficiencies of the ARR method is the absence of cashflow analysis. Payback, however, the second evaluation technique, uses cash flow as an input to asset selection. This method, sometimes called the payback period method, is defined as the number of years of cash flow required to recapture the original cost of an investment, normally without regard to salvage value. There are two methods of calculating payback. The first method is used when a project's cash flow is the same in each year of the project's life. The second method is used when a project's cash flow varies from year to year.

Table 8-4 contains earnings and cash flow data for a project with equal annual cash flows, an initial cost of $10,000, and a useful life of 10 years. The payback period is 6.25 years, obtained by dividing the original cost by the constant annual cash flow: $10,000/$1,600 = 6.25.

When annual cash flows vary, PB is calculated by analyzing the cumulative cash flow. Table 8-5 shows the unequal annual cash flows and cumulative cash flow for a project with a $15,000 initial cost and a 5-year useful life. The cumulative cash flows are the summation of the project's annual cash flows from its inception to that

Table 8-4   Earnings and Cash Flow for a Project

	Earnings	Cash Flow
Annual savings	$2,000	$2,000
Depreciation	1,000	—
EBT	1,000	—
Taxes @ 40%	400	400
EAT	$ 600	
Cash flow		$1,600

Table 8-5   Annual and Cumulative Cash Flows for a Project

Year	Annual Cash Flow	Cumulative Cash Flow
1	$2,000	$ 2,000
2	4,000	6,000
3	6,000	12,000
4	7,000	19,000
5	3,000	22,000

specific year. In year 3, the cumulative cash flow for the project is

$$\begin{array}{ccc} \text{Year 1} & \text{Year 2} & \text{Year 3} \\ \$2{,}000 + & \$4{,}000 + & \$6{,}000 = \$12{,}000 \end{array}$$

The cumulative cash flow at the end of the fourth year ($19,000) exceeds the initial cost of the investment ($15,000). Since the recovery of the investment falls between the third and fourth year, the payback period is 3-and-a-fraction years. To calculate the fraction, the amount of funds needed to recover the investment in year 4 is divided by the amount of cash flow in that year. Since the cumulative cash flow in year 3 is $12,000, we need another $3,000 to recover the total initial cost of $15,000. The annual cash flow in year 4 is $7,000; thus, the payback fraction is $3,000/$7,000, or .43. The payback period for the project, therefore, is 3.43 years.

The acceptance criterion for payback is usually determined by company policy as a function of funds availability. The acceptable payback period is usually decreased during times of funds shortages, and it is not uncommon for firms to have payback periods of only one or two years during periods of cash stringency.

Although payback is easily calculated, it disregards all cash flow beyond the payback period. Table 8-6 shows alternative projects with payback periods of two

Table 8-6   Initial Costs, Cash Flows, and Payback Periods for Two Projects

	Project A	Project B
Initial cost	$3,000	$3,000
Cash flow in year		
1	1,000	1,000
2	2,000	2,000
3	—	1,000
4	—	1,000
5	—	1,000
Payback period	2	2

Table 8-7 Initial Costs and Cash Flows for Two Projects

	Project A	Project B
Initial cost	$600	$600
Cash flow in year		
1	100	300
2	200	200
3	300	100

years. The projects differ, however, in the amount of cash flow generated after the second year. The cash flow for project A stops at the end of year 2, whereas the cash flow for project B continues into year 5. Most firms would prefer project B because of the continuing cash flow after the payback period. The PB method fails to take this into consideration.

Another deficiency is that payback does not differentiate between projects in terms of the timing of the cash flow, a problem similar to that encountered with the ARR. Some projects have high returns in their early years that then decrease; others start with lower yields but increase cash flow throughout their lives. Table 8-7 is a comparison of the annual cash flows of two such projects. Although both projects have the same $600 initial cost, the cash flows in years 1 and 3 differ by $200. The payback period for both projects is 3 years, but project B has the obvious advantage of supplying the firm with cash for reinvestment at an earlier time than project A.

Net Present Value

Net present value (NPV) is the first capital budgeting technique that incorporates a time factor when evaluating the costs and benefits of a project. NPV is defined as the summation of the present value of the annual net cash flows minus the present value of the initial cost. For example, a project with an initial cost of $10,000 with annual cash flows as indicated in Table 8-8 has an NPV of $363. The annual cash

Table 8-8 Project Annual Cash Flows

Year	Cash Flow	Discount Rate @ 14%*	Present Value
1	$6,000	.877	$ 5,262
2	4,000	.769	3,076
3	3,000	.675	2,025
Total			$10,363

*From the Appendix.

flows must be converted to present values by discounting them to the present using a discount factor, in this example, 14%. As explained in Chapter 1, discounting future cash flows is necessary because of the time value of money. The present value of the three net cash flows is $10,363 at 14%. The NPV of the project is thus $10,363 less $10,000, or $363.

The decision rule for a project under NPV is to accept the projects as long as the NPV is zero or positive. An NPV of zero implies that the original investment is recovered and that a return equal to the discount rate is earned on funds employed. Therefore, any project with a zero or positive NPV should be accepted.

A mathematical model of the NPV is given in Equation 8-2;

$$NPV = \frac{A_1}{(1 + i)^1} + \frac{A_2}{(1 + i)^2} + \cdots + \frac{A_n}{(1 + i)^n} - I_O \qquad (8\text{-}2)$$

where A is the cash flow in periods 1 to n, I_O is the initial cost of the investment, and i is the discount rate. All cash flows are in a summation series except the initial cost, and therefore Equation 8-2 can be simplified as shown in Equation 8-3:

$$NPV = \sum_{t=1}^{n} \frac{A_t}{(1 + i)^t} - I_O \qquad (8\text{-}3)$$

The discount rate used in the NPV calculation is the marginal cost of capital to the firm. An extended discussion of the cost of capital is included in Chapter 13. However, one point needs elaboration at this time; because the discount rate already incorporates a charge for all funds being used to finance projects, it is unnecessary to reduce the annual cash flows by any finance charges. To do so would, in effect, be double-counting the finance costs. Although a firm can finance a new project at 8%, if its cost of capital is 20% only the 20% discount rate is used and the 8% is completely disregarded. The rationale is that even if the firm can borrow for a specific project, it always has the option of taking those funds and paying off both the debt and equity charges (this is the firm's cost of capital) and saving 20%. The 20% charge thus includes provision for repayment of 8% money. Consequently, the method or cost of obtaining funds for financing a specific project should be ignored because a complete finance charge is included in the calculation of the cost of capital.

An example involving the use of the NPV technique to evaluate a complete project is now appropriate. Firm KLM is considering replacing a piece of equipment that originally had a book value of $50,000, qualified for the 10% ITC, and had a 5-year ACRS life. The current book value is $19,950, but it has no salvage value now and 2 years remain of its tax and economic life. Replacement equipment can be purchased with a book value of $100,000. It has a 5-year ACRS tax life and a 7-year economic life. Annual earnings before depreciation and taxes are expected to be

$20,000; the corporate tax rate is 40%; and the cost of capital is 10%. Should the company replace the equipment?

First, the initial cash expenditure must be determined:

Basis, new	$100,000
Less: Book loss, old asset—.4($19,950)	7,980
ITC, new asset—.1($100,000)	10,000
Plus: ITC recapture, old—.4($5,000)	2,000
Equals: Initial cost, new	$ 84,020

Since the old asset has no salvage value but a $19,950 book value, the book loss amounts to $7,980. The firm took a $5,000 ITC on acquisition of the old asset; and because it was sold prior to its 5-year ACRS life, 40% of the initial ITC is recaptured.

Second, the annual cash flows over the 7 years of the project's life must be computed as shown in Table 8-9. Third, the net present value must be computed as illustrated in Table 8-10. Since a negative NPV results, the proposal should be rejected.

In this illustration, the increased recovery charge resulting from the purchase of the new equipment is applied to the old, and a net recovery deduction is found as suggested by the discussion in Chapter 7. In some cases, a negative EBT will shelter the firm's other taxable income because the tax effects encountered in evaluation are based not solely on an individual project's earnings but on all projects' earnings. Consequently, a tax loss on an individual project will shelter earnings by the loss times the corporate tax rate. The tax savings from this loss are credited to net cash flows in each year.

Evaluation of the NPV Technique. NPV has three characteristics that make it a very attractive technique to use in evaluating new assets. First, it considers the time value of money; second, it focuses on the marginal cash flow of projects; third, a changing discount rate can be built into NPV calculations by altering the denominator of Equation 8-2. However, the NPV technique suffers from several drawbacks. First, by focusing only on cash flow, the importance of earnings is ignored. That is, no consideration is given to earnings, about which most managements are vitally concerned. Second, the use of NPV also necessitates calculating the cost of capital. This calculation is very complex, and most experts do not agree as to the exact method to be used.

Internal Rate of Return

The internal rate of return of a project (sometimes referred to as the discounted rate of return) is the discount rate (r) that equates the present value of the net cash

Table 8-9 Project Annual Cash Flow Computations

(1) Year	(2) EBDT	(3) Net Depreciation	(4) = (2) − (3) EBT	(5) = .4 × (4) Taxes	(6) = (4) − (5) EAT	(7) = (2) − (5) NCF
1	$20,000	$ 4,275*	$15,725	$6,290	$ 9,435	$13,710
2	20,000	10,925	9,075	3,630	5,445	16,370
3	20,000	19,950	50	20	30	19,970
4	20,000	19,950	50	20	30	19,970
5	20,000	19,950	50	20	30	19,970
6	20,000	—	20,000	8,000	12,000	12,000
7	20,000	—	20,000	8,000	12,000	12,000

*Net depreciation in year 1 = .15($95,000) − $9,975 = $4,275; year 2 = .22($95,000) − $9,975 = $10,925.

Table 8-10 Project NPV Computations

(1) Year	(2) NCF	(3) Interest Factor (10%)	(4) = (2) × (3) Present Value
1	$13,710	.90909	$12,464
2	16,370	.82645	13,529
3	19,970	.75131	15,004
4	19,970	.68301	13,640
5	19,970	.62092	12,400
6	12,000	.56447	6,774
7	12,000	.51316	6,158
Total of present values			79,969
Less: Initial cost			84,020
Equals: NPV			$ (4,051)

inflows with the initial cost of the project as shown in the following equation:

$$\sum_{t=1}^{n} \frac{A_t}{(1 + r)^t} = I_O \qquad (8\text{-}4)$$

Note that this equation is similar to Equation 8-3. The calculation of the internal rate of return is usually a trial-and-error process. That is, different discount rates must be tried until one is found that will make the NPV equal to zero. For example, a project with an initial cost of $1,000 has net cash flows of $700 and $500 in years 1 and 2, respectively. If a 20% discount rate is assumed for the first trial, a negative $70 NPV results. A negative NPV means that the present value of the cash flows is less than the initial project cost and the discount rate must be lowered to raise the present value of the net cash flows to zero. If an 8% discount rate is tried, the NPV is $77.

This positive NPV occurred because the present value of the net cash flows is in excess of the initial cost. To reduce this excess, the discount rate must be increased. If a 14% discount rate is used, the NPV is −$1. Since this is very close to an NPV or zero, the IRR of this project is just under 14%. The acceptance criterion for the IRR method is simply that any project having an IRR equal to or greater than a desired cut-off rate is accepted. Normally, this cut-off rate is the cost of capital to the firm. It is important to note that the IRR of a project is determined completely independently of the cost of capital. In this illustration, if the cost of capital were 10%, this project would be accepted.

The IRR criterion has advantages similar to those of the NPV technique in that it, too, considers the time value of money and focuses on the marginal cash flows of a project. In addition, it has an advantage over the NPV technique in that it produces a return on a project expressed as a percentage, which most practitioners prefer over a return expressed as a dollar amount. However, the IRR does have several disadvantages. First, it is relatively difficult to compute by hand because of the large number of trial-and-error procedures required. This is not a major problem, since most firms have access to computers that can compute the IRR very quickly. A second disadvantage is that the IRR, like the NPV, ignores project earnings and focuses only on cash flows. Third, if the annual net cash flows for a project are both positive and negative over the project's life, multiple IRRs may be produced.

A final deficiency of the IRR centers on the reinvestment problem. The reinvestment problem arises when the firm is either constrained by funds rationing or evaluating mutually exclusive projects. When either of these situations exists, it is necessary to rank the projects prior to selection according to some preference criterion other than the conventional accept-or-reject decision. Under these conditions, we are searching for the best project rather than accepting all projects that exceed the minimum acceptance level. Both the IRR and NPV will produce identical lists of accepted projects when there are no limitations, but they produce different selections when limitations are specified.

There seem to be two approaches to what causes the differences in ranking. The first suggests that present value calculations include the assumption that any intermediate cash flows received are going to be reinvested at the appropriate cost of capital or IRR. The second makes no reinvestment assumption but rather makes an assumption relating to an equivalent amount of funds today (present value) that could be reinvested to equal the future amount. It can be shown that these two views are mathematically equal.

The correct method to use when evaluating mutually exclusive projects is that technique that correctly reflects *current* opportunity costs. The fundamental question here is: If the firm did not invest in a given project now, what return could be expected on a viable alternative investment? IRR evaluation assumes that the current opportunity cost or the rate available on alternative investments is equal to the IRR. This interest rate does not normally resemble any actual present or future opportunity rate because it is generated numerically. The only technique that effectively implants current and future opportunity rates in the asset selection is the NPV. With this technique, the user specifies the rate that he or she actually anticipates. For this reason, the NPV is frequently preferred over the IRR method.

ANALYSIS OF RISK IN CAPITAL BUDGETING DECISIONS

In the preceding sections, it was assumed that risk does not exist in the measurement and evaluation of cash flows. This, however, is an unrealistic assumption. Risk does exist, and in the present context, it refers to the set of unique outcomes for a given event that can be assigned probabilities. Most decision makers are able to specify probabilities for unique outcomes of a given event. These estimates are subjective, and their exact specification rests with the decision maker. Subjective probabilities are based on the decision maker's experience with the real world. However, the task here is not to examine how real-world experience results in the formulation of these subjective probabilities. Rather, the concern of this section is, first, to indicate how sensitivity analysis can isolate sources of risk and their impact on the capital budgeting decision and, second, to illustrate techniques that can be used to evaluate risk in the capital budgeting decision.

Sensitivity Analysis In Capital Budgeting

Risk enters the capital budgeting decision from many sources, (e.g., annual revenue, annual expense, project life, and maintenance costs). Locating the potential sources of risk and measuring their impact help in the quantification of the total project risk.

One method currently being used for locating potential sources of risk and measuring their impact on project evaluation is sensitivity analysis. With this technique, potential sources of risk can be located by comparing the percentage deviation of that source with the change in the IRR brought about by that source deviation. For example, a project with an initial cost, annual net cash flows, salvage value, and project life of $14,960, $3,000, $3,000, and 10 years, respectively, is being considered. A potential source of risk might be a change in annual cash flows. That is, the single best estimate of the project's annual cash flows is $3,000, but it could be as low as $2,000 or as high as $4,000. These low and high estimates are used to compute the IRRs in Table 8-11. As the last two columns in this table indicate, a 33% change in annual cash flow results in more than 33% change in the IRR. Thus, as should be expected, deviations in annual cash flows are a major source of risk associated with any project.

In a probabilistic sense, salvage value may be much less certain than the value of the annual cash flow, but its impact on the IRR is fairly small. In this example, a 33% change in salvage value will cause less than a 10% change in the IRR. Even though salvage value is relatively large compared with the initial cost and it is more

Table 8-11 Sensitivity Analysis of Annual Cash Flows

Annual Cash Flow	IRR	Percentage Change in	
		NCF	IRR
$2,000	7.2%	−33	−56
3,000	16.4	—	—
4,000	24.2	+33	+48

uncertain than the annual cash flows, it is less critical. In general, for a given change in a risk source, the closer the percentage change in IRR is to zero, the less critical is the value of this source in the capital budgeting decision.

It is important to note that sensitivity analysis does not really evaluate risk. Rather, it merely shows which elements in the decision-making process could be most risk prone, even though these factors may not necessarily be more risk prone. While sensitivity analysis is a tool designed to locate the elements that are most risk sensitive, the probabilistic element of each component in the decision-making process must still be evaluated.

Risk Evaluation Techniques

Once the nature and sources of risk are understood, this comprehension must be incorporated into the decision-making process. A number of techniques are presented to allow inclusion of risk and to evaluate the impact of risk upon decisions.

Risk-Adjusted Discount Rate. One of the simpler techniques for incorporating risk into a capital budgeting decision is the risk-adjusted discount (RAD) rate. With this tecnhique, the amount of risk inherent in a project is incorporated within the discount rate used in the NPV calculation. Equation 8-3 defined the NPV as follows:

$$NPV = \sum_{t=1}^{n} \frac{A_t}{(1 + i)^t} - I_O \tag{8-3}$$

The i represents the cost of capital that is the desired return for the *average* project in a firm's portfolio of assets. However, the majority of projects evaluated are *not* average projects in terms of risk and return. Some projects have more risk and commensurately more return; other projects have less risk and return.

The RAD rate attempts to evaluate the impact of risk on various projects by varying the discount rate to account for the amount of risk imbedded in a project. For example, a very low RAD rate is used if the firm is considering the purchase of a risk-free asset such as Treasury bills. Similarly, a rate much higher than the cost of capital would be used if the firm were considering a product expansion into an untried market. The decision rule for the RAD rate method is to accept the project if its NPV discounted at the RAD rate is positive and to reject the project if the NPV is negative.

In mathematical notation, the net present value model using the RAD rate becomes

$$NPV = \sum_{t=1}^{n} \frac{A_t}{(1 + RAD)^t} - I_O \tag{8-5}$$

A good approximation for the RAD rate is the cost of capital for a firm that is solely in the business of the new project being considered. For example, a manufacturing corporation is considering diversifying into land development. The RAD rate to use would be approximately the cost of capital to firms that are engaged only in land development.

It is often impossible to obtain the cost of capital for a comparable firm when evaluating a new project. When this occurs, the decision maker must specify in quantitative terms the percentage change in risk for this new project as compared with the firm's total risk composition. For example, if a decision maker evaluates a new asset that is twice as risky as the average of the firm's total assets, and the firm's cost of capital is 10%, then the correct RAD rate is approximately 20%.

A complete example of the RAD rate net present value will clarify these concepts. A project under consideration by a firm is considered to be 50% more risky than the firm's average asset. The project has an initial cost, annual net cash flows, and estimated life of $12,000, $4,000, and 5 years, respectively. Since the firm's cost of capital is 10% and the project is 50% riskier than the average project, the RAD rate is .10(1.5), or 15%. Thus, the RAD rate–adjusted NPV is $4,000(3.3522) less $12,000, or $1,409, and the project should be accepted.

While the concept of a RAD rate is appealing for its simplicity, the user should be aware of its three shortcomings. First, the calculation of the exact RAD rate for each project is, in most cases, an art and subject to a great deal of error. Second, the RAD rate conceptually adjusts the wrong element. It is the future cash flows of a project that are subject to risk, not the cost of capital; but the RAD rate adjusts the discount rate and does not adjust the variable cash flows. Finally, the RAD rate does not use all the information available from a probability distribution of a project's cash flows.

Certainty Equivalents. Another approach to the incorporation of risk in project evaluation is certainty equivalents (CE). Recall that the purpose of the time adjustment (present value) of a project's future cash flows is to make the summation of the project's cash flows comparable at one particular point in time. Certainty equivalents operate in the same manner to eliminate risk from project comparisons so that the projects can be compared on a riskless basis.

The CE formulation is

$$\text{NPV} = \sum_{t=1}^{n} \frac{\alpha_t A_t}{(1 + RF)^t} - I_O \qquad (8\text{-}6)$$

The α_t represents the CE for the project's cash flow in period t. The CE is computed by comparing the risky cash flow with a riskless cash flow. Assume a risky cash flow of $1,000 in some future year and a $700 cash flow that management believes is comparably riskless. That is, management is indifferent to a $1,000 risky flow and a $700 riskless flow. The CE in this case is .7, because .7 multiplied by $1,000 produces the riskless flow. The CE then is a fraction (between 0 and 1) that, when multiplied by the risky cash flow, produces an equivalent riskless flow.

In the CE formulation of the NPV, the discount rate is RF, where RF equals the risk-free rate. Since risk is eliminated from the numerator of the present value equation, it must also be eliminated from the denominator by using this risk-free rate for purposes of comparison. The decision rule for CE evaluation is to accept the project if the NPV is positive and reject it if the NPV is negative.

An example using the CE will help to clarify the concepts. Assume that an asset has the following characteristics:

Initial cost	$20,000
Net cash flow in year 1	15,000
Net cash flow in year 2	20,000
Net cash flow in year 3	10,000

With CEs of α_1, α_2, and α_3 equaling .9, .8, and .5, respectively, the resultant modified NPV at a risk-free discount rate of 6% is

$$\text{NPV} = \frac{.9(\$15,000)}{(1.06)^1} + \frac{.8(\$20,000)}{(1.06)^2} + \frac{.5(\$10,000)}{(1.06)^3} - \$20,000$$
$$= \$12,736 + \$14,240 + \$4,198 - \$20,000$$
$$= \$11,174$$

Summary

This chapter first discussed four generally used evaluation techniques: payback, average rate of return, net present value and internal rate of return. Each technique was developed, numerical examples were provided, and the advantages and disadvantages discussed. Second, risk adjustments were incorporated into the NPV capital budgeting decision techniques. Specifically, the risk-adjusted discount rate and certainty equivalents were used to illustrate how risk can be quantified and incorporated into the NPV.

Questions

1. Define and evaluate each of the four evaluation techniques discussed in this chapter.
2. What distinguishes the ARR evaluation technique from the others?
3. What is the decision rule for project acceptance using the NPV evaluation technique?
4. What is the decision rule for project acceptance using the IRR evaluation technique? What drawback is encountered in its use?

5. How may sensitivity analysis be applied to the evaluation techniques discussed in this chapter?
6. Define and evaluate the following risk evaluation techniques: discount rate and certainty equivalents.

Problems

1. Rick Rack, president of Tacky Trim Company, is considering the purchase of a new machine to manufacture heat-set fabric trims. Mr. Rack requires a 20% accounting rate of return for any project accepted. If the cost of the machine is $20,000, salvage value is projected at $2,000 at the end of its 5-year life, and annual accounting earnings are $4,000, should Mr. Rack accept the machine?
2. Redd Barn, owner of a chain of fast-food restaurants, is considering installing ice cream machines in each of his restaurants. The machines will cost $50,000 each. After-tax cash flows in the first 3 years are expected to be $5,000, $7,500, and $10,000, with after-tax cash flows of $12,000 per year in the fourth and subsequent years. What is the payback period?
3. What is the payback period of a project that requires a $14,000 initial cash outlay and has successive net after-tax cash inflows of $3,000, $4,500, $6,000, $4,500, and $3,000 in years 1 through 5?
4. The Winding Creek Waterbed Company is considering two alternative projects. Project X has an initial cost of $125,000, an economic life of 8 years, and no salvage value. Project Y costs $200,000, has an economic life of 8 years, and an estimated salvage value of $25,000. Cash flows anticipated for each project before recovery allowances and taxes are:

	X	Y
Yr 1–4	$25,000/yr	$45,000/yr
Yr 5–8	20,000/yr	45,000/yr

The full 10% investment tax credit is taken with corresponding property basis reduction. Each property is 5 year ACRS property. Determine the net present value of each project using ACRS percentages, a 30% tax rate, and cost of capital of 10%.
5. If an investor purchased a piece of property for $20,000 7 years ago and sold it today for $45,000, what would its IRR and ARR be? (ignore all tax implications.)
6. Evaluate the following two proposals, using the IRR and NPV methods, if the cost of capital is 9%:

	A	B
Initial cost	$20,000	$15,000
Net cash flow, year 1	2,000	10,000
Net cash flow, year 2	7,000	8,000
Net cash flow, year 3	8,000	4,000
Net cash flow, year 4	9,000	2,000

7. What is the IRR of a project that has an economic life of 10 years, a $25,000 initial cost, and no salvage value? The project is 5-year ACRS property; the company uses ACRS percentages and takes the maximum allowable ITC. Annual cash flows before recovery allowances and taxes are $6,000. The corporate tax rate is 30%.

8. The Peter Pipe Company is considering two packaging alternatives for a new line of presmoked pipes. Method A, which is labor intensive, will require annual cash outflows, before taxes, of $16,000. Method B requires the purchase of automated packaging equipment with a 5-year economic life that has an initial cost of $40,000, is 5-year ACRS property, and has no salvage value. The firm uses the ACRS cost recovery percentages and the maximum allowable investment tax credit. Annual cash expenses associated with maintenance and operations are $8,000. The firm's cost of capital is 8%, and the corporate tax rate is 30%. Regardless of the method chosen, annual cash revenues are projected to be $18,000. Calculate the NPV of the two methods. Which method should be adopted?

9. Carolina Slim, the financial analyst for Maurice Phillips Corporation, is analyzing two alternative investment projects. The characteristics of these proposed investments are assumed to be:

	Investment A	Investment B
Initial cost	$60,000	$80,000
ACRS and Economic Life	5 years	5 years
Salvage Value	$5,000	$10,000
Annual cash revenues	21,000	24,000
Corporate tax rate	30%	30%
Recovery method	ACRS %	ACRS %
Cost of capital	10%	10%

Ms. Slim, however, is unsure of several of these estimates. Salvage value for each alternative could vary as much as 100% above or below the estimates and annual cash revenues could vary 25% above or below the estimates. How sensitive are the NPVs of each investment to these possible variances? What elements are the greatest source of risk?

10. A project has the following after-tax cash flows:

Initial cost	$7,500
Cash flow, years 1–3	2,000
Cash flow, years 4–6	1,500

Should the project be accepted if the cost of capital is 8%? If the project is twice as risky as the firm's average project, would the project be accepted using a risk-adjusted discount rate?

11. The certainty equivalents and net cash flows for a project with an initial cost of $24,000 are as follows:

Year	Certainty Equivalent	Net Cash Flow
1	1.00	$8,000
2	.95	8,000

Year	Certainty Equivalent	Net Cash Flow
3	.85	7,000
4	.75	7,000
5	.75	6,000
6	.75	6,000

BIBLIOGRAPHY

Gitman, Lawrence J., and John R. Forrester, Jr. "A Survey of Capital Budgeting Techniques Used by Major U.S. Firms." *Financial Management*, Fall 1977, pp. 66–71.

Grant, Eugene L., et al. *Principles of Engineering Economy*. New York: The Ronald Press Company, 1980.

Oblak, David J., and Roy J. Helm, Jr. "Survey and Analysis of Capital Budgeting Methods Used by Multinationals." *Financial Management*, Winter 1980, pp. 37–41.

Osteryoung, Jerome S. *Capital Budgeting*. Columbus: Grid, Inc., 1979.

Schall, Lawrence D., Gary L. Sundem, and William R. Geijsbeek. "Survey and Analysis of Capital Budgeting Methods. *The Journal of Finance*, March 1978, pp. 281–287.

_____, and Gary L. Sundem. "Capital Budgeting Methods and Risk: A Further Analysis." *Financial Management*, Spring 1980, pp. 7–11.

Five

ANALYTICAL TECHNIQUES FOR MAKING FINANCING DECISIONS

CHAPTER 9

Short-Term Financing

The investment decision, the first function of the financial manager, is covered in depth in the preceding chapters. Although the financing decision is often made simultaneously with the investment decision, from a pedagogical point of view, it is difficult to provide simultaneous coverage of both the investment and financing functions. Consequently, the remaining chapters center on the analytical techniques useful in making financing decisions. This chapter deals exclusively with the short-term financing decision and provides coverage of three basic areas. First, a general discussion or an overview of the various sources of financing is presented. Second, the basic methods used in computing interest are surveyed. Finally, the several sources of short-term financing are discussed. The remaining chapters present the tools required for long-term financing decisions.

AN OVERVIEW OF FINANCING

A firm's balance sheet can be thought of as a picture of the firm that shows its assets on the asset side and how these assets were obtained or financed on the liability and equity side. The most common means of categorizing the financing side of the balance sheet is by grouping sources of funds by maturity; (e.g., current liabilities, long-term liabilities, and equity). Current liabilities represent self-liquidating sources of funds, that is, as they mature and require payment, current assets or other current liabilities will in the normal course of business provide new funds to meet these obligations. Long-term liabilities are not self-liquidating but represent a more permanent source of financing that matures beyond the current period. The equity section contains sources of financing such as common stock which has no maturity date.

While differentiation of financial obligations by date of maturity is common for balance sheet presentations, other methods of differentiation may be more meaningful for the purpose of making financial decisions. The financial manager not only thinks in terms of the maturity structure of financing but also in terms of sources of financing and their costs. An alternative categorization of financing might be by sources of funds (i.e., from operations, interfirm sources, and financial market sources). The first and second groups in general do not carry an explicit interest cost; financing secured from financial markets almost always does.

Interfirm Sources

All firms purchase supplies and materials from other firms with some form of an agreement between the firms that payment is to be made at some specific time in the future. From the viewpoint of the firm making the credit purchase, an account or note payable is created; from the point of view of the firm selling on credit, an account or note receivable is created. There is normally no explicit interest charge to the purchasing firm; but, as discussed later in the chapter, if a cash discount for early payment is allowed by the selling firm that is not taken by the purchasing firm, an extremely high implicit interest charge can result.

Funds From Operations

Like accounts and notes payable, the firm does not pay explicit interest charge for funds retained in the firm. No payment is made to common stockholders when funds are retained by the firm instead of being paid out in the form of dividends. However, the owners of the firm (as will be developed in Chapter 12) expect common stock dividends and prices to increase over time. Thus, if the firm retains funds in the current period to invest in assets, owners expect these investments to produce profits and cash flow sufficient to increase dividends and common stock prices. This implied behavior can be measured and as such becomes a cost of funds retained by the firm.

For example, a firm's current dividend on its common stock selling at $50.00 a share is $2.00 and dividends are expected to grow at an annual rate of 5%. The firm's owners see a return on their $50.00 per share investment of ($2.00/$50.00) plus 5%, for a total of 9%. This firm must earn at least 9% on funds that are retained and reinvested to insure growth in dividends and share price. If the firm earns less than 9%, the investor always has the option of selling and reinvesting in another firm's common stock that will provide a 9% return. As investors sell, the firm's common stock price will fall, and the firm will find it difficult to raise new funds by selling new common stock. Consequently, while this 9% is not an explicit cost in the sense of paying 9% interest on debt, it is an implicit but very real cost to the firm.

Financial Markets

When a firm is unable to secure financing from its own operations or from interfirm sources, it becomes necessary to obtain funds through the organized financial markets. One factor that can be used to distinguish a mature economy from a fledgling economy is the existence of well-developed financial markets. The more developed an economy, the more developed the instruments and institutions that bring together the providers of capital with those who must seek capital from outside sources. Classification of financial markets can be accomplished in several ways.

Classifications of Financial Markets. Differentiation or classification of financial markets can be in terms of type of (1) market, (2) maturity, and (3) security. Financial markets may be differentiated by whether or not they are concerned with primary (new) or secondary (existing) securities. This text is principally directed at the firm's obtaining financing in the primary markets rather than its making temporary investments of its idle funds. However, as developed in Chapter 5, consideration of the secondary market is important to the firm, not only as a means of investing temporarily idle funds but also because an active secondary market is a basic requirement for a well-developed primary market. For example, an investor initially supplies funds to a firm by purchasing a new security. When the investor finds that the funds are needed to meet some unforeseen contingency, the securities must be resold in the secondary market. If the investor cannot sell this security to someone in the secondary market, in all likelihood a new security will not be purchased again. Consequently, a secondary market is an important requirement for the existence of an efficient primary market.

Both the primary and secondary markets can be further differentiated by maturity of the instruments handled. The money market deals with instruments that mature in the short term, a period of one year or less, while the capital market deals with instruments that mature in the long term, a period greater than a year. For example, when a firm issues commercial paper, a money market transaction is implied; however, if the firm issues a corporate bond instead, a capital market transaction results.

Finally, financial markets can be differentiated by type of security. Reference is often made to the bond market, equity market, mortgage market, Treasury bill market, and so on. These references are to the type of instruments or securities traded and are readily differentiated into money market (Treasury bills) and capital market (bonds, equity, mortgage) transactions. Without further qualification, it is not possible to distinguish which market operation is being referred to, the primary or the secondary market. The word "new" is usually used to differentiate a primary from a secondary transaction. For example, a reference to "new corporate bonds" suggests a primary market, as well as a capital market, transaction.

Regardless of how financial markets are classified for discussion and analysis, when a particular market is referenced, the reference is usually meant to include the instruments, institutions, procedures, and participants. From the financial manager's point of view, an understanding of these markets is necessary to ensure that funds are raised in a least cost fashion.

AN OVERVIEW OF INTEREST RATES AS A COST

Few single topics in the business world have generated as much discussion, concern, and political activity as interest rates have. Since money came into existence, interest rates have sparked discussions as to whether or not economically, morally, and religiously money could be charged for lending money. If so, why and what factors determine interest rates? What effect do interest rates have on business activity? Should there be legally imposed maximum interest rates? What methods should be used to compute such maximum rates? An examination of these and related questions would fill several volumes. The remaining chapters of this text will examine factors that determine various interest rates; the immediate discussion here is limited to the basic methods of computing interest.

Methods of Computing Interest

Interest can be defined as the payment received for lending money or the price paid to borrow money, depending on which side of the transaction one is on. The one doing the lending thinks of the interest rate as a rate of return on the money lent, while the one borrowing thinks of the interest rate as a cost expressed as a percentage of the money borrowed.

Simple Interest. The computational method that usually results in the least cost to the borrower is the simple interest method. With this method, interest (i) is charged only on the principal outstanding or unpaid balance (P), whether repayment is made in a single lump sum or in multiple repayments. When a single lump-sum repayment (F) is made at the end of the holding period ($n = 1$), the relationships among I, i, P, and n may be defined:

$$I = iPn \tag{9-1}$$

$$F = P + iPn = P(1 + in) \tag{9-2}$$

$$i = \frac{F - P}{P \cdot n} = \frac{I}{P \cdot n} \qquad (9\text{-}3)$$

where I = the dollar amount of interest paid
n = the number of periods associated with i; $n = 1$ when there is a single lump-sum repayment
i = the interest rate per period, not necessarily a year

To illustrate, if \$1,200 is borrowed for 1 year at 12%, Equation 9-1 indicates total interest of

$$I = (.12)(\$1{,}200)(1) = \$144$$

Substituting this value into Equation 9-2 yields the value of the future repayment (\$1,200 + \$144), or \$1,344. Alternatively, Equation 9-3 indicates how the interest rate can be calculated if only the amounts borrowed and repaid are known. The interest rate on borrowing \$1,200 and repaying \$1,344 a year later is \$144/\$1,200, or 12%.

If \$1,200 is borrowed at 12% with all interest and principal to be repaid at the end of the eighth year,

$$I = (.12)(\$1{,}200)(8) = \$1{,}152$$

and

$$F = \$1{,}200 + \$1{,}152 = \$2{,}352$$

and

$$i = \$1{,}152/\$9{,}600 = .12 \text{ or } 12\%$$

The computations are slightly more complicated if \$1,200 is borrowed for 1 year at 6% interest with repayment made in 4 equal monthly installments rather than a single lump-sum repayment. Equal quarterly payments are obtained by reducing P and I in a manner that forces the payback installments to be equal. The determination of equal end-of-quarter payments requires that a capital recovery interest factor (crf) or amortization factor be obtained first. The crf is then multiplied by the loan principal to determine the equal payments. This relationship is stated mathematically in Equation 2-5:

$$A = P\left[\frac{i(1 + i)^n}{(1 + i)^n - 1}\right] \text{ or } A = P[\text{crf}] \qquad (2\text{-}5)$$

The crf, the bracketed term for 3% and $n = 4$ is .26903 from the Appendix. Thus, the equal quarterly payments are

$$A = \$1,200(.26903) = \$322.83$$

The amortization schedule for this example is given in Table 9-1.

Mortgage lenders and credit unions commonly use simple interest with equal repayment schedules. In addition, commercial banks frequently use this method to compute interest on business and consumer installment loans.

Add-on Interest. Interest is computed on the *full* amount of the principal when the add-on interest method is used, regardless of the timing of the repayments. Equation 9-4 specifies how the repayments, A, are computed (A would be equal to F if repayment were made in one lump sum):

$$A = \frac{P + iPn}{m} \qquad\qquad (9\text{-}4)$$

where: $n =$ the number of years the principal, P, is borrowed
$m =$ the total number of repayments in n years

That is, A is found by adding to the amount borrowed the interest on the principal for the number of years involved and then dividing by the total number of installments over the life of the loan. For example, if a firm borrowed \$1,200 at 12% to be repaid at the end of 1 year, Equation 9-4 suggests that the single repayment is equal to \$1,344. It should be noted that this is the F value that Equation 9-2 would produce. Since $n = m = 1$ in Equation 9-4, it reduces to Equation 9-2.

However, the similarity between the simple and add-on interest methods (Equations 9-2 and 9-4) disappears when two or more repayments are to be made. If \$1,200 is borrowed at 12% but repayment is to be made in 4 equal installments, Equation 9-4 produces payments of

$$A = \frac{\$1,200 + (.12)(\$1,200)(1)}{4} = \frac{\$1,344}{4} = \$336.00$$

These payments are greater than the equal installments under the simple interest method because the add-on method assumes that the borrower has the *full* principal for the life of the loan. Interest is charged on the *full* principal each quarter even though part of it is repaid quarterly. Consequently, \$144 in interest is paid as compared with \$91.32 under the equal installment method of the simple method approach to the determination of interest.

The add-on method is used by finance companies and commercial banks on business and consumer loans. This method is commonly used when automobiles, trucks or heavy equipment are sold and financed with installment agreements.

Table 9-1   An Amortization Schedule

(1) Quarter	(2) Beginning Balance	(3) Payment	(4) = (2) × .03 Interest	(5) = (3) − (4) Principal Repaid	(6) = (2) − (5) Ending Balance
1	$1,200.00	$322.83	$36.00	$286.83	$913.17
2	913.17	322.83	27.40	295.43	617.74
3	617.74	322.83	18.53	304.30	313.31
4	313.44	322.83	9.39	313.44	—

Stated and Effective Rates. A comparison of the simple interest and add-on interest methods readily illustrates the higher installments and interest under the latter method. Consequently, the *effective* interest rate charged under the add-on method must be greater than 12%. The *effective* interest rate or the *annual percentage rate* (APR), as it is called under the truth-in-lending legislation, is defined as that annual interest rate that when used in the simple interest rate method will equal the amount of interest that would be paid under any other method.

For example, if $1,200 is borrowed at 12% add-on interest and is to be repaid in 4 equal installments of $336, the total interest is $(336)(4) less $1,200, or $144. To find the effective annual interest rate that will yield $144 in interest using the simple interest method, Equation 2-5 is used. Since P and A, at the add-on rate, are known, Equation 2-5 is solved for the capital recovery factor:

$$A = P[\text{crf}] \qquad (2\text{-}5)$$

$$\text{crf} = \frac{\$336}{\$1,200} = .28000$$

In the Appendix, the interest rate associated with a crf of .28000 is between 4% and 5%. Thus, the effective quarterly interest rate (i_e) is between

Percent per Quarter	crf
.04	.27549
i_e	.28000
.05	.28201

Interpolation produces an approximate quarterly effective interest rate of .04 + .10(.00451/.00652), or .046917, and an approximate effective annual interest rate or APR of (4)(.046917), or 18.8%.

It should also be evident from this analysis that the interest paid under the add-on interest rate method will always be $144, regardless of the number of payments made within the year. As the number of payments within the year increases beyond one, the borrower will have less and less use of the principal during the year. This causes the effective rate of interest to increase, approaching 24%, as the frequency of payments becomes continuous throughout the year.

Bank Discount Interest. The bank discount method is frequently used when business firms make short-term loans for periods of 1 year or less with no intermediate payments. Under the bank discount method, interest is calculated on the amount to be repaid, but the borrower receives only the difference between that amount and the calculated interest. There are two computational approaches to the bank discount method, depending on whether the borrower will accept an amount reduced by the interest charged or if the borrower must receive a stated amount. Under the first approach, the amount the borrower would receive (P) is given in Equation 9-5:

$$P = F - I = F - iFn' = F(1 - in').$$ (9-5)

That is, the borrower receives the difference between the amount to be repaid, F (F is also the face value of the loan), and I, the amount of interest. The amount of interest is found by multiplying the stated interest rate (i) by the loan's face value for the discount period (in years), n'. For example, if $1,200 at 12% is borrowed for 1 year, the amount repaid is $1,200; the amount of interest paid is $(.12)($1,200)(1)$, or $144, and the borrower receives $1,200 less $144, or $1,056.

The second approach is used when the borrower wants to receive the amount asked for, or $1,200 in this illustration. The face value or the amount to be repaid is found by solving Equation 9-6 for F:

$$F = \frac{P}{1 - i \cdot n'}$$ (9-6)

and in this example

$$F = \frac{\$1,200}{1 - (.12)(1)} = \$1,363.64$$

Consequently, the borrower receives $1,200 but at the end of the year must repay $1,363.64, which includes $(.12)($1,363.65)$, or $163.63, in interest.

Regardless of which computational approach to the bank discount method is used, the stated and effective interest rates will always be different because the stated interest is calculated on the amount to be repaid instead of the amount the borrower actually receives. For the $1,200, 1-year loan at 12% (the stated rate), $144 and $163.63 in interest were calculated on face values of $1,200 and

$1,363.64, respectively; however, the borrower receives only $1,056 and $1,200. The effective interest rate is the rate that when used with the simple interest method will produce the same amount of interest as under the method being examined. The effective rate can be found by dividing the amount of interest by the amount of funds the borrower receives, $144/$1,056 and $163.64/$1,200, yielding an effective rate of 13.64% for either computational approach. As a close inspection of Equations 9-5 and 9-6 indicates, regardless of the computational approach used, the effective rates will always be identical.

The effective interest rate should always be used to evaluate the cost of alternative sources of funds to ensure comparability. A simple interest 1-year loan of $1,200 at 12% cannot be compared with a bank discount 1-year loan of $1,200 at 12% on the basis of the 12% stated rates. A comparison of stated rates indicates the borrower is indifferent between a 12% simple interest loan and a 12% bank discount loan; but a comparison based on effective rates, 12% and 13.64%, respectively, indicates that the borrower would prefer the simple interest loan.

Compound Interest. If an amount is compounded, interest is computed not only on the principal but also on all interest to that point in time. For example, if $1,200 is compounded annually for 10 years at 6%, the caf, from the Appendix, is 1.79085 and the amount available at the end of year 10 is $2,149.02. The amount of interest added is the difference between beginning and ending amounts, or $949.02.

However, if interest is compounded for periods less than a year (365 days), the effective interest rate will always be greater than the stated rate because interest will be computed on principal plus interest that is added at shorter intervals. For example, $1,200 compounded semiannually at 6% means that interest of 3% is charged on $1,200 at the end of 6 months and another 3% interest charged on $1,236 at the end of the year. The amount of interest for the year is $73.08 instead of $72; consequently, the effective rate must be greater than 6%. When compounding over periods of less than a year, Equation 9-7 can be used to find the effective annual rate of interest:

$$i_e = [(1 + i)^n - 1].\tag{9-7}$$

In this example

$$i_e = [(1.03)^2 - 1] = 1.0609 - 1 = .0609 \quad \text{or} \quad 6.09\%$$

If 6% interest is compounded quarterly, the effective annual interest rate is

$$i_e = [(1.015)^4 - 1] = 1.06136 - 1 = .06136 \quad \text{or} \quad 6.136\%$$

Table 9-2 uses Equation 9-7 to compute the effective interest rate for several selected compounding periods of less than a year at a stated interest rate of 6%.

Table 9-2 Effective Interest Rates for Selected Periods When Compounding Exists and the Stated Rate Is 6%

Number of Compounding Periods	Effective Rates When Interest Is Computed On 365 Days
1	6.0000
2	6.0900
4	6.1364
12	6.1678
24	6.1757
52	6.1800
365	6.1831
Continuously	6.1837*

*When continuous compounding is applicable, Equation 9-7 becomes $i_e = (e^i - 1)$, where i = the stated annual rate, e = 2.718281828, and $i_e = [(2.718281828)^{.06} - 1] = .0618365$, or 6.1837%.

Alternatively, a capital recovery solution would produce the same results for these two examples.

SHORT-TERM FINANCING

Short-term financing consists of debt obligations with a maturity of 1 year or less. The major forms of short-term financing are trade credit, unsecured loans, and secured loans. Each of these forms of financing will be treated extensively in the following sections.

Trade Credit

When one firm purchases from another, the selling company often allows the buying firm some period of time before cash payment is required. Trade credit is primarily of this type and is referred to as an open account. Other forms of credit, such as notes payable and trade acceptances, are also used but to a much smaller degree. On open account, the seller ships the goods to the buyer accompanied by an invoice that lists the goods shipped, prices, and terms of sale. No legal instrument is drawn up that recognizes each transaction, as there would be for a note payable or trade acceptance.

Trade credit has the advantage of being widely available and flexible. Sellers use credit extension as part of their marketing strategy to increase sales (as discussed in Chapter 6), and consequently, their credit standards may not be as strict as those of financial institutions. Trade credit is for some firms a major source of funds. It provides flexibility because collateral is not required and restrictive covenants are not likely to be imposed. However, the cost of trade credit can be a disadvantage.

When a firm buys on open account, the selling firm is, in effect, granting a loan. Any time a loan is made, some form of interest is charged; there is no such thing as a free lunch. With this type of credit, however, the interest charge usually cannot be determined by the buying firm. By using cost-plus pricing (price found by determining costs and then adding some amount for profit), the selling firm can include its cost of obtaining funds in its selling price. To the extent then that the selling firm does include its financing costs in its selling price, the buying firm pays for the interbusiness loan.

The use of trade credit may or may not be beneficial to the buying firm. If the selling firm grants an immediate cash discount on cash sales that is larger than the buying firm's cost of borrowing, it would be to the firm's advantage to pay cash. For example, each month firm A purchases from firm B $10,000 worth of goods on credit terms of n 30 or cash terms of a 1% discount. If firm A purchases on credit, when the goods are all sold at the end of 30 days, firm A then pays firm B and makes another purchase. This cycle continues throughout the year. Firm B, however, grants a 1% discount from the face amount of the invoice on cash sales. Firm A then has the option of borrowing from the bank at an 8% discount rate (360 day year). If firm A continues to use trade credit, funds are rolled over every 30 days, and it pays $100 each month for the use of $10,000 in trade credit or $(365/360)(\$100/\$10,000)(12)$, an effective rate of 12.17%. With a bank loan, the firm must obtain $9,900 by borrowing at 8% (360-day year), or $(365/360)(.08)$ or 8.11%, on the 365-day year. It must repay $\$9,900/(1 - .08111)$, or $10,773.87, for an effective rate of ($873.87/$9,900), or 8.83%. Under these conditions, it is readily apparent that borrowing from the bank is the more profitable alterantive. If firm A's cost of borrowing is greater than 12.17%, it should use the trade credit alternative.

These alternatives may not readily exist; if no cash discount is given for a cash purchase, the buying firm should purchase on the selling firm's credit terms because the buying firm is paying for the credit terms anyway. However, when a firm buys on open account and a discount for early payment is included as part of the credit terms, it should consider the cost implications of not taking the discount.

Credit terms are expressed as 1/10, n 30; that is, deduct 1% from the invoice amount if paid in 10 days or pay the face amount in 30 days. A firm that pays in 30 days is incurring a 1% penalty for keeping its funds an additional 20 days. If a $5,000 invoice is paid on day 30, the full $5,000 must be paid. If payment is made within 10 days, only $4,950 is due. In effect, the selling firm is charging the buyer $50 to extend credit 20 days. This is the cost to the buying firm for not paying its bills promptly.

The percentage cost for not taking the allowed discount is \$50/\$4,950, or approximately 1.01%, for 20 days. However, for comparison purposes, this 20-day cost must be converted to an annual basis by multiplying by the number of 20-day periods in a 365-day year (365/20 = 18.25 periods). Equation 9-8 is one formula that may be used to find the effective annual interest rate:

$$i_e = \left(\frac{\text{interest charge}}{\text{principal}} \right) \cdot \left(\frac{365}{\text{days principal borrowed}} \right) \qquad (9\text{-}8)$$

This equation produces an effective annual interest rate of (.0101)(18.25), or 18.43%.

Alternatively, Equation 9-9 can be used to compute the cost of not taking the discount without knowing the invoice amount:

$$i_e = \left(\frac{\text{discount percentage}}{\text{principal in percent}} \right) \cdot \left(\frac{365}{\text{days principal borrowed}} \right) \qquad (9\text{-}9)$$

The principal in percent is equal to 1 minus the discount percentage. Equation 9-9 produces a cost of (1/99)/(365/20), or 18.43%, for the example as was calculated by using Equation 9-8.

Table 9-3 lists the effective annual costs of not taking various cash discounts as computed by Equation 9-9. When making these calculations, it was assumed that the invoice was paid on the due date if the firm missed the discount date.

If a firm misses the discount date but pays on day 11 instead of day 30 when terms are 2/10, n 30, then it is paying \$2 for the use of \$98 for just 1 day. Equation 9-9 indicates an effective rate of interest of 744.9%; (2–98)(365/1). Consequently, if the discount is missed, it is reasonable to withhold payment of the invoice until the due date.

It is also possible to "stretch" credit terms and lower the effective interest rate, provided that there is no penalty for late payment. The effective rate of interest is 9.3% in the preceding example if the firm misses the discount date and instead of

**Table 9-3   Credit Terms and the Effective
Cost of Missed Discounts**

Credit Terms	Effective Rate
1/10, n 20	36.9%
1/10, n 30	18.4
1/10, n 45	10.5
2/10, n 20	74.5
2/10, n 30	37.2
2/10, n 45	21.3

paying in 30 days, pays in 90 days (2/98)(365/80). By stretching trade credit, the firm pays only $2 for the use of $98 for 80 days. However, while the effective rate may be lowered, it may only provide a short-run benefit. The implicit charge for the resulting reduction in the firm's credit rating could raise the firm's future borrowing costs.

Unsecured Loans

The major source of unsecured, nontrade, short-term financing is commercial banks. Transaction loans, lines of credit, and revolving credit agreements are the forms this type of financing usually takes.

Transaction Loans. Transaction loans are negotiated each time the firm wants funds, usually for a specific purpose other than to meet seasonal needs. The bank discount method is usually used to compute interest, and in addition, compensating balances are often required. A compensating balance requires the firm to maintain a minimum balance in its checking account equal to a percentage of the loan. Compensating balances in the past have averaged 15%, but at this writing many banks are reported to have lowered this figure to 10%. A compensating balance may or may not increase the effective borrowing rate.

For example, a firm can borrow $100,000 for 90 days at 8%, using the bank discount method and a 360-day year, with a 10% compensating balance requirement. If the firm normally maintains an average demand deposit balance of $10,000, the effective rate of interest is (365/360)(4)($2,040.82/$100,000), or 8.3%. However, if the firm, because of this requirement, must maintain a balance of $10,000 more than it would ordinarily, the effective rate of interest is then (365/360)(4)($2,040.82/$90,000), or 9.2%

Line of Credit. A line of credit is an informal, short-term financing agreement between a firm and a commercial bank that allows the firm to borrow repeatedly during the year as long as the outstanding balance does not exceed a specified amount. The line of credit is established when a bank sends a letter to the firm outlining its willingness to provide financing and the terms of the relationship.

Terms of the relationship will include statements on interest rate, maximum credit, compensating balance, and covenants. The bank's best customers will be charged the prime interest rate; higher-risk firms will be charged progressively higher rates, with compensating balances frequently required. Firms are usually required to "clean up" (be free of borrowing) for some period of time during the year. Covenants, while not widespread, are required on some lines of credit with weak firms, specifying that they maintain a given liquidity position or eliminate or reduce dividends, and so on. Determination of the effective interest rate is identical to the procedure for a single transaction loan, with or without a compensating balance requirement.

Revolving Credit Agreement. A revolving credit agreement is similar to a line of credit but differs in three ways: (1) it is legally binding on the bank to supply the amount of funds stated in the agreement; (2) it can be made for a period longer than a year, quite often three years; and (3) it requires the firm to pay a commitment fee on the maximum amount of credit as well as the amount the firm actually uses. The interest rate the firm is charged is usually .25% to .50% higher than one obtainable under a line of credit. To this is added a commitment fee of, say, .5% per annum.

For example, a firm borrows an average of $70,000 for 90 days at an 8.3% interest rate on a $100,000 revolving credit agreement that has no compensating balance requirement but has a .5% commitment fee. The effective interest rate is (365/360)(4)($1,483.28/$70,000) + .005, or 9.1%. That is, the effective interest rate equals the effective bank discount rate plus the commitment fee.

Secured Financing

While many of a firm's assets may be used as collateral for a loan, accounts receivable and inventories are frequently used for short-term financing. Secured financing of this type must be used by firms whose credit ratings are too weak to obtain unsecured financing.

Accounts Receivable Financing. Accounts receivable can be used as collateral (pledged) or sold outright (factored) to provide the firm with short-term financing. Commercial banks, commercial finance companies, and factors are the three financial institutions that engage in pledging and factoring a firm's accounts receivable.

Pledging Accounts Receivable. When accounts receivable are pledged, commercial banks will lend 60% to 85%, and finance companies up to 90%, of the face amount of the receivables, depending on the financial strength of the firm involved, the size of each receivable, the borrowing firm's bad-debt experience, and so on. Interest is usually charged on a daily basis, with commercial banks charging 1% to 4% above the prime interest rate and the commercial finance companies charging 3% to 5% more than the banks. The higher commercial finance company rates reflect their willingness to accept more risk. Generally, there are no commitment fees, compensating balances, or clean-up requirements included in pledging agreements, which are normally negotiated for a 1-year period.

If the firm has a choice between a secured loan and an unsecured loan, a cost comparison should be made. Interest on an accounts receivable loan is computed daily on the actual funds borrowed. An unsecured loan is made for some period of time longer than 1 day with interest charged on the total amount borrowed regardless of whether or not the funds are needed each day. Presumably, when funds are not needed, they are invested in marketable securities, provided that the investment cost is less than investment income. Table 9-4 compares alternatives of secured and unsecured borrowing. A firm can borrow the amounts noted each day in

Table 9-4 A Comparison of Secured with Unsecured Borrowing

Day	Pledging Amount	Pledging Cost	Unsecured Borrowing Amount	Unsecured Borrowing Cost	Surplus Funds	Interest Earnings
1	$ 40,000	$ 15.56	$84,000	$ 23.52	$ 40,000	$ 6.67
2	50,000	19.44	—	23.52	30,000	5.00
3	60,000	23.33	—	23.52	20,000	3.33
4	80,000	31.11	—	23.52	—	—
5	40,000	15.56	—	23.52	40,000	6.67
Total	$270,000	$105.00	$84,000	$117.60	$130,000	$21.67

Table 9-4 at 14% interest per year by pledging accounts receivable. The loan is repaid the following day. Alternatively, the firm can borrow $80,000 on an unsecured loan at 10% interest per year for 30 days with a 10% compensating balance required, which is $4,000 above the firm's usual balance. To simplify the comparison, it is assumed that the firm borrows $84,000 to cover its peak needs as well as the $4,000 compensating balance requirement. The firm can earn 6% on its surplus funds and transacts business each day. In addition, all rates are based on 360 days in a year, and the bank discount method of determining interest is used for the unsecured loan.

The daily interest cost on secured borrowing is found by multiplying the daily interest rate (.14/360 = .000389) by the amount borrowed that day. Under the unsecured loan agreement, the firm borrows $84,000 for 1 month. It must repay $84,000/(1 − .00833), or $84,705.60, and the daily interest charge is $705.60/30, or $23.52. Each day's surplus funds are the difference between $80,000 and the funds actually needed that day as reflected by the amounts borrowed under pledging. The interest earned on the daily surplus funds is found by multiplying that amount by the daily rate on marketable securities (.06/360) = .000167).

A comparison of the two cost columns in Table 9-4 indicates that unsecured borrowing results in an interest cost of $117.60 versus $105.00 for secured borrowing. However, the net cost of unsecured borrowing is $117.60 less $21.67, or $95.93. If the firm's cost of investing surplus funds is under $105.00 less $95.93, or $9.07, the unsecured loan alternative would be preferred.

Factoring Accounts Receivable

Rather than pledge its accounts receivable, a firm can factor or sell its receivables to a commercial bank or a factor, with or without recourse. If the sale is made without recourse, the factor bears the risk of bad debts and the expense of collecting if a customer does not pay his or her account. The firm's customers may or may not be notified that a factor has purchased the firm's accounts receivable.

The number, quality, and size of each receivable as well as the degree of recourse, determine the service fee the factor charges. This fee ranges from 1% to 3% of the face amount of the factored receivable. In addition, since the firm is actually borrowing from the factor by receiving payment before the receivables are collected, the firm is charged interest at a rate 2% to 4% above the prime rate. The interest charge is on the actual amount of funds borrowed and is determined on a daily-use basis.

To illustrate, a firm has $30,000 in receivables on the first of the month, and on the average, this will be collected by the fifteenth of the month. However, if the firm needs the funds on the first (i.e., if the firm borrows for 15 days) a service fee of 3% is charged in addition to an interest rate of 14% on the amount borrowed. The service fee first reduces the amount the firm receives to .97 × $30,000, or $29,100. Furthermore, under the bank discount method, the firm only receives $29,100 less (.005833 × $29,100), or $28,930.36. The interest for the period is (.14/24)($29,100) = (005833)($29,100) = $169.74, inasmuch as there are 360/15 or 24 15-day periods in a 360-day year.

Inventory Financing

Most banks and commercial finance companies prefer accounts receivable to inventory financing because of the former's greater liquidity. However, inventories are used as collateral on loans in a variety of ways—public warehouse receipts, fieldhouse receipts, trust receipts, and chattel mortgages. Under a public warehouse agreement, the inventory is placed in storage in a public warehouse. The warehouse issues a receipt that the firm can then assign to the financing company, giving title to the inventory. If there is a fenced location, under the control of an independent warehouse operator, on the firm's property, the same results may be obtained as under public warehousing. Because of the high costs associated with warehousing, this method is used only when very large inventories are involved. A more common method of inventory financing is through the use of trust receipts. Trust receipts give the lender title to the inventory under a floating lien. This type of lien covers all the inventory even though it remains under the control of the firm. The sale of inventory results in a lien on the sale proceeds or a reduction in the loan. A chattel mortgage can be used only when the inventory can be identified by serial numbers. The lender holds title to the goods, and they can be sold only with his or her permission.

Financial institutions will lend amounts based on a percentage of the value of the inventory, valued at cost, depending on that value and the financial strength of the borrowing firm. Finished goods might have a loan value of 70% to 90% of cost, with raw materials having a value of 50% to 70%; semi finished goods, because they must be processed further, might have a loan value of 0% to 50%. Although interest rates are lower on loans secured by inventories because they are easier to administrate, rates are generally 1% to 2% above the prime interest rate charged on unsecured loans.

Summary

This chapter provides an overview of the sources of financing available to the firm. The four major methods of computing interest—simple, add-on, bank discount, and compound—were summarized. It was shown that the various methods used to compute interest result in different effective interest rates for a given stated rate. Thus, the effective interest rate is the only rate that should be used in comparing financing alternatives.

This chapter also emphasizes the more common methods used to compute interest, the difference between stated and effective rates of interest and short-term financing. The remaining chapters in the text emphasize long-term financing decisions.

Questions

1. How do funds obtained in the financial markets differ from funds provided by operations and from interfirm sources?
2. How may the financial markets be characterized?
3. Why is financing with short-term borrowing considered a more risky course of action?
4. How is interest computed under the simple interest method?
5. How is add-on interest determined?
6. What is the difference between the stated and effective rates of interest?
7. When and why is the effective interest rate for the add-on interest method higher than the stated rate?
8. Why does the effective interest rate exceed the stated interest rate for the bank discount interest method?
9. When will the effective interest rate exceed the stated interest rate under the compound interest method?
10. Interfirm financing (trade credit) may have an implicit cost. How may this implicit cost be determined?
11. What is the difference between a line of credit and a revolving credit agreement?
12. What is the difference between pledging and factoring accounts receivable?

Problems

1. If a firm's common stock is selling at $32 per share, the current annual dividend is $1.60, and the expected dividend growth rate is .06, what return must the firm earn to satisfy present shareholders?

2. If you borrowed $3,000 for 3 years at 8% interest:
   a. What lump-sum single repayment would be made at the end of the 3 years under the simple interest method?
   b. What lump sum single repayment would be made at the end of 3 years under the add-on interest method?
   c. Determine a schedule for three $1,000 annual principal payments plus interest under the simple interest method with unequal payments.
   d. Determine the amount of three equal principal plus interest payments under the simple interest method.

3. What is the effective interest rate if an $800, 1-year loan is repaid on equal monthly installments of $75.65?

4. If a buyer finances a $4,000 purchase for 36 months at a stated 5% interest rate, what will be his monthly payments if the add-on method is used to compute the interest?

5. Which financing alternative has the lowest cost?
   a. Four equal quarterly payments under simple interest
   b. Four quarterly payments under add-on interest
   c. One lump-sum payment at the end of the year under the simple interest method.
   d. One lump-sum payment at the end of the year under the add-on interest method. Illustrate with an example why you selected your answer using a principal of $1 and a 12% interest rate.

6. If you borrow $10,000 at 12% for 365 days, which of the following repayment alternatives would you prefer?
   a. Twelve equal monthly installments under simple interest
   b. A single year-end payment under simple interest with interest computed on a 360-day year
   c. Twelve equal monthly installments under add-on interest
   d. One year-end payment under compound annual interest
   e. A single year-end payment of $10,000, having received a lesser amount initially under the bank discount method

7. Which financing alternative has the lower financing cost: (a) failing to take the cash discount when trade credit terms are 1/20, n 60 or (b) borrowing $1,000,000 for 1 year, repaying $1,101,529.90?

8. Emma Beeyea, a recent college graduate, has been hired to assist the financial manager of Ricky Ticky Tack Company. Ms. Beeyea's first assignment is to review the company's policy toward discounts on trade accounts payable. A schedule of vendors, average monthly purchases and credit terms follows. If the firm can borrow from a bank at 8% interest (maximum borrowing = $125,000—face value with interest determined under the bank discount method) with a 15% compensating balance required (to be determined on the actual loan proceeds), should the company establish a policy of regularly taking discounts?

Vendor	Average Monthly Purchases	Terms
A	$30,000	2/10, n 30
B	5,000	n 30
C	3,000	3/15, n 60

Vendor	Average Monthly Purchases	Terms
D	18,000	1/5, n 20
E	12,000	3/20, n 45
F	28,000	5/20, n 90

9. The Chic-Chic Ski Company needs $4 million for 60 days to finance a seasonal increase in inventory. The following financing alternatives are available:
   a. Borrowing from a bank at 10% discount interest with the bank requiring a 10% compensating balance.
   b. Foregoing the trade discount from its suppliers who offer terms of 5/10, n 70
   c. Issuing commercial paper at an annual interest cost of 9% and a placement cost of $3,000.
   Which alternative has the lowest annual cost?
10. The Fandango Fan Company needs $100,000 for 90 days. It can borrow from its present bank at 10% interest with a 10% compensating balance required, or it can borrow from a new bank at 11% with no compensating balance. Both banks use the bank discount method to determine interest. Which alternative should Fandango choose?

BIBLIOGRAPHY

Bonker, Dick. "The 'Rule of 78,' " *Journal of Finance,* June 1976, pp. 878–888.

LaPorte, Anne Marie. "ABCs of Figuring Interest." *Business Condition,* Federal Reserve Bank of Chicago, September 1973, pp. 3–11.

CHAPTER 10

Analysis of Term Loans and Leases

The evaluation of lease agreements has elements of both financing and investment decisions. A firm may have the alternative of purchasing an asset outright, financing it with a term loan that is repaid in annual installments, or leasing the asset and making annual lease payments. If the lease alternative is chosen, the firm loses, for example, the annual depreciation tax shield and the investment tax credit that are a part of the investment decision. Thus, the two types of financial management decisions become entwined.

The various types of leases are discussed first in this chapter; second, the cost of the debt alternative is considered; next, a technique to determine the cost of leasing is developed; fourth, an illustration of the comparison between debt and lease alternatives is provided; finally in the last section, qualitative factors in lease analysis are noted.

TYPES OF LEASES

A lessee and lessor can enter into one of two types of leases: operating or financing leases. A certain amount of confusion arises in this area, however, because the definitions of operating and financing leases for accounting purposes differ from that for tax purposes. For accounting purposes, a financing lease is one that meets certain criteria that indicates a shift in the risks of ownership to the lessee from the lessor; thus, the accounting records of both the lessor and lessee will reflect the sale of the asset by the lessor to the lessee. All other leases are operating leases that simply require the recognition of the periodic lease payments by the lessee as rent and as rental income by the lessor.

It is the tax effects of whether a lease is treated as a financing or an operating lease that are important to the lease or buy decision since this governs the deductibility of lease payments and who is entitled to the investment tax credit (ITC) and depreciation deductions. A similar, but not identical, situation exists for tax purposes; that is, if a lease is a financing lease, the lessee is considered to have purchased the leased asset and is allowed the investment tax credit and periodic charges to income through depreciation rather than a deduction for the periodic rental payments. Operating leases permit the lessee to deduct the periodic rental payments as the leased assets are used.

In the analysis of the lease or buy decision, the implicit assumption is that the lease is an operating lease or a financing lease that qualifies for operating lease treatment; that is, the lessor is considered the owner of the asset with the lessee making periodic lease payments. It is also implicitly assumed that if the lessee chose to purchase the asset rather than lease it, he or she would be able to take full advantage of the ITC in the year of acquisition and has sufficient earnings to absorb all cost recovery allowances in the years of use. If this second assumption does not hold, the lease model developed in the subsequent section would require modification. In a financing lease, treated as such for tax purposes, the lessee is treated as if he or she had purchased the asset, and the analysis would parallel that for purchased assets except that the cost of capital in net present value (NPV) analysis would be the interest rate imbedded in the lease agreement.

TERM LOANS AND THEIR COSTS

In Chapter 9, the basic methods used in computing interest on installment loans were introduced. A term loan is defined as a loan with a maturity of more than 1 year, to be repaid in installments or amortization payments. The primary lenders of business term loans are commercial banks and life insurance companies. Commercial banks prefer restricting their loans to maturities of 3 to 5 years; insurance companies prefer maturities of 5 to 15 years.

Amortization Schedule

The basic skills needed to determine the amortization payments or installments were developed in Chapter 9. The only difference to be noted here for term loans is that multiple payments are to be made annually instead of monthly, and so on. The capital recovery factor is used to compute the borrowing firm's before-tax repayment schedule as indicated by Equation 2-5:

$$A = P\left[\frac{i(1 + i)^n}{(1 + i)^n - 1}\right]$$ (2-5)

where A = the firm's before-tax annual payment
P = the principal borrowed or the amount to be repaid
i = the annual interest rate
n = the number of annual payments

The annual payments are the same in each year and are assumed to be made at the end of each year.

For example, a $500,000, 5-year loan at 8% interest is associated with a crf of .25046. This figure is obtained from the Appendix or by solving the term in brackets in Equation 2-5. Thus the equal year-end payments are:

A = $500,000(.25046)
    = $125,230

By repaying the principal of $500,000 in five annual installments of $125,230, the lender receives an 8% return on the annual declining principal balance. Columns 1 through 5 of Table 10-1 illustrate this conclusion. Dividing the annual interest payment in any year by the balance due in the preceding year, which is the principal outstanding for that year, equals an 8% return.

Loan Cost

While the 8% return on the declining principal balance represents a source of income to the lender, it is the before-tax cost to the borrowing firm. The before-tax cost of debt (k_d^*) is defined by Equation 10-1 in two alternative forms:

$$P = \sum_{t=1}^{n}\frac{A_t}{(1 + k_d^*)^t} = \sum_{t=1}^{n}\frac{I_t + R_t}{(1 + k_d^*)^t}$$ (10-1)

where P = the principal or amount borrowed
I_t, R_t = the interest paid and principal repayment in year t
n = the loan maturity
A_t = the sum of the principal and the interest paid in year t

That is, the present value of five $125,230 principal-plus-interest payments at 8% is equal to $500,000. Equation 10-1 states that the before-tax cost of debt is that interest rate that equates the present value of the annual principal and interest payments to the amount borrowed. The before-tax cost of debt, then, is the IRR,

Table 10-1 Loan Amortization Schedule

(1) Year	(2) Annual Payment	(3) = .08 × (5) Annual Interest	(4) = (2) − (3) Principal Repayment	(5) Balance Due	(6) = .6 × (3) Interest after Tax	(7) = (4) + (6) After-Tax Cash Flow
0	—	—	—	$500,000	—	—
1	$125,000	$40,000	$ 85,230	414,770	$24,000	$109,230
2	125,230	33,182	92,048	322,722	19,909	111,957
3	125,230	25,818	99,412	223,310	15,491	114,903
4	125,230	17,865	107,365	115,945*	10,719	118,084
5	125,230	9,276	115,954*	—	5,566	121,520

*Totals do not equal $500,000 because of rounding.

which equates the present value of the cash outflows necessary to pay off a loan to the initial amount of funds borrowed.

Because of the difference in tax treatment between debt costs and lease payments, it is necessary to divide the cash outflows, A_t, into I_t and R, using the extreme right-hand side of Equation 10-1. This difference in tax treatments also requires that Equation 10-1 be restated on an after-tax basis. Interest payments are tax deductible, but payments on the principal are not. This can be incorporated into Equation 10-1 as shown in Equation 10-2:

$$P = \sum_{t=1}^{n} \frac{I_t(1 - T) + R_t}{(1 + k_d)^t}$$

(10-2)

where T = the corporate tax rate and
k_d = the after-tax cost of debt.

Table 10-1 also includes the value of $I_t(1 - T)$ from the preceding example based on a 40% corporate tax rate in column 6 and $I_t(1 - T) + R_t$, the after-tax cash outflow from the firm, in column 7.

The after-tax cost of debt, k_d, is defined as the percentage (or IRR) that equates the sum of the present values of the after-tax cash outflows to the amount borrowed. Although the principal payments remain the same in both the before- and after-tax cost of debt models, I_t is greater than $I_t(1 - T)$; thus, k_d must be smaller than k_d^*. In fact, k_d can be determined to be 4.8% by using Equation 10-3 directly or by using Equation 10-2 and interpolating:

$$k_d = k_d^*(1 - T)$$

(10-3)

This means that the present value of the cash outflows in column 7 at a 4.8% rate will be equal to $500,000.

The present value factors at 4.8% can be approximated by interpolation between 4% and 5% or by using Equation 2-4. The computations required to demonstrate the validity of Equation 10-3 are shown in Table 10-2. Thus, Equation 10-3 defines the after-tax cost of debt.

THE COST OF LEASING

A model to determine the cost of leasing can be developed in a manner similar to that used to develop the model for the cost of debt. However, there are several underlying assumptions that must be explicitly stated. First, the cost of leasing must be insensitive to alternative debt charges; that is, the firm's cost of leasing does not change regardless of whether it can borrow at an interest rate of 5% or 8%. Second, the lease model can be developed in terms of the NPV and IRR.

The models used to determine the cost of leasing and debt differ in several respects. The first notable difference is that when an asset is leased rather than purchased, the firm loses the benefits of the depreciation tax shield and salvage value. However, it gains the tax shield associated with the cost of leasing, with the lost depreciation tax shield and salvage value benefits being charged to the cost of the lease. Second, annual lease payments are usually made 1 year in advance while the loan payments are made at the end of each year. For example, a 5-year lease requires payments in $t = 0, 1, 2, 3,$ and 4; a 5-year loan would have payments in $t = 1, 2, 3, 4,$ and 5. Consequently, the cash outflow of the annual lease payments precedes the tax benefits by 1 year, whereas the debt cash outflow and tax benefits occur in the same year.

Lease Cost: Basic Model

The basic model to determine the after-tax cost of leasing, incorporating these distinctions between debt and lease financing, can be developed in a series of steps. For each year the lease is in effect, the firm's after-tax cash outflow (CFO) due to the lease payments is:

$$\text{CFO} = L_t - (L_{t-1})(T) + D_t(T) \tag{10-4}$$

where L_t = the lease payment in year t
L_{t-1} = the previous year's lease payment
D_t = the depreciation charge in year t
T = the corporate tax rate

The term $L_t - (L_{t-1})(T)$ means that the lease payment in year t is reduced by the amount of the reduction in taxes in year t that results from the deductibility for tax

Table 10-2 PV of Loan After-Tax Cash Flows

Year	pvf @ 4.8%	After-Tax Cash Flows	Present Value
1	.95420	$109,230	$104,227
2	.91049	111,957	101,936
3	.86879	114,903	99,827
4	.82900	118,084	97,892
5	.79103	121,520	96,126
Total			$500,000*

*Total does not equal $500,000 because of rounding.

purposes of the previous year's lease payment. The value $D_t(T)$ is interpreted as the depreciation tax shield that is forgone because the asset was not purchased; the positive sign denotes that this amount increases the cash outflow from the firm.

Step 2 in the model's development requires incorporating the values of each of the terms in Equation 10-4 for each year of the life of the lease, the time value of money and the initial cost of the asset. The initial cost of the asset (P_0) is the amount the firm would have to pay if it purchased the asset instead of leasing it. Since the initial cost, lease payments, lease tax shield, and depreciation tax shield cash flows occur in different time periods, the concept of the time value of money dictates recognizing this fact. Equation 10-5 is a restatement of Equation 10-4 to account for these factors:

$$\text{NPV}_L = \sum_{t=0}^{n-1} \frac{L_t}{(1 + k_d)^t} - \sum_{t=1}^{n} \frac{L_{t-1}(T)}{(1 + k_d)^t} + \sum_{t=1}^{n} \frac{D_t(T)}{(1 + k_d)^t} - P_0 \qquad (10\text{-}5)$$

NPV_L is the net present value of leasing and is computed by subtracting the initial cost of the asset (P_0) from the present value of annual leasing costs. The discount rate to use is the after-tax cost of borrowing.

To compute the IRR of the lease analysis, Equation 10-6 is solved for r_L:

$$P_0 = \sum_{t=0}^{n-1} \frac{L_t}{(1 + r_L)^t} - \sum_{t=1}^{n} \frac{L_{t-1}(T)}{(1 + r_L)^t} + \sum_{t=1}^{n} \frac{D_t(T)}{(1 + r_L)^t} \qquad (10\text{-}6)$$

In Equation 10-6, r_L is the after-tax cost of the lease; that is, it is the rate that equates the present value of the lease payments less the present value of the lease tax shield plus the present value of the forgone depreciation tax shield to the asset's initial cost.

Step 3 takes into consideration the benefits of salvage value that the firm forgoes because the asset is leased instead of purchased. If this value is not considered, r_L or NPV_L will be understated because forgone salvage benefits are part of the cost of leasing. Equations 10-7 and 10-8 add the present value of the forgone salvage value to Equations 10-5 and 10-6.

$$NPV_L = \sum_{t=0}^{n-1} \frac{L_t}{(1 + k_d)^t} - \sum_{t=1}^{n} \frac{L_{t-1}(T)}{(1 + k_d)} + \sum_{t=1}^{n} \frac{D_t(T)}{(1 + k_d)^t}$$

$$+ \frac{\alpha_s S - (\alpha_s S - BV)T}{(1 + k_d)^n} - P_0 \tag{10-7}$$

$$P_0 = \sum_{t=0}^{n-1} \frac{L_t}{(1 + r_L)^t} - \sum_{t=1}^{n} \frac{L_{t-1}(T)}{(1 + r_L)^t} + \sum_{t=1}^{n} \frac{D_t(T)}{(1 + r_L)^t}$$

$$+ \frac{\alpha_s S - (\alpha_s S - BV)T}{(1 + r_L)^n} \tag{10-8}$$

where α_s = a certainty equivalent coefficient that adjusts the salvage value for risk
   S = the estimated salvage value in year n
   BV = the book value of the asset in year n

The term $(\alpha_s S - BV)T$ adjusts the actual salvage value for the tax effect of salvage value differing from the asset's book value (asset cost less recovery allowances to date of disposal). With the ACRS depreciation charges, book value will generally be zero unless the asset is disposed of before the expiration of its cost recovery life; for example, a 5-year recovery period asset is disposed of in year 4. Since ACRS lives are artificially short, a book value at disposal is unlikely, but not impossible. For example, if an asset is disposed of for $100 when the book value is $200, the corporate tax rate is 40%, and the certainty equivalent (CE) is .8, the total salvage value is .8($100) − [(100).8 − 200].4, or $128. This represents the actual cash inflow as well as the reduction in taxes due to the loss on disposal, which is a forgone benefit to the firm.

The example presented in Table 10-3 illustrates the cash flows presented in the right-hand side of Equations 10-7 and 10-8. A firm is considering leasing an asset that, if purchased, would cost $100,000. Under the conditions of the lease, the firm would make five annual lease payments of $27,000, with the payments made in advance. The firm's tax rate is 40%, the ACRS life is 5 years, and the estimated actual salvage value is $10,000, with a CE of .8. If the firm can borrow money to finance the project at 14%, then

$$K_d = .14(1 - .4) = 8.4\%$$

Using this 8.4% discount rate in Equation 10-7, the NPV_L is

Table 10-3 Computations of the Cash Flow of a Lease

(1) Year	(2) Lease Payment L_t	(3) Lease Tax Shield $L_{t-1}(T)$	(4) ACRS* Depreciation D_t	(5) Depreciation Tax Shield $D_t(T)$	(6) (2) − (3) + (5) Annual Cash Outflow
0	$27,000	—	—	—	27,000
1	27,000	$10,800	$15,000	$6,000	22,200
2	27,000	10,800	22,000	8,800	25,000
3	27,000	10,800	21,000	8,400	24,600
4	27,000	10,800	21,000	8,400	24,600
5	—	10,800	21,000	8,400	2,400†

*Assumes 100% of asset cost recovered through ACRS depreciation with reduction in ITC.
†Includes the forgone salvage benefit, $10,000(.8) − ($10,000[.8] − 0)(.4), which is equal to $4,800. However, the forgone salvage benefit is offset by the lease tax shield, so that the net cash flow in year 5 is an outflow of $2,400.

$27,000 + $20,479 + $21,275 + $19,312 + $17,816 + $1,603 − $100,000 = $7,485.

The general rule for the NPV model is to lease the asset if the NPV is negative and to borrow if the NPV is positive. In this case the firm should borrow since the NPV_L is positive.

Using Equation 10-8, the IRR that equates the present value of the annual cash outflows with the asset's initial cost is the after-tax cost of the lease, r_L. If a 10% rate is used, the net present value of the annual cash flows is $1,257; a discount rate of 13% yields a net present value of −$336; by interpolating between these two percentages, the after-tax cost of the lease is 12.9%. In developing the complete model in the balance of the chapter, both the NPV_L and r_L of leasing will be determined.

Lease Cost: The Complete Model

The basic model presented in Equations 10-5 and 10-6, and expanded to include forgone salvage value in Equations 10-7 and 10-8, will now be completely developed to include the forgone investment tax credit and any normal operating expenses that may be avoided through the lease agreement. Frequently under a true operating lease agreement, the lessor will provide all maintenance and repairs as part of the lease agreement. If this is the case, this relieves the lessee of an expense that would have to have been borne if the asset were purchased. For example, the lessor of a computer may provide maintenance at no additional lease cost, relieving the lessee of these costs. Not all leases, particularly the financing-type lease treated as an operating lease, have this provision, and the proposed lease agreement would have to be examined to determine the specific terms. In addition, a maintenance contract with a separate cost could be provided by the lessor, but the purchase of the maintenance contract in this case constitutes a separate decision apart from the lease or buy decision. If, however, maintenance is provided by the lessor for no added cost, the model must be adjusted for maintenance expenses avoided by the lessee. Since maintenance expenses are subject to some uncertainty and are deductible when a firm owns the asset, the risk-adjusted, after-tax expense is $\alpha_t E(1 - T)$. This is a benefit to the leasing firm, and its present value must be subtracted from the right-hand side of Equations 10-7 and 10-8.

In addition, if a firm leases equipment, it generally forgoes the investment tax credit (ITC) since the ITC is usually available only to the asset's owner, which in this case, is the lessor.[1] Presumably, the lessor passes the advantage provided by the ITC on to the lessee in the form of lower lease payments; but since the ITC was originally considered in the investment decision, the loss of it must be considered in the financing decision. The loss is treated in a manner similar to the depreciation tax shield; it is added to and considered an expense of leasing.

Equation 10-9 is Equation 10-8 restated to incorporate the benefit of forgone maintenance expenses and the loss of the ITC in the IRR model format:

$$P_0 = \sum_{t=0}^{n-1} \frac{L_t}{(1 + r_L)^t} - \sum_{t=1}^{n} \frac{L_{t-1}(T)}{(1 + r_L)^t} + \sum_{t=1}^{n} \frac{D_t(T)}{(1 + r_L)^t} - \sum_{t=1}^{n} \frac{\alpha_t E_t(1 - T)}{(1 + r_L)^t}$$

$$+ \frac{\alpha_s S - (\alpha_s S - BV)T}{(1 + r_L)^n} + ITC \tag{10-9}$$

Equation 10-10 is the adjusted NPV model:

$$NPV_L = \sum_{t=0}^{n-1} \frac{L_t}{(1 + r_L)^t} - \sum_{t=1}^{n} \frac{L_{t-1}(T)}{(1 + r_L)^t} + \sum_{t=1}^{n} \frac{D_t(T)}{(1 + r_L)^t} - \sum_{t=1}^{n} \frac{\alpha_t E_t(1 - T)}{(1 + r_L)^t}$$

$$+ \frac{\alpha_s S - (\alpha_s S - BV)T}{(1 + r_L)^n} + ITC - P_0 \tag{10-10}$$

Note that the sign for maintenance expense is negative in both Equations 10-9 and 10-10, indicating that it is a benefit of leasing or an expense incurred only if the asset is owned or debt financed. The positive sign on the ITC suggests that it is a cost of leasing because it is a benefit received only through ownership.

[1]Under the safe harbor leasing provisions of ERTA, it was possible for leasing agreements to be structured in such a way that the ITC and/or ACRS depreciation charges could be given to either the lessor or the lessee. While the model developed here is capable of handling these alternatives, a complete discussion of the format of these lease agreements is beyond the scope of this text.

The comprehensive example following illustrates the complete leasing model of Equations 10-9 and 10-10. A firm can lease a $25,000 forklift truck for 5 annual payments of $7,000 each, with payments made in advance in each year the lease contract is in effect, assuming a 46% corporate tax rate. The lessor provides all maintenance, which is estimated at a cost of $1,000 per year with a CE of .9 in each of the 5 years. The forklift is 3-year ACRS recovery property subject to a 6% ITC. The firm chooses to reduce the cost of the asset by one-half of the ITC for ACRS deduction purposes rather than reduce the ITC to 4%. The forklift's salvage value is estimated at $3,000 with a CE of .8 at the end of the asset's 5-year life. Table 10-4 shows the annual cash flows associated with the lease of this equipment.

THE DEBT-LEASE DECISION

When the investment decision indicates that an asset should be accepted, the firm may also have the option of leasing the asset rather than purchasing it through debt financing. The debt-lease decision model states that the firm should lease the asset if r_L is lower than k_d; conversely, the asset should be debt financed if the after-tax cost of debt k_d, is lower than r_L. For the example, as illustrated in Table 10-4, the after-tax cost of leasing (r_L) is 14.5%.

If the firm uses the NPV_L evaluation technique, then a net present value decision criterion is substituted. For example, if a commercial bank offers to lend the firm the necessary funds to purchase the asset at $16\frac{2}{3}\%$ on a 5-year term loan, then Equation 10-3 produces an after-tax cost of debt of .1667 (1.0 − .46), or 9%. Using the after-tax cost of debt in the NPV_L formation yields an NPV_L of $1,792. Since the NPV_L of debt financing is positive, the firm should acquire the asset by purchase, financing it through the loan rather than leasing it. If, however, the NPV_L model using the after-tax cost of debt as the discount rate yielded a negative NPV_L, then the firm would be better off leasing the asset.

QUALITATIVE FACTORS IN THE DEBT-LEASE DECISION

Most cash flows that must be considered in the debt-lease decision can be estimated with certainty, such as the asset's initial cost, amount financed or leased, debt repayment, lease payments, and depreciation. However, maintenance and salvage values are highly uncertain. In a situation where k_d and r_L are very close, the final decision to lease or buy could very well depend on estimates of maintenance expense and salvage value. Sensitivity analysis of r_L to changes in these two factors can provide insights into their impact.

Technological obsolescence appears to be a critical factor in the lease or buy decision. With technology expected to increase at a faster rate each year, evaluation of the effects of obsolescence becomes more and more important. For example, fourth-generation computers are currently being used, with the fifth generation on

Table 10-4 Lease Cash Flow Calculation

(1) Year	(2) Lease Payments L_t	(3) Lease Payment Tax Shield $L_{t-1}(T)$	(4) ACRS Depreciation (based on 97% of $25,000) D_t	(5) Depreciated Tax Shield $D_t(T)$	(6) ITC and After-Tax CE Adjusted Maintenance	(7) $[(2) - (3) + (5) - (6)]$
0	$7,000	—	—	—	—	$7,000
1	7,000	$3,220	$6,062.50	$2,789	$(1,014)*	7,583
2	7,000	3,220	9,215	4,239	486	7,530
3	7,000	3,220	8,972.50	4,127	486	7,421
4	7,000	3,220	—	—	486	3,294
5		3,220	—	—	486	(2,410)†

*The 6% ITC available on 3-year ACRS property provides a $1,500 ITC that is forgone by leasing; the net cost is $1,014 when adjusted for maintenance.
†Includes the forgone benefit of salvage equal to {$3,000(.8) − [$3,000(.8) − 0].46} or $1,296. The lease tax shield, adjustment for maintenance and the forgone salvage yield a net cash inflow of $2,410.

180

its way. However, it is doubtful that the costs associated with technological obsolescence can be eliminated through leasing, as some advocates proclaim. The rapidly eroding value of an asset through obsolescence must be planned for in the lessor's determination of the lease payments; consequently, any apparent risk of obsolescence that is assumed by the lessor is generally compensated for through higher lease payments.

Summary

Lease financing has become very important in recent years as a method to acquire and finance new assets. Consequently, a knowledge of leasing and its cost is important to the thorough understanding of financial management. This chapter advances a decision criterion for the debt-lease decision. The financing alternative selected is the one with the least cost.

Questions

1. Define operating and financial leases.
2. Why is it necessary to determine the after-tax cost of debt?
3. In the complete cost of leasing models, explain what and why items other than the actual lease payments by the lessee to the lessor are included.
4. What are the decision rules for deciding between leasing or purchasing an asset?
5. What nonquantitative factors must be considered in the lease or buy decision?
6. Evaluate the statement that leasing transfers the risk of obsolescence from the lessee to the leasing company.

Problems

1. The following data are applicable to Problems 1(a), (b), and (c).

	Situation 1	Situation 2	Situation 3
Principal borrowed	$200,000	$1,500,000	$475,000
Simple interest rate	6%	10%	12%
Length of loan	3 yr	6 yr	5 yr
Tax rate	20%	40%	30%

   a. Using these data, what equal annual installment payments would be required for each situation?
   b. Using these data, prepare loan amortization schedules for each situation, including the after-tax cash flow.
   c. Using these data, what is the after-tax cost of debt for each situation?
2. The Hum Tea Company can lease or purchase a particular asset. If purchased, the asset would cost $100,000, is 5-year ACRS property, and has no salvage value. If leased,

annual lease payments, paid in advance, would be $25,000 for 5 years. The firm has a corporate tax rate of 30%. What is the after-tax cost of the lease? Use the full ITC.

3. The Dum Tee Corporation can lease a plastic fabricating machine for 6 annual lease payments of $40,000, paid in advance. Alternatively, the firm could purchase an equivalent asset for $200,000. The asset is 5-year ACRS property, and has an estimated salvage value of $40,000 with a .5 certainty equivalent factor. What is the after-tax cost of the lease if the corporate tax rate is 40%? Use the full ITC.

4. The Seine Filter Company is evaluating a machine that can be either purchased or leased. If purchased, initial cost is $25,000, it is 5-year ACRS property, and it has an estimated salvage value of $3,000 with a certainty equivalent factor of .75. If leased, annual lease payments, paid in advance, of $6,500 are required. What is the after-tax cost of leasing if the corporate tax rate is 20%? The company normally reduces the ITC.

5. What is the after-tax cost of leasing for the following proposed project?

> Initial cost = $8.000
> ACRS classification = 5 yr
> Annual maintenance expenses = $600
> CE (maintenance expenses paid by the lessee) = .8
> Estimated salvage value = $2,000
> CE (salvage value) = .6
> Corporate tax rate = .40
> ITC = Full 10%
> Annual lease payments (paid in advance) = $2,500

6. The Slip Slide Company must decide whether to lease or buy an asset. If the asset is purchased, funds equal to the initial cost can be borrowed at 12% interest on the unpaid balance. The lease alternative will require annual lease payments of $7,000, paid at the beginning of the year, for 5 years; the lessor will pay all maintenance expenses. Other data are:

> Initial cost = $30,000
> ACRS life = 5 yr
> Maintenance costs = $1,500/yr
> CE (maintenance) = .7
> Salvage value = $10,000
> CE (salvage) = .5
> Corporate tax rate = 20%
> ITC = full 10%

Which alternative should the company choose?

7. Al Truistic, of Weldon General Hospital, must decide whether to lease or buy a new automated meal delivery system for the patients. If the hospital buys the system, it will be required to borrow 100% of the initial cost at 10% simple interest. The lease alternative will require annual lease payments, paid in advance, for 6 years, of $40,000. The lessor will pay all maintenance expenses. Weldon General is not a tax-exempt organization and is subject to a corporate tax rate of 20%. Other data pertaining to the purchase are

> Initial cost = $180,000
> ACRS life = 5 yr
> Maintenance costs = $12,000/yr
> CE (maintenance) = .6
> Salvage value = $28,000
> CE (salvage) = .6
> ITC = full 10%

Which alternative should Al Truistic select?

11

Long-Term Debt

There are two primary sources of long-term capital for a firm to use in the financing of the assets of the corporation. First, the firm can issue long-term debt, the subject of this chapter, or, second, the firm may obtain equity, the subject of Chapter 12.

When issuing long-term debt, the firm must decide on exactly how to structure the debt instrument. That is, the firm must devise a bond with specific characteristics (e.g., year of maturity) that will minimize the firm's debt cost and yet retain a degree of financial flexibility.

Sometimes a firm is forced to call in an old bond issue and reissue a new bond because of a change in interest rates. This refunding process is an important part of long-term debt management.

This chapter is divided into three sections. The first describes the unique characteristics of bonds and the second develops a yield-to-maturity model as a methodology for evaluating the costs of alternative debt instruments. The final section is a model for the evaluation of the bond refunding decision.

COMPONENTS OF A BOND

In issuing a bond, an indenture agreement is specified between the firm and the bondholder. The trustee is responsible for overseeing the interests of the bondholder. In the indenture agreement are the restrictive or protective covenants specifing the restrictions (e.g., specific financial ratios) and obligations to which the firm must adhere. It is up to the trustee to verify that these protective covenants have not been violated.

A corporate bond is a long-term debt instrument that pays both a fixed semiannual interest amount and the face amount of the bond (generally $1,000) at maturity. These two elements are the costs a firm has to pay to receive the proceeds from the bond issue.

Interest payments are a function of the coupon rate, specified on the bond. The semiannual interest payment is this coupon percent divided by 2 and the resultant multiplied by the face value. A bond that has a coupon of 12% will have a semiannual interest payment of $60.

Most corporate bonds are term bonds. A term bond issue means that all the bonds from a specific bond issue have the same set maturity date. That is, a $100 million bond issue of a firm will have all the $1,000 bonds maturing at the same time.

If one issue of bonds has several maturity dates, it is called a serial bond. The issuer redeems a certain portion of the bonds at specified maturity dates, rather than redeeming the entire issue at one time. This permits the issuer to pay off the bond issue in small increments. If a firm issues term bonds, it may be required to set aside funds in a sinking fund. The purpose of the sinking fund is to protect the bondholder by forcing the firm to save sufficient funds so that firm can retire the bonds at maturity by paying off the face value. Generally, the corporation makes annual deposits in the sinking fund. The trustee, administrator of the bond issue, may redeem some of the outstanding bonds by using the call provision or by buying the bonds in the open market if the bonds are selling below face value.

Corporate bonds frequently have a call provision. A call provision allows the firm to call in (redeem) bonds after a specific period of time has elapsed after the date of the original issue. To call in the bond, the firm has to pay a call premium. A call premium is an amount over the face value that a firm must pay a bondholder if the firm decides to call in or redeem the bond prior to maturity.

There are six types of bonds; they differ predominantly because of the collateral backing of the bond. Mortgage bonds have as collateral specific fixed assets (e.g., buildings and land). Debentures are unsecured bonds of a firm except for the credit reputation of the firm. The creditor receives funds in case of bankruptcy after the mortgage bondholder. The lowest claim on assets is the subordinated debenture. This bond is an unsecured bond that ranks behind a debenture.

The other three types of bonds are used only in specific cases. First, there are income bonds. With income bonds, the firm is obligated only to pay interest when it is earned, and no payment is required in the case of insufficient cash. A convertible bond can be converted from an interest-bearing instrument into common stock at the discretion of the holder up to the call date.

The final type of bonds are industrial development and pollution control bonds. With these bonds, the issuer is really a local government. Though the local government issues these bonds for the direct benefit of the firm, the firm pays all the costs of these bonds. If certain requirements are met these bonds are tax-exempt, and the interest rate is less than the rate the firm would normally have to pay.

COMPUTATION OF THE COST OF LONG-TERM DEBT

The cost of long-term debt is computed using an internal rate-of-return model. This internal rate of return is the before-tax cost of the debt to the firm, the discount rate that equates the net proceeds from the bond issue to the semiannual interest payments over the life of the bond plus the recovery of the face value of the bond at its maturity. After the before-tax cost of the bond issue is computed, it is then multiplied by 1 minus the rax rate to compute the after-tax cost of the bond.

The general formula for computing the before-tax cost of debt k_d^* is first to compute the IRR of the bond and then convert it to its after-tax cost. The before-tax cost formula for a bond is

$$NP = B(1 - f) = \sum_{t=1}^{n} \frac{C}{(1 + k_d^*)^t} + \frac{F}{(1 + k_d^*)^N} \qquad (11\text{-}1)$$

where
NP = net proceed the firm receives from the sale of the bond after any flotation costs
B = selling price of the bond to the public in dollars
f = flotation costs of the bond issuance in percentage
C = semiannual interest payment
F = face value of the bond (usually $1,000)
k_d^* = yield to maturity
t = specific semiannual period
N = the last semiannual period for the bond issue

To compute the after-tax cost of k_d, multiply k^*_d by $(1 - T)$. If we let k_d equal the after-tax cost of debt, then the equation for computing the after-tax cost of issuing long-term debt is:

$$k_d = k_d^* (1 - T) \qquad (11\text{-}2)$$

To demostrate how to compute the after-tax cost of debt, suppose that a firm was considering issuing a bond with a 12% coupon paid semiannually. This firm would receive $900 for each bond issue (the underwriter and other issuing costs would absorb 10%). The bond matures in 10 years, and there are 20 interest payments to be made. The first step in this analysis is to compute the net present value of this bond offering at different discount rates. The discount rate that gives a net present value of zero is the before-tax yield to maturity. To find the present value of the interest payments, look up or compute the pvf A for the number of payments and the discount rate being used. For example, in this problem, if 14% discount rate is being evaluated, then use the annuity factor for 20 years and 7% to compute the present value of the interest payments. Table 11-1 shows the computations for various discount rates.

The exact before-tax cost of the bond is computed by trial and error. Whenever the NPV goes from positive to negative, the IRR lies in the interval. In this case, the before-tax cost of debt (k_d^*) is approximately 13.9%. Assuming a 46% tax rate produces an after-tax cost (k_d) of about 7.1%.

FACTORS THAT IMPACT ON BOND COST

One important factor that impacts on the after-tax cost of debt is the riskiness of the debt issue. Riskiness is defined here as the probability that the issuing firm will go bankrupt.

Both Moody's and Standard & Poor's rate bond issues as a function of the bonds risk. The top-quality bonds are rated Aaa, and the worse grades bonds are rated C or D. Table 11-2 shows Moody's bond ratings and their meaning. Besides the bond rating, numerous other factors impact on the after-tax cost of debt. These

Table 11-1 Computation of Long-Term Debt Cost

	13%	14%	15%
Proceeds of issue	$900	$900	$900
PV of interest	(661)	(636)	(611)
PV of face	(284)	(258)	(235)
NPV	(45)	(6)	(54)

Table 11-2 Moody's Bond Ratings and Their Meaning

Bond Rating	Meaning
Aaa	Prime quality
Aa	High grade
A	Upper medium grade
Baa	Lower medium grade or speculative
B	Speculative
Caa & Ca	Very speculative
C	Lowest grade

factors include year of maturity, coupon rate, year of call, call premium, collateral, general level of interest rates, and other miscellaneous factors.

Many factors impact on the cost a firm has to pay to issue long-term debt. It is the financial manager's job to pick and choose among the various debt components and put together a package low in cost and minimal in risk to the firm.

REFUNDING A DEBT ISSUE

Frequently, a firm issues a bond and then interest the rate drops, and it is advantageous to replace or refund the old bond issue with a new one at a lower interest cost. Refunding a long-term debt issue is a problem that can be adapted readily to capital budgeting techniques discussed earlier. However, while using the methodology of capital budgeting, bond refunding is a financial decision.

Refunding decisions normally arise when interest rates drop after the bond was issued. For example, if a firm issued a bond two years ago with a coupon rate of 8% but equivalent issues of equal value are now selling with an interest rate of 6%, the firm should evaluate whether it is wise to refund (or replace) the 8% issue with new 6% bonds.

The IRR methodology is adequate for this decision methodology. Specifically, the IRR model will determine the discount rate that equates the interest saving from the refunding operation to its initial cost.

The general decision model of bond refunding is structured to find the internal rate of return of the refunding and then compare that rate with the after-tax cost of the new bond financing. If the internal rate of return of the refunding exceeds the after-tax cost of the new bond, then the refunding should be accomplished; otherwise, the refunding operation should not be initiated. The after-tax rate of new bond issue is used as the hurdle rate, since it is the rate the firm will have to pay if the new bonds are issued.

The following example demonstrates how the refunding decision is made. Ace Chemical has $10 million of 9% debentures outstanding that have 20 years remaining to maturity. It could refund these bonds currently with a new 20-year bond issue sold to the public at par ($1,000) with a 7% coupon rate. Total gross spread will be 2%. (This is the amount the firm must pay the underwriter out of proceeds of the new issue for issuing the bonds.) There will be an additional $40,000 worth of issuing expenses in connection with the issuance of the new 7% debt. The old bonds have an unamortized discount of $500,000 (the old bonds were originally sold at a discount that has not been fully expensed for tax purposes). All other expenses of issuing the old bonds have been amortized fully, and the old issue has a call price of $105 (bonds can be called in for redemption, but the firm must pay $1,050 for each $1,000 bond). The corporate tax rate is 40 percent, and a 1-month overlap period between the issue of new bonds and the call of the old issue is planned. The firm can invest any idle funds for the period between issue date and call date in Treasury bills with an annual yield of 6%.

Before we proceed to the solution, several points need to be made. First, for tax purposes, the unamortized issue expenses on the old bonds, the call premium, and the unamortized discount on the old bonds are deductible in the year of refunding. Second, the period of overlap is the lag time between the time the new bonds are sold and the old bonds are called. Funds from the sale of new bonds are usually invested in Treasury bills for this overlap period. During this overlap period, however, the firm is paying interest on both issues.

The specific methodology used to solve this problem is to calculate the IRR that equates the marginal cost of issuing the new debt to the annual savings of new bonds over the old bonds. If the IRR of the refunding decision exceeds the after-tax yield of the new debt issue, the refunding should be accomplished; otherwise, the old bonds should be kept intact.

The marginal cost of issuing the new bonds is basically the call price of the old issue minus the net proceeds of the new issue. This difference is then further reduced by the tax benefits occurring if the old issue is called. Table 11-3 outlines the calculations of the marginal initial costs of refunding the 9% of debt with new 7% debt.

Table 11-3   Initial Costs of Bond Refunding

Cost of calling old bonds at $105		$10,500,000
(10,000 bonds × $1,050)		
Proceeds of new issue	$10,000,000	
Gross spread (2% of $10,000,000)	−200,000	
Net proceeds of new issue		9,800,000
Initial cost difference		$ 700,000
Initial Revenues and Expenses		
Treasury bill return		(48,000)
($9,800,000 − $40,000) × (6% ÷ 12)		
New bond issuance expense		40,000
Interest expense during overlap		75,000
(9% ÷ 12 × $10,000,000)		
Additional cost of issuing before taxes		$ 766,200
Initial Tax Consequences		
Overlap interest	(75,000)	
Call premium deduction	(500,000)	
Unamortized discount	(500,000)	
Treasury Bill revenue	48,800	
Net taxable expenses	$ (1,026,200)	
Tax saving at 40%		(410,800)
Net cost of issuing new bonds		$ 355,720

The amount of $355,720 represents the net initial investment that would have to be made to refund this issue.

The second step in the refunding decision is to calculate the annual cash flow from servicing the interest expense from both the old and new issue. This second step in the numerical calculations is given in Table 11-4.

It is important to note that redemption of the bond at face value in the year of maturity is not considered in this analysis since both issues mature in the same time period and their redemption values are equal ($10,000,000).

The third and final step in the refunding decision is to compute the IRR that equates the initial investment of $355,720 to the marginal annual flow for 20 years of $114,000 ($530,000 − $416,000). This refunding rate of return is that rate of return at which the annual flow of $114,000 for 20 years will equal $355,000. By the trial-and-error IRR procedure, this rate can be ascertained and is approximately 32%. Since this rate greatly exceeds the after-tax rate on the new debt issue (7% × 40% = 4.2%), the refunding should be undertaken.

Another way in which to perform the analysis is to compute the NPV of the bond refunding. With this approach, the NPV is the present value of the annual interest savings ($114,000) minus the initial cost of $355,720. The discount rate to use in this NPV analysis is the after-tax cost of the new bond 4.2%. In this case, the NPV of the refunding is $1,166,497. Since the NPV is positive, the refunding should be accomplished.

Table 11-4 Annual Net Cash Outflows from Refunding

Old Bonds (9%)		
Interest expense (9% × $10,000,000)		$900,000
Less: Tax savings		
Interest expense	$900,000	
Amortization of bond discount ($500,000/20)	25,000	
Total deductible expenses	925,000	
Tax savings ($925,000 × 40%)		−370,000
Annual net cash outflows for old issue		$530,000
New Bonds (7%)		
Interest expenses (7% × $10,000,000)		$700,000
Less: Tax savings		
Interest expense	700,000	
Amortization of bond discount ($200,000/20)	10,000	
Total deductible expenses	$710,000	
Tax savings ($710,000 × 40%)		−284,000
Annual net cash outflows for new issue		$416,000

Summary

In this chapter, three main points are discussed. First, there was a review of the major factors that impact on long-term debt, including the role of the trustee to the alternative collateral requirements. Then a model was developed for measuring the after-tax cost of long-term debt. With this model, the firm can evaluate alternative types of debt configuration to ascertain the lowest-cost alternative. The model developed here is an IRR model adjusted for taxes. Finally, IRR and NPV models were developed for long-term debt refunding operations. With these models, the firm can ascertain the financial soundness of calling in old bonds and issuing the new bonds.

Questions

1. Define:

term bonds	call premium
serial bonds	mortgage bonds
call provision	debenture

2. What is the internal rate of return of a bond?
3. What risk faces a purchaser of bonds?
4. Why would a firm "refund" a bond issue?
5. Briefly explain the techniques available for evaluating the bond refunding decision.

Problems

1. What is the after-tax cost of debt under the following circumstances?

Yield to Maturity	Tax Rate
12%	30%
14%	46%
8%	18%
10%	40%

2. What are the net proceeds of the following bond issues?

Selling Price	Flotation Costs
$3,000,000	6%
$4,500,000	$200,000
$10,000,000	3%

3. What is the after-tax cost of debt for the following bond issue?

Selling price = $2,000,000
Flotation costs = 2% of selling price

Annual interest rate = 10% paid semi-annually
Maturity date = 10 years
Face value = $2,200,000
Corporate tax rate = 30%

4. $8 million of 12% bonds which mature in 20 years can be replaced with 8% bonds selling at $1,000 face value. The old bonds have an unamorized discount of $100,000 and a call price of $1,060. A gross spread of 4% and $70,000 of other issuing expenses will be incurred if the new issue is sold. There is a 1 month overlap between the issuing of the new bonds and the calling of the old bonds. Idle funds may be invested at an annual rate of 7%. If the corporate tax rate is 20 percent, what is the marginal cost of issuing the new bonds?

5. A company can replace $10 million of 18% bonds maturing in 20 years with 12% bonds maturing at the same time and priced to sell at par($1,000). The old bonds have an unamortized discount of $200,000 and a call price of $1,050. A 3% gross spread and $90,000 of other issuing expenses are necessary for the sale of the new bonds. In addition, a month overlap is expected between the issuing and refunding. Proceeds from the sale can be invested at a 10% annual rate. A 40% corporate tax rate is applicable. Should the old bonds be recalled?

6. The Middleburg Radiator Corporation is considering refunding a $4,000,000 issue of 10 year, 15% bonds. The bonds sold originally at par ($1,000) and can be recalled for $1,030. New 10% bonds can be sold for $1,000 (par) but require a 4% spread plus other issuing expenses amounting to $80,000. A month overlap is expected during which time the proceeds of the sale can be invested at 5%. The company uses a 30% corporate tax rate. Should the refunding operation take place?

BIBLIOGRAPHY

Ang, James S. "The Two Faces of Bond Refunding." *Journal of Finance*, June 1975, pp. 869–874.

Bierman, Harold, Jr. "Expected Short-Term Interest Rates in Bond Refunding." *Financial Management*, Spring 1974, pp. 75–79.

Bowlin, Oswald D. "The Refunding Decision: Another Special Case in Capital Budgeting." *Journal of Finance*, March 1966, pp. 55–68.

Kalotay, A. J. "On The Advanced Refunding of Corporate Debt." *Financial Management*, Summer 1978, pp. 14–18.

Oaks, John. "Corporate Debt Decisions: A New Analytical Framework." *Journal of Finance*, December 1978, pp. 1297–1315.

Sibley, A. M. "Some Evidence on the Cash Flow Effects of Bond Refunding." *Financial Management*, Autumn 1974, pp. 50–53.

Weingartner, H. Martin. "Optimal Timing of Bond Refunding." *Management Science*, March 1967, pp. 511–524.

12

Common Stockholders'
Wealth and Leverage

This chapter is the last that develops the analytical techniques designed to facilitate long-term financing decisions. Prior to examining these techniques, however, it seems appropriate to explicitly define the financial manager's objective when making a decision between the various sources of funds. This objective is discussed briefly in Chapter 1 as it relates to the overall finance function, and it must be emphasized that it is still the basic criterion for making the financing decision as it was for the investment decision. However, a detailed examination of this topic was deferred to this chapter to maintain the continuity of defining that objective with the analytical techniques appropriate to achieving that objective.

Consequently, a detailed development of the financial manager's decision-making objective is the first topic of this chapter. The concepts of break-even and operating leverage are then explained, followed by an examination of financial leverage; finally, the combined effects of operating and financial leverage on the decision criteria are explored.

VALUATION AND MAXIMIZATION OF STOCKHOLDERS' WEALTH

Chapter 1 asserts that the financial manager's objective is to make both investment and financing decisions in a manner that maximizes the current wealth of the common stockholders. The current wealth of the common stockholders is defined in terms of the current market price of common stock. The current price of common stock is influenced by market forces, largely beyond the control of management, and forces that are under their influence. The latter set of forces are of interest because they constitute the factors that determine the intrinsic value of the firm. This intrinsic value, or value based on all the facts appropriate to that firm, is related to the current and expected profitability of the firm as well as its risk, which in turn determine the trend in the price of the firm's common stock.

A widely used method of placing an intrinsic value on common stock can be developed in the following manner. The price of a share of common stock today depends on its future selling price and any dividends to be received. If a share of stock is purchased today, held one period, and then sold, the current price is equal to the selling price one period later plus the dividend received at the end of the period, both discounted to the present at a rate of return (r) required by the purchaser. In general the determination of the current value of a share of common stock held for n periods is a function of the PV of its dividends plus the PV of its future selling price, both found by discounting at the common stockholder's required rate of return. Because there is no maturity date on common stock, as there is on corporate debt, and if the stockholder were never to sell the stock, the price or wealth of the shareholder is the PV of a perpetual stream of dividends.

Critical to the understanding of the determination of the current price of common stock is an analysis of the dividend stream. Most investors purchasing common stock expect dividends (and stock price) to increase over time. That is, they expect $D_n > \cdots > D_3 > D_2 > D_1 > D_0$, where D_0 is the dividend just paid. For example, if g is the constant growth rate of dividends expected by investors and is equal to 5%, and the dividend just paid (D_0) is $1.00, then[1]

Period	Dividends in Symbolic Form	Dividends in Dollars
0	D_0	$1.00
1	$D_1 = D_0 + gD_0 = D_0(1 + g)^1$	1.05
2	$D_2 = D_1 + gD_1 = D_0(1 + g)^2$	1.1025
3	$D_3 = D_2 + gD_2 = D_0(1 + g)^3$	1.157625
.	.	.
.	.	.
.	.	.

[1]This chapter assumes a constant growth rate of dividends. If other growth rates are expected, see Fred Weston and Eugene Brigham, *Managerial Finance*, 7th ed. (Hinsdale, Ill.: The Dryden Press, 1981), for the computations involved in calculating share price.

It can be shown that the current price of a share of common stock given this behavior of dividends can be expressed as follows:

$$P_0 = \frac{D_1}{r - g} \qquad (12\text{-}1)$$

An equation of the form $V = (A/r)$ expresses the current or present value (V) of any asset in terms of a perpetual stream of dollar returns (A) discounted at a required rate of return (r). Consequently, the current price of common stock is equal to the expected stream of dividends discounted at the stockholders' required rate of return less the growth rate.

For example, if the expected dividend next period is $1.05, the stockholders' required rate of return is 10%, and the growth rate is 5%, the current price of common stock is:

$$P_0 = \frac{\$1.05}{.10 - .05} = \frac{1.05}{.05} = \$21$$

Note also that, for a given value of r and g, any change in the expected dividend implies a change in the current price of common stock and, consequently, the current wealth of the common stockholders. An expectation of a $1.10 dividend suggests an increase in stockholders' wealth from $21 to $22 per share. Conversely, an expectation of a $1.00 dividend yield decreases wealth from $21 to $20 per share of common stock.

Past, Current, and Future Eps, Dividends, and Stock Prices

Expected dividends, as well as r and g, are important determinants of the current wealth of the common stockholders. An investor's expectation of future dividends are influenced by the firm's past and current dividends, which are often influenced by past and current earnings per share (EPS).

Table 12-1 contains actual and estimated data for EPS, dividends, and prices of common stock for a company for the years 1976 to 1987. The price of common stock for 1984 cannot be computed until a determination of the expected dividend in 1985 is made, nor can the price of common stock for 1984 or any later year be determined until g is estimated, assuming that r is known.

The Growth Rate

The data in Table 12-1 can be used to estimate g by utilizing present value or compounding techniques. If dividends were $.80 in 1976 and are currently $1.18 per share, then:

**Table 12-1   Past, Current, and Future
EPS, Dividends, and Stock Prices**

Year	EPS	Dividends	Stock Prices
1976	$2.00	$ .80	$16.80
1977	2.10	.84	17.60
1978	2.21	.88	18.60
1979	2.32	.92	19.40
1980	2.44	.97	20.40
1981	2.56	1.02	21.40
1982	2.69	1.07	22.40
1983	2.82	1.12	23.60
1984	2.96	1.18	—
1985	2.96	1.18	24.80*
1986	3.11*	1.24*	26.00*
1987	3.27*	1.30*	†

*Estimated values.
†Cannot be estimated until dividends for 1988 are estimated.

$$\$1.18 = \$.80(1 + g)^8$$

or

$$1/(1 + g)^8 = \$.80/\$1.18$$
$$= .67797$$

In the Appendix, .67797 is associated at $n = 8$ with an approximate growth rate of 5%. That is, dividends from 1976 through 1984 have grown at about a 5% rate. Furthermore, EPS and common stock prices have grown over the 8-year period at about the same 5% rate.

This 5% growth rate and an assumed required rate of return of 10% can be used to estimate the 1982 price of common stock. The expected dividend (D_1) in 1983 is $1.18(1.05), or $1.24. Using Equation 12-9, the current market price of common stock is $1.24/(.10 − .05), or $24.80. This procedure can continue to be used to forecast EPS, dividends and the price of common stock as illustrated in Table 12-1 or beyond.

The Required Rate of Return

Solving Equation 12-1 for r yields

$$r = \frac{D_1}{P_0} + g \tag{12-2}$$

That is, the required rate of return on common stock is equal to the dividend yield plus the growth rate of the price of common stock. For example, if the expected dividend, current market price per share, and growth rate are $1.24, $24.80, and 5%, respectively, then the return is equal to 10%. Five percent of this return is the dividend yield ($1.24/$24.80), and 5% is from the appreciation in market price. Stated another way, when an investor purchases a share of common stock for $24.80 and 1 year later receives a $1.24 dividend just prior to selling the share for $26.04, the dividend yield is $1.24/$24.80, or 5%, and the capital gain is ($26.04 − $24.80)/$24.80, or 5%. The $24.80 current investment produces $2.48 1 year later, a 10% total return.

While this analysis is a truism (i.e., an observable fact), it does not explain why r must be equal to 10%. The components of the required rate of return necessary to induce an investor to buy or continue to hold the firm's common stock are summarized in Equation 12-3:

$$r = RF + BR + FR \tag{12-3}$$

This equation states that the rate of return on equity (r) necessary to induce an investor to buy or hold a firm's common stock is equal to the risk-free return (RF) plus a premium for business risk (BR) plus a premium for financial risk (FR). For example, a 5% risk-free return plus a 3% premium for business risk and a 2% premium for financial risk yields a required rate of return of 10%.

The 10% common stockholders' required rate of return used in the earlier examples (e.g., to make calculations for Table 12-1), was based on several assumptions: that the debt-equity ratio remained constant, that the growth rate of EPS and dividends was constant, and that a constant dividend policy existed. It must be stressed that if these assumptions do not hold, r must change because BR and/or FR premiums will change.

The premium for business risk results from the variability of future earnings before interest and taxes, whereas the premium for financial risk is related to the dispersion of expected future earnings available to common stockholders. The total of these two types of risk accounts for the overall risk that investors associate with a firm's common stock. The greater these premiums, the lower the common stock price, other factors remaining the same. The factors influencing these risk premiums are considered in the remaining sections of this chapter.

THE CONCEPTS OF LEVERAGE

As just noted, risk to the common stockholders occurs because of changes in earnings that revise expected dividends, the expected growth rate, and the price of common stock. Risk from variability in earnings can be divided into two sources, business risk and financing risk, with business risk defined as the variation in EBIT caused by changes in sales revenue and/or costs, and financing risk defined as the change in earnings available to the common stockholders due to change in earnings per share (EPS) or rate of return on equity (r_e) resulting from a change in EBIT. Business risk is associated with operating leverage, sometimes referred to as first-stage leverage; financing risk is associated with financial leverage or second-stage leverage.

Operating Leverage

If product price and costs are held constant, operating leverage can be defined as the change in EBIT brought about by a change in units of output sold. The following equations are helpful in analyzing operating leverage by defining revenue (R), cost (C), and EBIT:

$$R = pQ \qquad\qquad\qquad (12\text{-}4)$$

$$C = F + vQ \qquad\qquad\qquad (12\text{-}5)$$

$$EBIT = R - C \qquad\qquad\qquad (12\text{-}6)$$

where p = product unit price
        Q = units of output produced and sold
        F = total fixed costs (i.e., costs that do not change as units of output change)
        v = a constant average variable cost per unit

Equations 12-4 and 12-5 are then substituted into Equation 12-6. If we next set EBIT (and Equation 12-4) equal to zero, we define the BEQ (break-even quantity) as that quantity of output where revenues exactly equal total costs. This sequence simplifies to Equation 12-7:

$$EBIT = R - C = 0$$
$$= pQ - F - vQ = 0$$
$$= Q(p - v) - F = 0$$

$$BEQ = \frac{F}{p - v} \qquad\qquad\qquad (12\text{-}7)$$

That is, the break-even output or quantity level is equal to the dollar fixed costs divided by the difference between per unit product price and per unit variable cost (sometimes called the contribution margin).

For example, a firm in its plans for a new facility is considering two production technologies, A and B. Technology A involves higher variable cost techniques; technology B relies on higher fixed cost production techniques. The unit product price, average variable cost, and fixed costs for technology A are $.50, $.25, and $100, respectively; for technology B these values are $.50, $.10, and $200, respectively. The BEQs for the two alternatives are as follows:

$$\text{BEQ}_A = \frac{\$100}{\$.50 - \$.25} = 400$$

$$\text{BEQ}_B = \frac{\$200}{\$.50 - \$.10} = 500$$

The relationships among revenue, costs, EBIT and BEQ for these two alternatives are illustrated in Figure 12-1.

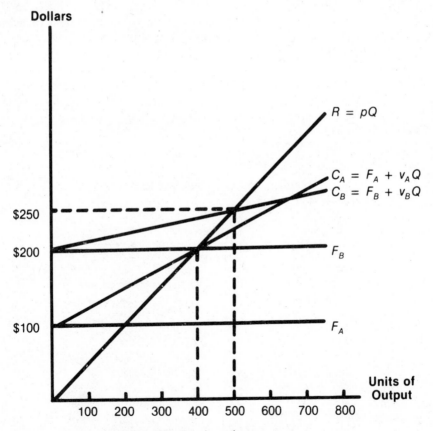

Figure 12-1. Break-even analysis for two alternatives.

If technology A is chosen by the firm, losses are less for levels of output below the BEQ, and the BEQ is lower than under technology B. However, once output goes beyond approximately 700 units (the indifference point between technologies A and B), the vertical distance between the total revenue line and the total cost line is greater for technology B; because that vertical distance represents EBIT, technology B would provide a higher level of earnings. These conclusions can also be obtained by analyzing Table 12-2.

It should be noted that changes in product price, average variable costs, and fixed costs will change the BEQ. If the unit selling price increases (decreases), variable costs per unit fall (rise) or fixed costs decrease (increase), the BEQ will be lower (higher) under either technology.

However, even if these factors were known constants, a firm would still have to know with certainty its sales volume before it could determine which of the mutually exclusive technologies to use. If the firm were certain that unit sales would remain in excess of 700 units, technology B would be preferred because earnings available to the common stockholders would be higher. Higher earnings imply expectations of an increased dividend stream and thus a higher current common stock price. Conversely, if the firm were not certain of the level of unit sales or if unit sales tend to fluctuate about 700 units, technology A might be preferred.

These conclusions become apparent when the risk the common stockholders undertake is examined to determine its influence on the values of BR premium and r in Equation 12-3. This risk can be visualized by examining the sensitivity of EBIT to a change in unit sales or by examining the degree of operating leverage (DOL). The DOL is defined by Equation 12-8:

Table 12-2   Output, Revenue, Costs, and EBIT Under
Technologies A and B

Units of Output	Total Revenue	Technology A Total Costs	Technology A EBIT	Technology B Total Costs	Technology B EBIT
—	—	$100	$(100)	$200	$(200)
100	50	125	(75)	210	(160)
200	100	150	(50)	220	(120)
300	150	175	(25)	230	(80)
400	200	200	—	240	(40)
500	250	225	25	250	—
600	300	250	50	260	40
700	350	275	75	270	80
800	400	300	100	280	120
900	450	325	125	290	160

$$DOL = \frac{\text{percentage change in EBIT}}{\text{percentage change in } Q} \qquad (12\text{-}8)$$

Substituting Equations 12-4 and 12-5 into Equation 12-6 and simplifying yields Equation 12-9:

$$EBIT = Q(p - v) - F \qquad (12\text{-}9)$$

This equation states that EBIT is directly proportional to Q, with p and v remaining constant. Thus if Q changes, EBIT changes in the same direction. F can be omitted because by definition F does not change as Q changes. Thus, this equation can be written as Equation 12-10:

$$\Delta EBIT = \Delta Q(p - v) \qquad (12\text{-}10)$$

The percentage change in EBIT is obtained by dividing the right-hand side of Equation 12-10 by the right-hand side of Equation 12-9. The percentage change in Q is equal to $\Delta Q/Q$. Consequently,

$$DOL = \frac{\Delta Q(p - v)}{Q(p - v) - F} \cdot \frac{Q}{\Delta Q}$$

or

$$DOL = \frac{Q(p - v)}{Q(p - v) - F} \qquad (12\text{-}11)$$

The degree of operating leverage defined in this manner allows us to calculate the sensitivity of EBIT to a change in the quantity of output at any output level very easily.

For example, the DOL at 700 units of output under technology A is calculated as follows:

$$DOL = \frac{700(.50 - .25)}{700(.50 - .25) - 100} = 2.33$$

If sales, in units, fall by 100%, the change in EBIT is 233%, or (2.33)($75) is equal to $175, the decrease in EBIT. Thus, such a fall in output reduces EBIT from a positive $75 at 700 units of output to a negative $100 at zero units of output. The DOL can also be interpreted for different percentage changes in output; for example, a 10% change in unit sales results in a 23.3% change in EBIT. In either case, however, the DOL indicates that a small change in output results in a much larger or magnified change in EBIT.

A close inspection of Equation 12-11 also suggests that there is a direct relationship between fixed costs and the degree of operating leverage. That is, the larger the fixed costs, given p and v, the larger the DOL and the greater the magnification of EBIT. This point can readily be seen if a comparison is made with technology B where fixed costs are $200, twice the fixed costs associated with technology A. The DOL at 700 units of output under technology B is:

$$\text{DOL} = \frac{700(.50 - .10)}{700(.50 - .10) - 200} = 3.5$$

Thus, a 100% decrease in units of output implies a 350% decrease in EBIT, or EBIT falls by 3.5 × $80, or $280, from a positive $80 to a negative $200. It should be noted that the DOL is really a form of sensitivity analysis; it shows how sensitive EBIT is to a change in output.

If the firm's management can be certain that sales will remain at or above 700 units, technology B would be the preferred alternative because the wealth of the common stockholders, in terms of the price of common stock, would be higher. That is, at all units of output equal to or greater than 700 units, earnings would be higher for technology B, suggesting that the stream of expected dividends would also be higher. Thus, the common stock price would be higher than under technology A. For example, assume that the company's dividend payout ratio is 2% of EAT, a corporate tax of 40% is used, the dividend growth rate is 5%, the stockholders' rate of return is 10%, and unit sales are 700. Equation yields the following common stock prices under technologies A and B:

$$\text{Technology A:} \quad P_0 = \frac{0.2(1 - .4)(\$75)}{.10 - .05} = \frac{.90}{.05} = \$18$$

$$\text{Technology B:} \quad P_0 = \frac{.02(1 + .4)(\$80)}{.10 - .05} = \frac{.96}{.05} = \$19$$

Although some firms (e.g., public utilities) can rely on sales being to the right of the BEQ and stable, other firms in other industries cannot be so confident. Firms with high fixed cost technologies, coupled with fluctuating sales, exhibit considerable earnings and stock price variations. Such variations can be perceived as increasing the amount of business risk and, if such is the case, Equation 12-3 suggests that the stockholders will assign a higher BR premium to the firm's common stock or they will require a higher value of r to purchase and hold the stock of a firm with higher fixed costs than that of a firm with lower fixed costs.

For example, if the firm decides on technology A, with lower fixed costs, the price of common stock could readily sell at $18 per share even with fluctuating sales because earnings are less sensitive to these fluctuations. However, if the firm chooses technology B, with higher fixed costs and fluctuating sales, investors would require a higher BR premium, and thus a higher required rate of return, to purchase the common stock of the firm because earnings are much more sensitive to sales fluctuations. The value of r might be 15%; that is, 10% plus a 5% risk premium because of the higher fixed costs and widely fluctuating sales. Furthermore, investors may feel that the growth rate is equal to zero because varying sales and high fixed costs imply alternating periods of lower profits and higher losses which allow no discernible expectations to be formed regarding earnings and dividend growth. Equation 12-1 now suggests a stock price under fluctuating sales and technology B of:

$$P_B = \frac{.02(1 - .4)(\$80)}{.15} = \frac{.96}{.15} = \$6.40$$

Consequently, the stockholders' wealth would be lower under technology B because of the greater required rate of return resulting from a higher BR premium brought on by the higher fixed cost technology coupled with fluctuating sales.

The Theory of Financial Leverage

Not only do the variability of sales and the proportion of fixed cost to total costs affect earnings and risk, but the amount of debt also has an important influence on earnings available to and risk assumed by the common stockholders. In general, the higher the amount of debt financing (both short and long term) to total financing, the greater is the impact on earnings available to the common stockholders, all else being equal.

This conclusion can be examined by recasting the income statement into symbolic notation:

$$EAT = EBT - T(EBT) = EBT(1 - T) \tag{12-12}$$

where EAT, EBT, and T are earnings after taxes, earnings before taxes and the corporate tax rate, respectively. EBT is equal to EBIT $- I$, where I is equal to an interest rate index (i) on short- and long-term debt multiplied by the amount of debt financing (D). Substituting these values into Equation 12-12 produces Equation 12-13:

$$EAT = (EBIT - iD)(1 - T) \tag{12-13}$$

Dividing both sides of Equation 12-13 by E, the dollar amount of equity in the firm, and letting EAT/E equal r_e, the after-tax return on equity, yields Equation 12-14:

$$r_e = \left(\frac{\text{EBIT}}{E} - i\frac{D}{E} \right) \cdot (1 - T) \qquad (12\text{-}14)$$

Multiplying the right side of this equation by A/A, where A is the dollar amount of total assets, and rearranging terms, suggests Equation 12-15:

$$r_e = \left(\frac{\text{EBIT}}{A} \cdot \frac{A}{E} - i\frac{D}{E} \right) \cdot (1 - T) \qquad (12\text{-}15)$$

Since the balance sheet equation is $A = D + E$, $D + E$ can be substituted for A as follows:

$$r_e = \left(\frac{\text{EBIT}}{A} \cdot \frac{D}{E} + \frac{E}{E} - i\frac{D}{E} \right) \cdot (1 - T)$$

Letting $\text{EBIT}/A = r_a$, the return on assets before interest and taxes, and rearranging terms produces Equation 12-16:

$$r_e = \left[r_a + (r_a - i)\frac{D}{E} \right] \cdot (1 - T) \qquad (12\text{-}16)$$

That is, the after-tax rate of return to the common stockholders depends on the rate of return on assets before interest and taxes, the difference between this before-tax and interest rate of return and the interest rate, the interest rate on debt, the proportion of debt to equity used to finance assets and the corporate tax rate.

The essence of financial leverage is captured in the term $(r_a - i)(D/E)$. If $r_a >$ i, then the higher the D/E ratio, the larger are the returns available to the common stockholders. If the firm can borrow at rate i to purchase assets that provide a return higher than i, then the larger the amount of debt financing, the more the earnings will exceed the fixed interest costs and the greater will be the residual accruing to the common stockholders. The example in Table 12-3(a) illustrates this point. A firm with a 40% tax rate can borrow funds at 6% and purchase assets with these funds that will earn a return of 14% before interest and taxes. The higher the proportion of debt used in the operation of the firm, the greater the return to the common stockholders, r_e.

Table 12-3(b) illustrates the case of $i = r_a$, where no financial leverage exists. Regardless of the D/E ratio, funds borrowed at 6% earn a 6% return sufficient to pay interest, taxes, and a return to the common stockholders, (r_e) of 3.6%. As the D/E ratio rises, the greater is the amount of earnings required to cover the higher interest expense and the smaller the amount of earnings available to the residual owners. Since the amount of equity is falling, however, the rate of return to the common stockholders remains at a constant 3.6%.

Table 12-3   The Impact of Financial Leverage on r_e

(1) $I - T$	(2) D/E	(3) i	(4) r_a	(5) $(r_a - i)D/E$	(6) $r_a + (r_a - i)D/E$	(7) $r_e(6 \times 1)$
				$11\text{-}3(a)\text{: } i < r_a$		
.6	0	.06	.14	0	.14	.084
.6	1	.06	.14	.08	.22	.132
.6	3	.06	.14	.24	.38	.228
				$11\text{-}3(b)\text{: } i = r_a$		
.6	0	.06	.06	0	.06	.036
.6	1	.06	.06	0	.06	.036
.6	3	.06	.06	0	.06	.036
				$11\text{-}3(c)\text{: } i > r_a$		
.6	0	.06	.02	0	.02	.012
.6	1	.06	.02	$-.04$	$-.02$	$-.012$
.6	3	.06	.02	$-.12$	$-.10$	$-.060$

Furthermore, financial leverage would be unfavorable if the interest rate is greater than the return on assets, as shown in Table 12-3(c). The higher the D/E ratio, the lower the return to the common stockholders and the more unfavorable the use of debt becomes. The stockholders would be better off if the firm had no debt, because a 2% return on assets would provide a positive 1.2% return after taxes. The more debt the firm has, the less likely it is that its earnings will be able to cover the higher interest costs. Consequently, the rate of return to the common stockholders decreases, even becoming negative in this case. The influence of financial leverage on r_e for the three levels of r_a is shown graphically in Figure 12-2.

EAT and EPS Sensitivity to Financial Leverage. The degree of financial leverage (DFL), at a given EBIT, is the percentage change in EAT or EPS resulting from a percentage change in EBIT. That is:

$$DFL = \frac{\text{percentage change in EPS}}{\text{percentage change in EBIT}} \tag{12-17}$$

EPS is equal to

$$EPS = \frac{(EBIT - I)(1 - T)}{N} \tag{12-18}$$

where N = the number of outstanding shares of common stock.

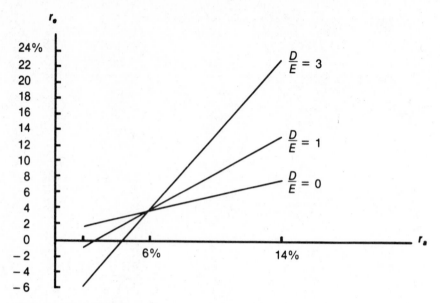

Figure 12-2. Graphical illustration of financial leverage.

The change in EPS is equal to

$$\Delta EPS = \frac{(\Delta EBIT)(1 - T)}{N} \tag{12-19}$$

Since I does not change as EBIT changes (i.e., it is a fixed cost), it is ignored in Equation 12-19. The percentage change in EPS may be obtained by dividing Equation 12-19 by Equation 12-18. Since the percentage change in EBIT is $\Delta EBIT/EBIT$, Equation 12-20 simplifies to this definition of DFL at any particular EBIT:

$$DFL = \frac{[(\Delta EBIT)(1 - T)/N] \cdot [N/(EBIT - I)(1 - T)]}{\Delta EBIT/EBIT} = \frac{EBIT}{EBIT - I} \tag{12-20}$$

That is, for any level of EBIT, the larger the value of I (i.e., the higher the fixed interest expense), the more sensitive EPS are to a change in EBIT.

For example, if interest expenses for firm A and firm B are $25 and $40, respectively, and EBIT are $80 for each firm, then the DFL for each firm is

	Firm A	*Firm B*
EBIT	$80	$80
EBIT − I	$55	$40
DFL	1.45	2.0

If EBIT for both firms increase by 10%, the increase in EPS for firm A is 14.5%, and the increase in EPS for firm B is 20%, Firm B is more highly leveraged than firm A, and consequently, EPS for firm B are more sensitive to change in EBIT than are the EPS of firm A. A decrease in EBIT for the firms would also cause a greater decrease in EPS for firm B than for firm A.

EBIT-EPS Analysis

Frequently, the relationship between EBIT and EPS is constructed when several financing methods are to be investigated. For example, a firm can raise $800,000 by selling new 20-year, 10% bonds at face value ($1,000) or 8,000 shares of common stock at $100. Table 12-4 shows the relationship between EBIT and EPS under these two alternatives, assuming that (1) EBIT range between $250,000 and $450,000, (2) there are 12,000 shares of common stock existing, (3) interest expense is currently $100,000, and (4) the corporate tax rate is 40%.

At EBIT closer to $250,000, the sale of common stock would be the more favorable alternative from the common stockholders' viewpoint. Conversely, at EBIT close to $450,000, the sale of debt would be more favorable to the stockholders.

To gain further insight into the financing decision, it is necessary to find the level of EBIT at which the common stockholders would be *indifferent* to the debt and stock financing alternatives (identical EPS under the alternatives). This indifference in EBIT is found using Equation 12-21:

$$EPS_1^* = \frac{(EBIT^* - I_1)(1 - T)}{N_1}$$

$$EPS_2^* = \frac{(EBIT^* - I_2)(1 - T)}{N_2}$$

By definition $EPS_1^* = EPS_2^*$, then

$$\frac{(EBIT^* - I_1)(1 - T)}{N_1} = \frac{(EBIT^* - I_2)(1 - T)}{N_2}$$

and

$$\frac{EBIT^* - I_1}{N_1} = \frac{EBIT^* - I_2}{N_2} \qquad (12\text{-}21)$$

where EPS^*, $EBIT^*$ = EBIT and EPS, respectively, at the indifference point between two financing alternatives

I_1, I_2 = the interest expense under two financing options

Table 12-4 Computations of EPS under Several Financing Options

	Common		Debt		Preferred	
EBIT	$250,000	$450,000	$250,000	$450,000	$250,000	$450,000
Interest	100,000	100,000	180,000	180,000	100,000	100,000
EBT	150,000	350,000	70,000	270,000	150,000	350,000
Taxes @ 40%	60,000	140,000	28,000	108,000	60,000	140,000
EAT	90,000	210,000	42,000	162,000	90,000	210,000
Preferred dividends	—	—	—	—	88,000	88,000
Earnings Available to Common	$ 90,000	$210,000	$ 42,000	$162,000	$ 2,000	$122,000
Number of Shares	20,000	20,000	12,000	12,000	20,000	20,000
EPS	$4.50	$10.50	$3.50	$13.50	$.10	$6.10

N_1, N_2 = the number of shares of common stock outstanding under two financing options

T = the corporate tax rate

If the numerical values of the two alternatives are substituted into Equation 12-21, the value of EBIT* is obtained:

$$\frac{(\text{EBIT*} - \$100{,}000)}{20{,}000} = \frac{(\text{EBIT*} - \$180{,}000)}{12{,}000} = \text{EBIT*} = \$300{,}000$$

EBIT* of $300,000 produce an EPS* of $6.00.

This indifference point allows construction of an indifference chart, Figure 12-3, for the two financing alternatives. Favorable financial leverage is clearly illustrated at any EBIT to the right of $300,000 because raising funds by debt results in higher EPS by an amount equal to the vertical distance between the debt and the common stock lines.

Committed and Uncommitted Earnings. If the debt alternative is used, the funds must be made avaiable to cover interest expense, principal repayment, and any

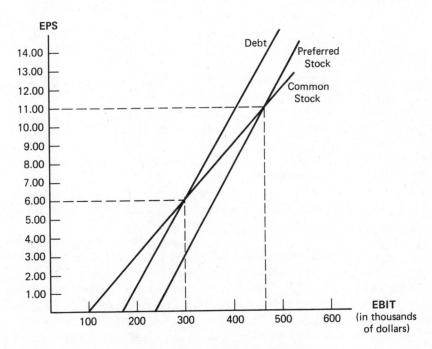

Figure 12-3. Indifference chart for several financing alternatives.

contributions to a sinking fund. Any EBIT-EPS discussion should be concerned with all items that require a commitment of earnings be it a before- or after-tax requirement.

For example, interest and lease payments are tax-deductible items, but preferred stock dividends, contributions to a sinking fund, and principal repayments are not. These types of commitments are of a contractual nature and should be included in any EBIT-EPS analysis. An item is of a contractual nature if it is a fixed expense. Suppose that the firm sold 8,000 shares of 11%, $100 par value preferred stock at par. The dividend amounts to .11($800,000), or $88,000. In Table 12-4 for EBIT of $250,000 and $450,000, EPS are $.10 and $6.10, respectively. That is, for any level of EBIT, EPS will be lower than the debt alternative. The reason is the tax deductiblity of interest. Conversely, for the preferred stock option, EBIT would have to be higher to yield the same EPS as the debt alternative. The reason is the nondeductibility of preferred stock dividends. This conclusion is shown in Figure 12-3.

An indifference point between the common and preferred stock alternatives as illustrated in Figure 12-4 can be found by broadening the definition of the I term in Equation 12-21. If I is defined as any before-tax commitment of a contractual nature, the EBIT-EPS analysis is more complete. An after-tax value can be converted to a before-tax amount as follows,

$$\text{Before-tax amount} = \frac{\text{after-tax amount}}{1 - T}$$

where T is the corporate tax rate. The before-tax amount of the preferred stock dividend is $88,000/(1 - .4)$, or $146,667. If this amount is added to the $100,000 in interest expense the firm currently has, an indifference EBIT (with the common stock alternative) of $466,667 is computed (using Equation 12-11). At this level of EBIT, EPS is $11.00.

Some financial leverage is, no doubt, desired by equity investors because the favorable influence implies a higher expected dividend stream and value of g. The value of r might even fall and the price of common stock increase as a result of their expectations. Unfavorable financial leverage is illustrated by any level below an EBIT of $300,000.

Through EBIT-EPS analysis, various financing plans or degrees of financial leverage can be examined in relation to their influence on EPS. However, while the information is helpful, the final decision of which financing plan to adopt depends upon the future level of EBIT and future financing needs. If EBIT tends to vary about $300,000, financial risk to the common stockholder rises, implying, from Equation 12-3, a higher value of r and from Equation 12-1 a lower common stock price. Likewise, if debt is used now, future financing needs met by more debt will further increase the debt-equity ratio and, consequently, the financial risk and r, thus lowering the price of common stock. These arguments are illustrated in Table 12-5.

The Interest Rate and Leverage. While the influence of financial leverage has been considered from the viewpoint of the common stockholders, a similar influence applies to creditors. Short-term creditors, long-term creditors, and preferred stockholders are also concerned with the proportions of debt and equity used to finance the firm's assets. The higher the debt-equity ratio, the greater the risk these suppliers of funds assume, the higher the fixed costs, and the greater their concern over the ability of the firm to generate earnings. Thus, their required rates of return may be higher, also reflecting higher BR and FR premiums. For example, Equation 12-3 could be restated as Equation 12-22, expressing factors that influence the creditors' required rate of return:

$$r_d = RF + BR + FR \tag{12-22}$$

As the use of debt rises relative to equity, say, above an industry average, r_d increases.

Combined Leverage

When financial leverage is combined with operating leverage, a small change in sales will cause a larger magnification of EPS than results if only one type of leverage is employed. This conclusion can be shown as follows:

$$DCL = \frac{\text{percentage change in EPS}}{\text{percentage change in } Q} \tag{12-23}$$

The percentage changes in EPS and Q are $(\Delta EBIT)/(EBIT - I)$ and $\Delta Q/Q$, respectively, so that Equation 12-23 can be written as Equation 12-24:

$$DCL = \frac{\Delta EBIT}{EBIT - I} \cdot \frac{Q}{\Delta Q} \tag{12-24}$$

Table 12-5   Possible Influences of Financial Leverage on g, r and P_0

D/E	r	g	P_0
0	10%	5%	$12
1	9	6	20
3	20	2	3

By substituting Equation 12-9 and 12-10 into Equation 12-24, Equation 12-25 results:

$$DCL = \frac{\Delta Q(p - v)}{Q(p - v) - F - I} \cdot \frac{Q}{\Delta Q} = \frac{Q(p - v)}{Q(p - v) - F - I} \quad (12\text{-}25)$$

Since F and I are subtracted from $Q(p - v)$, the larger their combined value for given values of Q, p, and v, the higher will be the value of the DCL.

For example, output, product price, average variable cost, fixed costs, and interest expense for firm A are 700 units, $.50, $.25, $100, and $25, respectively. For firm B these values are 700 units, $.50, $.10, $200, and $40, respectively. The DCL for each is:

$$DCL_A = \frac{700(\$.50 - \$.25)}{700(\$.50 - \$.25) - \$100 - \$25} = 3.5$$

$$DCL_B = \frac{700(\$.50 - \$.10)}{700(\$.50 - \$.10) - \$200 - \$40} = 7.0$$

That is, a 1% increase in output results in a 3.5% increase in EPS for firm A and a 7.0% increase in EPS for firm B.

In summary, this analysis implies that a firm with a large amount of combined leverage and variable sales may have a higher degree of risk than a firm operating under the opposite conditions. If so, Equation 12-3 suggests that a higher combined risk premium and required rate of return would be assigned to this firm.

Summary

This chapter has explored the influence of operating, financial, and combined leverage on the wealth of the common stockholders. The wealth of the common stockholders, defined as the current price of a firm's common stock, is determined by the expected dividend stream, dividend growth rate, and stockholders' required rate of return. Operating leverage is the percentage change in EBIT resulting from a percentage change in sales; financial leverage is the percentage change in EPS caused by a percentage change in EBIT. Combined leverage, the product of operating and financial leverage, is the percentage change in EPS caused by a percentage change in sales. It was shown how such changes affect the risk to the common stockholders, thus influencing the price of common stock.

Questions

1. Since owners' wealth is defined in terms of the current market price of common stock, what are the factors that influence this price?

2. How can the intrinsic value of a firm be determined?
3. Of what value are past and current dividends if the intrinsic value of the firm is determined by the expected dividend?
4. What factors influence the investor's required rate of return that is a determinant of a firm's intrinsic value?
5. Define operating leverage. What is the degree of operating leverage (DOL)?
6. What is financial leverage? What is the degree of financial leverage (DFL)?
7. How does an EBIT indifference chart help the financial manager decide between alternative sources of funds?
8. What is the degree of combined leverage?

Problems

1. **a.** Tom Collins requires a 10% return on any investments. He is interested in a particular stock that normally has end-of-period dividends of $2.00 per share; in addition, he anticipates that the stock will sell for $27.50 per share at the end of the current period. How much would Tom be willing to pay for the stock today?
   b. Tom's brother, John, also requires a 10% return on his investments. He, however, is interested in a stock for its dividend growth rather than share price appreciation. If dividends on a particular stock are currently $4.50 with anticipated annual growth of 4%, how much would John be willing to pay for the stock today?

2. If a stock's next period dividend is expected to be $3.60 per share and shareholders require a 12% return, determine how their wealth will change under the following dividend growth conditions:

   (a) 2%   (b) 6%   (c) 10%   (d) −4%

3. If shareholders require an 8% rate of return and expect dividends to grow at a 4% annual rate determine how their wealth would change under the following expected dividend conditions:

   (a) $0.80/share   (b) $2.50/share   (c) $4.00/share

4. **a.** If a firm's stock has a current market price of $37.00 per share, the expected dividend is $2.00, and the dividend growth rate is 4%, what is the required rate of return?
   b. If a firm's current market price per share, expected dividend, and dividend growth rate are $50, $4.50, and 10%, respectively, what is the required rate of return?
   c. How sensitive is the required rate of return on a stock if the expected dividend of $2.50 could vary in either direction by 20%, the growth rate is 4% and the current market price is $75?

5. The Sleazy Mattress Company makes only one type of mattress—supersoft. The mattress is sold to distributors at $37.50; annual distribution is 10,000 units, annual fixed costs are $50,000 and variable costs are $12.50 per unit. What are Sleazy's break-even output and EBIT for its annual distribution?

6. The Snow Fun Company is considering a possible addition to its line of sleds, toboggans, and skis. Data on these products are:

	Product L	Product O
Unit price	$25.00	$12.50
Average variable costs	5.00	4.00
Fixed costs	15,000.00	5,000.00

Construct and analyze a break-even analysis chart for the two products for output of 0 to 1,000 units.

7. Using the data from Problem 7 for products L and O, determine the DOL for each product.

8. The Ball Game Company manufactures an electronic game that sells to distributors at $15.00 each. Fixed costs are $250,000 annually, variable costs are $6.00 per game, annual sales are 40,000 units, and the corporate tax rate is 30%. The firm has an investment in total assets of $800,000. If the firm can borrow at an annual interest rate of 10%, what is the effect on the return to common stockholders, r_e, if the debt-equity ratio is:

(a) .5   (b) 1.0   (c) 1.5   (d) 2   (e) 2.5

9. Compare the DFL for three firms with the following characteristics:

	Firm A	Firm B	Firm C
Outstanding shares	20,000	60,000	2,000
EBIT	$105,000	$475,000	$45,000
Interest expense	$30,000	$125,000	$10,000
Tax rate	.3	.4	.2

10. Calculate the degree of combined leverage (DCL) for the following firms and interpret the results:

	Rose Blossom	Apple Orchard	Spring Tulip
Output	300,000	75,000	500,000
Fixed costs	$350,000	$700,000	$75,000
Variable unit costs	$1.00	$7.50	$.10
Interest expense	$25,000	$40,000	—
Selling price	$3.00	$25.00	$.50

BIBLIOGRAPHY

Chen, Andrew H., and Kim E. Han. "Theories of Corporate Debt Policy: A Synthesis." *Journal of Finance,* May 1979, pp. 371–384.

Ferri, Michael G., and Wesley H. Jones. "Determinants of Financial Structure—A New Methodological Approach." *Journal of Finance,* June 1979, pp. 631–644.

Gahlon, James M., and James A. Gentry. "On the Relationship Between Systematic Risk and the Degrees of Operating and Financial Leverage." *Financial Management,* Summer 1982, pp. 15–23.

Seitz, Neil. "Shareholder Goals, Firm Goals and Firm Financing Decisions." *Financial Management,* Autumn 1982, pp. 20–26.

Weston, Fred J., and Eugene F. Brigham. *Managerial Finance,* 7th ed. Hinsdale, Ill.: The Dryden Press, 1981.

CHAPTER 13

The Cost of Capital

The cost of capital is extremely important in financial management. If either the NPV or the IRR evaluation technique is used in the capital budgeting decision, the cost of capital is the discount rate used in the NPV calculations and the hurdle rate used as the IRR accept-reject criterion. The cost of capital also can be used in leasing and capital-structure decisions, and so on.

What is the cost of capital and how is it calculated? At least four different definitions of the cost of capital are used. First, it is the average cost of the existing capital structure; i.e., the firm's historical cost of financing. Second, it is the average cost of obtaining new funds. Third, it is the marginal cost of securing new financing. Finally, it is the average cost of the target capital structure. The purpose of this chapter is to delineate, compare and compute these costs of capital. Because all costs are a weighted average of the various funds in the capital structure, methods of determining the cost of the components, debt, preferred stock, and common equity are developed first.

COST OF CAPITAL COMPONENTS

A firm can obtain long-term funds from debt, preferred stock, internal sources and common stock. Each of these sources has a cost that must be determined as an after-tax cost to the firm. Since the common stockholders and preferred stockholders received their dividend payments with after-tax dollars, it is necessary for all component costs to be on an after-tax basis. The only component not normally measured on an after-tax basis is debt.

The Cost of Debt

Term loans and bonds are sources of debt funds, and their after-tax cost to the firm (k_d) is determined by Equation 13-1:

$$k_d = k_d^*(1 - T) \tag{13-1}$$

where k_d^* is the before-tax cost of debt and T is the corporate tax rate. A discussion of the cost of term loans was included in Chapter 10, this chapter will focus on determining k_d, the after-tax cost of a bond. The reader should refer to Chapter 11 for a complete explanation of calculations involved in this cost computation.

The before-tax cost of a bond depends on the selling price of the bond, (B); the interest, (C_t), expressed in equal dollar amounts over t time periods; the term of the bond, (n); the face value of the bond, (F); and the brokerage fees, (b), paid when the bond is issued and expressed as a percentage of B. Equation 13-2 expresses these relationships mathematically:

$$B(1 - b) = \sum_{t=1}^{n} \frac{C_t}{(1 + k_d^*)^t} + \frac{F}{(1 + k_d^*)^n} \tag{13-2}$$

The value of k_d^* that equates the left side with the right side is the before-tax cost of the bond.

If a firm can sell 10% (annual coupon rate), 20-year bonds with a $1,000 face value for $950 less a 10% flotation fee, Equation 13-2 would appear as follows:

$$\$950(1 - .10) = \sum_{t=1}^{20} \frac{\$100}{(1 + k_d^*)^t} + \frac{\$1,000}{(1 + k_d^*)^{20}}$$

The trial-and-error methodology discussed in Chapter 8 to find the IRR must be used to compute k_d^*. If a bond is selling at less than face value ($855 after brokerage and flotation costs, in this example) then the discount rate that will satisfy this equation must be greater than the coupon rate of 10%. Using pvfA and pvf in the Appendix for 12% and 20 periods produces

$$\$100(7.46944) + \$1,000(.10367) - \$855 = \$-4$$

A negative amount indicates that the 12% discount rate is too high; using an 11% discount rate produces a positive $65. Interpolation yields an approximate before-tax cost of the bond 11.1%. Note that this cost is based upon the $855 *net* proceeds received by the firm.

Equation 13-1 must then be used to convert this before-tax cost to an after-tax cost. If the corporate tax rate is 40%, the after-tax component cost of debt is equal to approximately 6.6%.

Cost of Preferred Stock

Preferred stock is a hybrid between debt and equity. It normally pays a constant annual dividend, but its claim on income and assets is subordinate to debt; however, it has a higher claim to these items than do the common stockholders. In addition, since the firm is not allowed to deduct as an expense any preferred dividends, no tax adjustment to the cost of preferred stock is necessary.

Unlike most bonds, preferred stock does not mature; rather, once it is sold, the firm expects to pay dividends for an infinite number of periods. The after-tax cost of preferred stock (k_p) is equal to the annual dividend (D_p) divided by its price (V) adjusted for any brokerage and flotations costs (f) and is calculated according to Equation 13-3:

$$k_p = \frac{D_p}{V(1 - f)} \tag{13-3}$$

If 9% preferred stock with $100 par value can be sold for $98 less a 12% flotation fee, its after-tax cost is $9.00/[$98(1 − .12)], or 10.4%. Note that this cost is based on the proceeds received by the firm and not the price the investor pays for the stock.

The Cost of Internal Funds

Frequently, the term "retained earnings" is used to refer to internally generated funds. However, this can be misleading. Retained earnings can be defined as either the historical accumulation of after-tax earnings (less dividends) that appears in the common-equity section of the balance sheet or as the current period's contribution to that accumulation. The definition of retained earnings used in the context of the cost of capital is the amount of cash, after taxes and common stock cash dividends, that is currently retained by the firm and is available to finance assets during the period. The central concept in computing a cost of internal funds is what rate of return would the common stockholder have earned on these funds if they had been paid out in the form of dividends rather than retained by the firm. The corporation must earn a rate of return on internal funds at least equal to the rate that the shareholder could earn on these funds to justify their retention.

This rate of return may be estimated through the use of the traditional dividend model as presented in Chapter 12, which states that the value or price of a share of common stock is related to the expected dividend, dividend growth rate, and the rate of return required by the shareholders. In symbolic notation, Equation 12-1 rewritten as Equation 13-4, defines this relationship:

$$P_0 = \frac{D_1}{r - g} \tag{13-4}$$

If Equation 13-4 is solved for k, Equation 13-5 states that the required rate of return the shareholder must receive is the dividend yield (D_i/P_0) plus the constant growth rate (g):

$$r = \frac{D_1}{P_0} + g \tag{13-5}$$

The presumption is that if the firm pays dividends, the shareholders could purchase additional shares of the firm's common stock and earn a return, r. Consequently, when the firm retains and invests funds, they must provide a return at least equal to r to ensure the growth of dividends and share price. If a return less than r is earned on retained funds, the market price of common will fall.

For example, if the expected dividend is $1.37, the growth rate is 8%, and the current market price is $17.13, Equation 13-5 yields a stockholder's required rate of return equal to 16%. It should be noted that, since the firm is not issuing new common stock, the price of common stock is not adjusted for a corporate flotation cost.

The Cost of Common Stock

The cost of issuing common stock is the minimum rate of return the firm must earn on that portion of an investment financed by common stock that prevents a decline in the market price of common stock. When a firm sells common stock, the current and potential shareholders require a return, r, to continue to hold or induce them to purchase shares. A portion of any investment financed with common stock must earn at least the return r to ensure future dividends and growth. If not, the common stock wealth maximization model developed in Chapter 12 indicates that the price violates the firm's objective of maximizing owners' wealth; the cost of issuing common stock must be at least equal to r.

However, in most cases the firm's cost of issuing common stock is more than r if the firm incurs flotation costs when it issues new common stock. The investor must pay amount P_o for a new share of common stock, but the firm's new proceeds are equal to the price paid by the investor (P_o) less these flotation costs. Thus,

Equation 13-5 modified for these costs produces Equation 13-6, the component cost of new common stock:

$$k_e = \frac{D_1}{P_0(1 - f)} + g \qquad (13\text{-}6)$$

The cost of common stock is almost always higher than any other source of funds; consequently, firms are reluctant to raise funds by selling new common stock.

When firms do sell common stock, k_e can be computed by utilizing Equation 13-6. For example, the current market price of common stock is $17.13, the flotation fee for issuing common stock is 10% and the dividend just paid was $1.27. The dividend paid six years ago was $.80. The dividend growth rate is found by dividing $1.27 by $.80 and examining the Appendix for the interest rate at $n = 6$ associated with this factor of 1.58750. The interest rate is approximately 8%. The expected dividend (D_1) would be ($1.27)(1.08), or about $1.37. The cost of new common stock is then [$1.37/($17.13)(1 − .10)] + .08, or 16.9%.

THE WEIGHTED COST OF CAPITAL

This discussion concerns the four definitions of the cost of capital noted at the very beginning of the chapter. A cost of capital is the weighted average cost of the component costs. Thus, weights are of paramount importance to the calculations and understanding of the issues involved.

Book Versus Market Weights

Weights can be defined as the percentage of funds raised from one source divided by the total amount of funds raised. The total amount raised from all long-term financing sources is called the capital structure. For example, suppose that a firm has raised $1,000,000 from debt sources and $10,000,000 from all sources (the value of the capital structure). The debt proportion is $1,000,000/$10,000,000, or 10%. Likewise, the proportion of preferred stock and equity to the total could be found in the same manner.

There are several potential ways in which to compute these weights. First, the firm might raise new funds in the same proportion as was done historically; that is, the firm could use book weights or proportions. If this were done, the answer for debt would be 10% as just computed. Second, instead of using book weights, the firm might raise new funds in the current period using market weights. That is, it would take the market values of each source and then divide by the total market value of all sources. If the market value of the $1,000,000 in debt is $1,500,000 while the market value of the total capital structure is $12,000,000 (instead of

$10,000,000), then the firm should raise about 12.5% of its new funds from debt sources. Finally, the firm could use weights or proportions that are consistent with its target capital structure.

The target capital structure contains a debt weight or proportion producing the lowest-cost capital structure. That is, the objective of the firm is to raise funds from different sources in such a fashion as to minimize the cost of financing. Consequently, instead of raising 10% or 12.5% from debt sources in the current period, the firm might raise 20% from debt. If debt is to supply 20% of the new funds because the lowest cost is produced, then it can be said that *target weights* are being used.

The risk implications of debt financing or financial leverage were discussed in Chapter 12. The concepts of financial leverage and target capital structure are combined in the last section of this chapter. To help in understanding the relationships involved, however, it may be beneficial to discuss weights and the existing capital structure of the firm.

The Existing Capital Structure

Table 13-1 contains the existing capital structure (at market value) and its weights, which are the percentage of each source of the total of all sources. Bonds and preferred stock have each supplied $1,000,000 of the total $10,000,000 of financing; thus, the proportion of bonds or preferred stock to the total is .10, or 10%. Common stock and retained earnings, that is, equity, account for 80% of the total $10,000,000 in financing.

It is possible to use these weights with the component costs of each source to calculate a cost of this existing capital structure. Why should such a computation be done? There is little or no reason to compute such a cost; the cost of the existing capital structure is an historical value. There is nothing that management can do to change what has occurred in the past. What the firm wants to measure is the cost of raising new funds currently.

To make a computation of the cost of raising new funds, a decision must be

Table 13-1   A Firm's Capital Structure and Cost of Capital Weights

Sources	Values or Amounts	Weights
Bonds	$ 1,000,000	10%
Preferred stock	1,000,000	10
Common equity	8,000,000	80
Total	$10,000,000	100%

made to raise funds using the same weights or proportions as exist currently. If new funds are raised in the same proportions as exist in the present capital structure, it means that by so doing, the firm is raising funds with the amount of financial leverage that yields the lowest weighted average cost of capital (WACC). Weights that produce the lowest WACC are defined as target weights. For the moment, it is assumed that the weights in the existing capital structure are those that produce the least cost of raising new funds (i.e., they are target weights).

The Weighted Average and Marginal Cost of Capital

Suppose, for example, that a firm plans to raise $1,000,000 in new funds during the year. Since the new $1,000,000 is used to finance new project this year, the firm desires to know the cost of these new funds. As noted, the existing capital structure of $10,000,000 does have an overall cost, but this cost is the firm's historical cost of raising funds; as such, it does not indicate the cost to the firm of raising $1,000,000 in new fund this year. Consequently, the cost of the existing capital structure is ignored, and the cost associated with raising new funds during the year is examined in detail.

The cost of capital is the rate of return that must be earned so that the market price of a share of common stock does not decline; as such, it is the cost of raising new funds from debt, preferred stock, and equity sources in the current period. It is a weighted average cost because the target weights are multiplied by their associated component costs and the products are summed. It is also an additional or marginal cost because additional funds are to be raised that increase or add to financing costs.

The Weighted Average Cost of Capital. For the example, suppose that a firm has $600,000 of internal funds available to support the new financing. Table 13-2 shows the computations for the weighted average cost of capital, assuming both the component costs and target weights indicated. Note that the target weights differ from the weights in the existing capital structure. Because the $600,000 in internal funds is part of equity, no new common stock need be sold to obtain the target proportions of

Table 13-2   Computations of the WACC and WMCC

(1) Sources	(2) Amounts	(3) Weights	(4) Costs	(5) Product of (3) and (4)
Debt	$ 200,000	.20	.09	.018
Preferred stock	200,000	.20	.10	.020
Common equity	600,000	.60	.18	.108
Total	$1,000,000	WACC = WMCC		.146

20% debt, 20% preferred stock, and 60% equity financing. The cost of these new funds (WACC) is 14.6%. That is, the average cost of raising $1,000,000 is 14.6%.

The Weighted Marginal Cost of Capital. However, the marginal or additional cost to the firm for the $1,000,000 in new financing is also 14.6%. The marginal cost of capital shows the relationship between the WACC and the total amount raised in a year. If the firm sells no new common stock this year (i.e., It raises only $1,000,000 this year), the WACC equals the WMCC (the weighted marginal cost of capital).

Since 14.6% represents the weighted cost of financing the purchase of the new assets, it is also the interest rate that should be used in determining the NPV of each asset or to compare with each asset's IRR. Investment projects should be evaluated using the cost of funds that the project must earn to allow the firm to pay future interest on debt, dividends on preferred stock, and dividends on common stock. If a project is accepted that earns 14.6%, it will provide these necessary funds. If a project earns more than 14.6%, the residual belongs to the common stockholders because interest and preferred stock dividends are fixed commitments. In these cases, the market price of the common stock should not decrease. Consequently, if the WMCC is used to evaluate projects, the market price of common stock, and hence the wealth of the shareholders, is maximized.

Consider the cost if the firm were to raise $2,000,000, an additional $1,000,000 under the assumption that the component costs of financing remain as shown in Table 13-2 and that the component cost of new common stock is 20%. Once internally generated funds are consumed, a firm must raise equity funds by selling higher-cost common stock, which causes the WMCC to rise above what it would be if only $1,000,000 were raised. That is, 60% of the second $1,000,000 must be obtained by selling common stock and the WMCC is 15.8% as computed in Table 13-3.

In general, a *break* in the WMCC schedule occurs when internal funds are exhausted and common stock must be sold to maintain the target weights. The break or point at which new common stock must be sold is found as follows:

Table 13-3 Computation of the WMCC: $1,000,000 to $2,000,000

(1) Source	(2) Weights	(3) Costs	(4) Product of (2) and (3)
Debt	.20	.09	.018
Preferred stock	.20	.10	.020
Common equity	.60	.20	.120
		WMCC =	.158

$$\text{New common stock break point} = \frac{\text{internal funds}}{\text{equity target weights}}$$

$$= \frac{\$600,000}{.60}$$

$$= \$1,000,000$$

Consider still a third possibility in which the firm might raise $3,000,000 in new funds during the year. When a required amount is this large, it is realistic to assume that the component costs will rise, but for reasons not associated with a general rise in market interest rates. When a firm attempts to raise a large amount of new funds relative to its existing capital structure, the capital market questions whether the firm will be able to generate sufficient future cash to pay interest, preferred dividends, and common dividends; that is, operating or business risk increases. As discussed in the previous chapter, when risk increases, investors' required rates of return on debt, preferred stock, and common stock increase because of the higher risk premiums required.

Table 13-4 shows these higher component costs and WMCC computations. Note that the weights remain the same for debt, preferred stock, and common stock for the computations. Again, the WMCC is the cost that should be used in making investment decisions.

The Target Capital Structure and Cost of Capital

For the development and discussion of the WMCC, it was assumed that the proportions of debt and equity in the capital structure were optimal; that is, the existing capital structure combined debt (bonds and preferred stock) and equity in such proportions as to produce the lowest average cost of capital overall.

In Chapter 12 the effects of leverage on the cost of debt, equity, and market price of a firm's common stock were explored. The conclusion drawn was that the optimal capital structure or mix of debt and equity is the one that maximizes share

Table 13-4   Computation of the WMCC: $2,000,000 to $3,000,000

(1) Source	(2) Weights	(3) Costs	(4) Product of (2) and (3)
Debt	.20	.10	.020
Preferred stock	.20	.11	.022
Common equity	.60	.21	.126
		WMCC =	.168

price. Such a capital structure is the target capital structure because it maximizes share price and the lowest cost of capital is produced. A target capital structure provides the weights the firm should use in raising new funds and is the capital structure the firm desires to maintain over time.

Table 13-5 illustrates various debt-asset ratios, associated component weights, component costs and the resulting WACC. The WACC can be computed by using Equation 13-7:

$$\text{WACC} = \sum_{j=1}^{m} w_j k_j. \qquad (13\text{-}7)$$

As the proportion of debt to equity first increases, the component cost of all funds remains fairly constant while the WACC falls. This is due to the favorable influence of financial leverage, as developed in Chapter 12. However, once the debt-asset ratio of 40% is reached, further substitution of debt for equity brings the unfavorable effects of financial leverage into play, causing the financial risk premium to rise. This in turn increases the investor's required rate of return, the firm's component costs, and the WACC. Consequently, the target capital structure should consist of 40% debt and 60% equity.

Summary

This chapter developed various cost concepts and computational techniques to compute the overall cost of obtaining new funds. The overall costs were shown to be a weighted average of the firm's individual sources of funds. The cost of the existing capital structure, however, is not relevant for making investment decisions.

Table 13-5   The Effects of the Debt-Asset Ratio on the Cost of Capital

(1) Debt-Asset Ratio	(2) w_d	(3) w_p	(4) w_e	(5) k_d	(6) k_p	(7) k_e	(8) WACC
.0	0	0	1.0	.05	.06	.13	.130
.1	.05	.05	.9	.05	.06	.13	.123
.2	.10	.10	.8	.05	.06	.13	.115
.3	.15	.15	.7	.05	.06	.13	.108
.4	.20	.20	.6	.05	.06	.13	.100
.5	.25	.25	.5	.07	.08	.14	.108
.6	.30	.30	.4	.09	.10	.15	.123
.7	.35	.35	.3	.11	.13	.16	.132
.8	.40	.40	.2	.12	.14	.20	.144

The WMCC is the only cost relevant for current investment decisions because it represents the firm's cost of obtaining new funds for current investments. It was shown that through the use of the WMCC as the minimum acceptable rate for new investments, the per share market price of common stock will be maximized. If a firm is not at its target capital structure, however, then the WMCC should be computed using the target weights in the WMCC computations regardless of the actual weights.

Questions

1. What is meant by the cost of capital?
2. What are the components of the cost of capital?
3. How is the after-tax cost of debt determined?
4. What is the cost of retained earnings?
5. How is the cost of a new issue of common stock determined?
6. What is meant by the weighted cost of capital?
7. Of what value is the WMCC for new funds?
8. Define the target capital structure.

Problems

1. Determine the after-tax cost of debt under the following conditions:
   a. A noninterest-bearing note of $10,000 face value payable in 6 months; the proceeds received are $9,400. The tax rate if 40%.
   b. A 2-year installment loan of $5,000, repayable in equal monthly installments of $235.35. The tax rate is 30%.
2. Determine the after-tax cost of bond financing if $300,000 in 10%, 10-year $1,000 face value bonds can be sold at face value less a 5% flotation fee. The applicable tax rate is 20%.
3. Determine the after-tax cost bond financing if $1,000,000 in 8%, 20-year, $1,000 face value bonds can be sold to yield $960,000 less $7\frac{1}{2}$% flotation fees. The applicable tax rate is 40%.
4. Compare the following bond financing alternatives for a corporation with a 30% tax rate:

	Alternative A	Alternative B
Total face value of debt	$750,000	$800,000
Stated interest rate	12%	9%
Flotation fee	2%	3%
Proceeds (before flotation fee)	$760,000	$760,000
Time to maturity	10 yr	10 yr

5. What is the after-tax cost of preferred stock for a corporation that has a 30% tax rate if $200,000 of 5%, $100 par value stock can be sold for $185,000 less a 5% flotation fee?
6. Compare the following financing alternatives for a corporation with a 40% tax rate:

a. $100,000 in 10%, 10-year, $1,000 face value bonds that can be sold to yield $92,000 less 2% flotation costs.

b. $100,000 in 6%, $100 par value preferred stock that can be sold to yield $85,000 less a 1% flotation fee.

7. What is the after-tax cost of retained earnings as a financing alternative if the next period's expected dividend is $2.50, the dividend growth rate is .05, the current market price per share is $45.00 and the average brokerage fee an investor pays is 4%?

8. What is the after-tax cost of issuing new common stock as a financing alternative if annual dividends have grown from $1.00 10 years ago to a current $3.00, flotation costs are 6%, and the current market price of the common stock is $24.00 per share?

9. If a firm with a 40% tax rate can borrow $100,000 at an effective interest rate of 11% and can sell $50,000 of new common stock at a cost of 15%, what is the weighted average cost of the $150,000 obtained? What is the weighted marginal cost of these funds?

10. The Warren Warmer Corporation wishes to invest in additional plant facilities. The firm's _present_ capital structure and after-tax costs are:

	Market Value	Cost
Debt	$400,000	5.25%
Preferred stock	150,000	7.00
Common stock	650,000	13.00

To expand, the firm can issue $300,000 in new debt at an after-tax effective interest rate of 8.4% and $200,000 in preferred stock at an after-tax cost of 10%. What cost of capital would be used in either NPV or IRR evaluation procedures?

11. Holding the amount of common stock in a capital structure at 30%, vary the debt and internal funds in 10% increments to determine the optimum capital structure, assuming the costs of funds do not change. There is no preferred stock.

$$k_d = .064$$

$$k_e = .15$$

$$k_r = .12$$

BIBLIOGRAPHY

Ang, James S. "Weighted Average vs. True Cost of Capital." *Financial Management,* Autumn 1973, pp. 56–60.

Arditti, Fred D. "The Weighted Average Cost of Capital: Some Questions on Its Definition, Interpretation, and Use." *Journal of Finance,* September 1973, pp. 1001–1008.

———, and Milford S. Tysseland. "Three Ways to Present the Marginal Cost of Capital." *Financial Management,* Summer 1973, pp. 63–67.

———, and Haim Levy. "The Weighted Average Cost of Capital as a Cutoff Rate: A

Critical Analysis of the Classical Textbook Weighted Average." *Financial Management*, Fall 1977, pp. 24–34.

Boudreaux, K. J., et al. "The Weighted Average Cost of Capital: A Discussion." *Financial Management*, Summer 1979, pp. 7–23.

Gup, Benton E., and Samuel W. Norwood III. "Divisional Cost of Capital: A Practical Approach." *Financial Management*, Spring 1982, pp. 20–24.

Scott, David F., Jr., and Dana J. Johnson. "Financing Policies and Practices in Large Corporations." *Financial Management*, Summer 1982, pp. 51–59.

Weston, J. Fred, and Eugene F. Brigham. *Managerial Finance*, 7th ed. Hinsdale, Ill.: The Dryden Press, 1981.

CHAPTER 14

Dividend Policy and Internal Financing

A key component of the cost of capital examined in the preceding chapter is the cost of internal or retained funds. The concept of internal funds is a cash flow concept rather than an earnings concept. Most firms have an amount of cash available after all cash transactions have been satisfied but before the payment of dividends, to stockholders and/or investment in new projects, (i.e., a residual of cash transactions that is available either to divide among common stockholders as dividends or to be used to finance new investment). This chapter is devoted to the topic of this division of internal cash between dividends and reinvestment.

Three major areas must be investigated to gain analytical insight into the division of internal funds between dividends and reinvestment. Again, as in all other chapters, these areas will be examined under the assumption that the firm makes decisions that maximize the wealth of the common stockholder. Consequently, the first section of this chapter discusses the analytical framework for the dividend-reinvestment decision from the viewpoint of the investor. Conversely, the second section investigates this decision from the viewpoint of the firm and its constrained environment. Finally the concluding section of the chapter examines alternative dividend policies.

THE ANALYTICAL MODEL

Financial management assumes that all decisions are made with the objective of maximizing the wealth of the common stockholders. Wealth of the common stockholder is defined in terms of share price of common stock. In Chapter 12, it was shown that share price (P_o) is the present value of a perpetual stream of dividends that have constant growth rate, (g). This perpetual stream of dividends produces a current price of

$$P_0 = \frac{D_1}{r - g} \qquad (14\text{-}1)$$

The next period's expected dividend, (D_1), is the proxy for the perpetual dividend stream, and r is the stockholders' required rate of return. If the next period's expected dividend is $.85, the required rate of return 10%, and the dividend growth rate 6%, a share price of [.85/(.1 − .06)], or $21.25, is obtained.

Equation 14-1 provides a useful framework with which to analyze the division of internal funds between dividends and reinvestment. Table 14-1 gives earnings per share (EPS), dividends per share (DPS), and common stock prices for the Cody Company under two alternative dividend policies. With the low dividend policy, an r of 10%, a g of 6%, and a payout ratio equal to 40% are assumed. The payout ratio is defined as that fraction of EPS that is paid out to the common stockholder in the form of cash dividends. Under the high dividend policy, $r = 8.5\%$, $g = 3\%$, and the payout ratio is 50%. These two dividend policies represent extremes; various policies in between are possible, but these are used to illustrate the issues involved.

A low dividend policy implies that the firm is paying smaller cash dividends and retaining more money for investment in new assets. Such a policy may yield growth in EPS and DPS greater than the high dividend policy, because growth of EPS and DPS is necessarily a function of investment in new assets, and their rate of return as earnings results from asset utilization. Asset growth must be financed with funds, from either internal or external sources or a combination of the two. Thus, all else being equal, the low dividend policy provides more internal funds, higher asset growth, and higher EPS and DPS growth.

However, the low dividend policy may cause common stockholders to demand a higher required rate of return. That is, if stockholders give up higher dividends, they may, in return, want a higher share price. Conversely, the higher dividends might be traded for the lower share price usually associated with a high dividend policy.

Columns 4 and 7 in Table 14-1 are constructed using Equation 14-1. For example, in year 1 the share price is computed as follows:

$$P_0 = \frac{\$.80}{.1 - .06} = \$20.00$$

Likewise, the share price in year 1 for the high dividend policy would be

Table 14-1   CODY COMPANY EPS, DPS, and Price of Two Dividend Policies*

	Low Dividend Policy			High Dividend Policy		
(1)	(2)	(3)	(4)	(5)	(6)	(7)
Year	EPS	DPS	Price	EPS	DPS	Price
1	$2.00	$ .80	$20.00	$2.00	$1.00	$18.18
2	2.12	.85	21.25	2.06	1.03	18.73
3	2.25	.90	22.50	2.12	1.06	19.27
4	2.38	.95	23.75	2.19	1.09	19.82
5	2.52	1.01	25.25	2.25	1.13	20.55

*EPS, DPS, and price grow at a compound rate; for example, EPS in the third year for the low dividend policy are $2.00(1.06)^2$, or $2.2472, rounded to $2.25. Rounding errors cause some disagreement in results. EPS and DPS are end-of-year values; prices are beginning-of-year values.

$$P_0 = \frac{\$1.00}{.085 - .03} = \$18.18$$

The remaining prices in columns 4 and 7 were calculated in a similar manner.

Because the wealth of the common stockholders is defined in terms of the current share price, the low dividend policy (high funds retention rate) produces the higher common stockholders' wealth for all years. That is, if a stockholder had a 1-year holding period (the stock is purchased at the beginning of year 1 and sold at the beginning of year 2), the low dividend policy would produce an $.80 cash dividend and $21.25 in cash from the sale of the share at the end of the year, for a total of $22.05. The high dividend policy produces a combined value of $19.73. The present value of $21.25 received in 1 year at the 10% required rate of return is $22.05/1.1, or $20.00 (rounding errors in Table 14-1 produce $20.05). The present value of $19.73 is $19.73/1.085, or $18.18, for the high dividend policy and a 1-year holding period. The $1.82 difference between the present values of the stock prices ($20.00 less $18.18) is maintained regardless of the length of the holding period. If the investors have a 2-year holding period, the low dividend policy produces a current share price (present value) of $\$.80/(1.1)^1 + \$.85(1.1)^2 + \$22.50/(1.1)^2$, or $20.00. An $18.18 share price is obtained in the same manner for the high dividend policy and a 2-year holding period, using a present value of 8.5%.

A firm should also consider the impact of personal income tax and capital gains tax rates on the wealth of the common stockholders when it formulates dividend policy. It can be argued that these tax rates favor a low dividend payout policy for two reasons. First, a low dividend policy postpones the payment of ordinary income taxes on larger dividends either indefinitely or at least for some time into the future.

Second, ordinary dividend income is converted into capital gains income via higher share prices when the stock is sold in the future, as illustrated in Table 14-2.

The calculations in Table 14-2 assume that an investor has a 2-year holding period, a 30% personal income tax rate on ordinary income (dividends), and a 10% capital gains rate. If the firm implements the low dividend policy, the present value of the future cash flows is $21.46. The stockholder purchases the stock for $20.00, receives dividends of $.80 and $.85 in years 1 and 2 (after taxes, $.56 and $.59), and then sells it at the beginning of year 3 (end of year 2). The capital gain is the difference between the selling and the purchase price: $22.50 less $20.00, or $2.50. The present value is found using the 10% required rate of return to discount the after-tax values. The same procedure is used to find the present value for the high dividend policy. The low dividend policy has a $3.00 advantage over the high dividend policy.

Although this analysis only compares the two extremes of low and high dividend policies, it does indicate some of the issues involved. To find the optimal dividend policy, all possible payout ratios should be analyzed. However, the principles just discussed would apply to all possible payout ratios. First, the dividend policy adopted by the firm should maximize the current wealth of the shareholders by maximizing the current share price of common stock. Second, a low payout ratio (high retention rate) is usually associated with a higher common stockholders'

Table 14-2   Personal Income and Capital Gains on Two Dividend Policies

Item	(1) Amount	(2) Tax Rate	(3) = (1) × (2) Tax	(4) = (1) − (3) After Taxes	(5) Present Value*
Low dividend policy					
Dividend, year 1	$ .80	$.30	$.24	$ .56	$ .51
Dividend, year 2	.85	.30	.26	.59	.49
Capital gain:					
$22.50 − $20.00 =	2.50	.10	.25	2.25	1.86
Selling price				22.50	18.60
Present value					$21.46
High dividend policy					
Dividend, year 1	$1.00	$.30	$.30	$ .70	$ .65
Dividend, year 2	1.03	.30	.31	.72	.61
Capital gain:					
$19.27 − $18.18 =	1.09	.10	.11	.98	.83
Selling price				19.27	16.37
Present value					$18.46

*At 10% and 8.5% discount rates for the low- and high-dividend policies, respectively.

required rate of return. Third, the preferential tax treatment of capital gains favors the low payout ratio (high retention rate).

These factors consider the effects of dividend policy from the viewpoint of the common stockholders only and largely ignore the constraints confronting the firm. The issues facing the firm as it formulates a dividend policy are discussed next.

FIRM'S VIEWPOINT: FACTORS INFLUENCING DIVIDENDS

In the previous section, it was assumed that the firm's desire and ability to pay dividends was compatible with either a low or a high dividend payout ratio. There are, however, many factors influencing a firm's willingness and ability to adopt various dividend policies. These influences are discussed in the paragraphs that follow.

Legal Influences

Certain legal restrictions establish the framework within which a firm must formulate its dividend policy. Generally, state laws place three constraints on the firm for the protection of its creditors. First, the net profit rule requires the firm to pay dividends only from retained earnings, the accumulation of profits to date. The balance sheet of Glass Manufacturing Company is shown in Table 14-3. The net profit rule restricts the company's dividend payments to retained earnings, or $50,000. Second, the capital impairment rule prohibits the payment of dividends from the capital account in excess of retained earnings. That is, the Glass Manufacturing Company cannot reduce the $100,000 capital stock account by paying a total dividend of more than $50,000. This rule is designed to protect the creditors by maintaining a capital cushion.[1] Third, the insolvency rule also protects the creditors because it prohibits dividend payments when the firm is insolvent, (i.e., when liabilities exceed assets). If a dividend payment is made when liabilities exceed assets, the common stockholders would receive funds on which creditors have a prior claim. While these legal constraints provide a framework for dividend policy decisions, economic and financial factors also influence dividend policy.

---

[1]A liquidating dividend, clearly stated as such, can be paid. Such a dividend returns to the common stockholders the capital they paid into the firm. These dividends are usually associated with bankruptcy proceedings, but in 1979 several companies were considering voluntary liquidation. That is, several firms were considering selling all assets and subsequently paying a liquidating dividend because it would be much higher than the selling price of a share of common stock. See *Business Week*, "When a Company is Better Dead," March 26, 1979, page 88.

Table 14-3   GLASS MANUFACTURING COMPANY
Balance Sheet March 31, 1981

Fixed assets	$150,000	Common stock	$100,000
		Retained earnings	50,000
Total	$150,000		$150,000

Liquidity Considerations

Current accounting income or the accumulation of net income in the retained earnings account may be totally unrelated to the cash available within the firm to pay dividends (or, in fact, to pay anything), as shown in Table 14-3. The only assets held by the Glass Manufacturing Company are fixed assets. Thus, a firm with a past record of earnings, as indicated by the retained earnings account, may not be able to pay a cash dividend because of its liquidity position. That is, the firm, as illustrated by the data in Table 14-3, does not have any cash with which to pay a dividend.

Even if the firm's balance sheet indicates sufficient cash, it may still be unwise to pay a cash dividend. If the Glass Manufacturing Company's balance sheet appeared as it does in Table 14-4, $50,000 cash would be available to pay the maximum legal dividend. However, the firm also has $50,000 of current liabilities that must be paid, with cash, in the near future. Consequently, $50,000 is not sufficient to pay both $50,000 in dividends and $50,000 in current liabilities. To determine the amount of cash available for dividends, a cash budget is required.

Several possible cash budgets for the Glass Manufacturing Company appear in Table 14-5. The total cash available during the second quarter is the summation of the beginning cash balance, cash sales and collections on accounts receivable. Total disbursements is the summation of all uses of cash during the quarter. Since dividends are a use of cash, alternative dividend payments are listed under disbursements. Cash budget A indicates that the firm can pay the legal maximum dividend, if it so desires, and still have the minimum cash balance of $50,000 to begin the third quarter.

Table 14-4   GLASS MANUFACTURING COMPANY Balance Sheet
March 31, 1981

Cash	$ 50,000	Current liabilities		$ 50,000
Fixed assets	150,000	Common stock	$100,000	
		Retained earnings	50,000	150,000
Total	$200,000			$200,000

Table 14-5 GLASS MANUFACTURING COMPANY Alternative Cash Budgets Second Quarter, 1981

	Cash Budget			
	A	B	C	D
Beginning cash balance	$ 50,000	$ 50,000	$ 50,000	$ 50,000
Receipts				
Cash sales	75,000	75,000	75,000	75,000
Collections	175,000	175,000	175,000	175,000
Miscellaneous	—	—	10,000	14,000
Total cash available	300,000	300,000	310,000	314,000
Disbursements				
Purchases	180,000	180,000	180,000	180,000
Wages	15,000	15,000	15,000	15,000
Rent	5,000	5,000	5,000	5,000
Dividends	50,000	50,000	10,000	14,000
Miscellaneous	—	50,000	50,000	50,000
Total disbursements	250,000	300,000	260,000	264,000
Cash available end of period	50,000	—	50,000	50,000
Less: Required minimum balance	50,000	50,000	50,000	50,000
Surplus (shortage)	$ —	$(50,000)	$ —	$ —

Although cash budget A does indicate the firm can pay a maximum dividend, there are still other considerations influencing dividend policy that must be considered. A major factor in the firm's decision of how much cash to pay out in the form of a dividend is the rate of return on assets and the growth rate of assets.

Asset Growth Rate

If the firm has and expects to take advantage of future profitable investment opportunities, cash budget A overstates the amount of cash available for dividends. Ample present and future investment opportunities indicate a relatively high asset growth rate. Such an asset expansion level suggests a greater need for the firm to retain cash. A high retention rate necessarily implies a low dividend payout rate. Consequently, cash budget A does not represent a viable option under these conditions.

If Glass Manufacturing Company has investment opportunities totaling $50,000 during the quarter, cash budget B indicates the results of the firm's acquiring both the $50,000 (a miscellaneous use of cash) in assets and paying the $50,000 dividend. As shown by cash budget B, a $50,000 cash shortage results. If this is the alternative followed, the firm must seek external funds. Access to financial markets is still another influence on dividend policy.

Access to Financial Markets

A shortage of funds under these conditions suggests that the firm must go outside for $50,000 to pay both dividends and acquire the assets. If the firm has a strong past profit record, it may have easy access to external sources. However, if the firm is new or small, or has a weak past profit performance, it may be denied access to financial markets because of the high risk to investors. Under these conditions, the firm would have to either eliminate the $50,000 dividend entirely to acquire the $50,000 in new assets, or it could reduce both the dividend and asset acquisitions for the period. That is, a firm that does not have access to financial markets will normally be forced to retain more cash and pay lower dividends.

A firm that has access to the financial markets could raise the additional $50,000 by selling new common stock. Firms are reluctant, however, to sell new common stock for three reasons: new common stock represents the source of funds with the highest cost, it dilutes control of the dominant group, and it dilutes earnings per share. With a greater number of shares outstanding, the potential exists for a new group to obtain more shares and take control. In addition, with more shares outstanding, earnings must increase significantly to keep earnings per share from falling. As a consequence, a lower dividend payout ratio is favored.

A second external source of funds available to firms with access to financial markets is debt. Debt contracts, however, can impose constraints on dividends. Generally, debt contracts, especially long-term debt contracts, specify that dividends must be paid from current earnings and that net working capital (current assets minus current liabilities) *cannot* fall below a specified amount. Another source of financing, cumulative preferred stock, also specifies that common stock dividends *cannot* be paid until all accrued preferred stock dividends have been paid.

Thus the Glass Manufacturing Company has to compromise its dividend policy. If it chooses to issue debt instead of new common stock, the debt contract may force the company to limit its common stock dividend to current earnings, $20,000. The management of the firm, given these new considerations, may agree to a $10,000 dividend.

Cash budget C in Table 14-5 indicates the cash position of the firm under these conditions. The firm purchases the $50,000 in new assets by using $40,000 from internal sources (which reduces the cash dividend from $50,000 to $10,000) and $10,000 in long-term debt (listed as a miscellaneous source of cash). It is possible that the dividend could be more or less than the $10,000 dividend illustrated, depending on the stability of earnings.

Stability of Earnings

If a firm's earnings are relatively stable, it can forecast future earnings more accurately. Consequently, the firm might opt for a higher dividend payout ratio. In cash budget C (Table 14-5), a 50% payout ratio (dividend/earnings, $10,000/$20,000) is shown. Cash budget D, however, illustrates a 70% payout ratio. This cash budget assumes that the firm's earnings are relatively stable and that lenders are indifferent to lending $10,000 or $14,000.

While there are perhaps other factors influencing the firm's dividend policy, the major factors have been discussed and illustrated. These influences provide the background and framework for a discussion of alternative dividend policies in the next section.

ALTERNATIVE DIVIDEND POLICIES

Firms must consider the factors just discussed when formulating dividend policy. In addition, it can be observed that firms tend to maintain a relatively stable dividend policy. Even though earnings after taxes may be quite volatile, dividends will not rise and fall with earnings. That is, dividends per share tend to remain fairly constant, increasing only when firms believe the higher dividend can be sustained.

There is no conclusive empirical proof that stable dividends lead to higher common stock prices, but there are several conceptual reasons why this might occur. First, investors are more likely to consider firms with stable dividends less risky than firms whose dividends fluctuate. When dividends fluctuate, even though their average is the same as that of stable dividends, investors are more likely to require a higher rate of return. A higher required rate of return reduces the price of the stock. Second, many stockholders rely on dividends to provide income to meet living expenses. Fluctuating dividends are an inconvenience to such stockholders, suggesting a lower stock price. Third, one of the requirements for a firm's stock to be on the *legal list* is stable dividends. The legal list contains those securities that regulatory agencies allow mutual savings, insurance companies, pension funds, and so on to buy. Thus, the legal list encourages interested firms to maintain stable dividends. Finally, the behavior of dividends is thought to convey information about the profitability of the firm. A stable dividend implies permanent and stable profits; an increasing dividend suggests a permanent increase in profitability; a decreasing dividend indicates a reduced level of profitability.

Stable dividends seem to be an observable fact of corporate behavior, and the reasons just offered are an explanation of why. The first alternative dividend policy to be discussed, however, involves a fluctuating dividend. This first policy is referred to as the residual theory of dividends.

Residual Theory of Dividends

The idea behind the residual theory of dividends as an alternative dividend policy is very simple. Residual means "left over." Thus the residual theory states that the amount of funds left over after all profitable investments have been funded is paid out in dividends.

The key to formulating a dividend policy based on the residual theory concept is the definition of a profitable investment. Funds should be invested in assets as long as the rate of return on these assets is greater than or equal to the rate of return the investor could obtain if he or she received the funds as dividends and invested them in a project of comparable risk. For example, if a firm can earn 15% on invested funds, but the investor could earn only 10% on these funds if he or she received them in the form of dividends, then the investor is better off if the firm retains the funds and reinvests them. However, as the discussions in Chapter 13 on the cost of capital and in Chapter 8 on the internal rate of return capital budgeting evaluation technique both indicate, the investment accept-reject criterion requires comparison of the IRR and WMCC.

As long as the IRR is greater than or equal to the WMCC, funds should be committed to the investment project. Since the common stockholder's required rate of return is part of the WMCC computation, the decision criterion ensures that funds retained will be invested at a return rate equal to what the stockholder could have earned if he or she had received the funds in the form of dividends.

Another key to formulating a dividend policy under the residual theory of dividends is the concept of the target capital structure developed in Chapter 13. The target capital structure is that proportion of debt to equity, or the debt-asset ratio, that minimizes the firm's average cost of capital. The optimal debt-asset ratio for the firm must first be determined because this optimal debt-asset ratio provides the lowest WMCC. Dividend policy should then be formulated so that the optimal capital structure is obtained.

Perhaps an example can illustrate the use of these ideas and how a dividend policy would be developed. The Kentucky Bourbon Company has an optimal debt-asset ratio of 50%. The firm has $30,000 in internally generated funds available for new projects if it does not pay dividends and another $30,000 can be obtained from new debt. The Firm's WMCC of 10% is constant to $60,000. If the firm raises funds beyond $60,000, it would have to sell new, more expensive common stock, raising the WMCC to 12%. The firm's capital budgeting department developed Table 14-6, which shows new investment opportunities ranked by IRRs under three different sets of economic conditions.

These IRR schedules can be related to the WMCCs and the appropriate investment levels determined. When investment opportunities are fair, $30,000 should be invested; when conditions are good, $50,000 should be invested; when conditions

Table 14-6 KENTUCKY BOURBON COMPANY IRRs and Investment Opportunities under Various Conditions

	IRR		
Investment	Fair	Good	Best
$10,000	12%	15%	18%
20,000	11	14	17
30,000	10	13	16
40,000	9	12	15
50,000	8	10	14
60,000	7	9	13
70,000	6	8	12
80,000	5	7	11

are best, $70,000 should be invested. These values are found by comparing the 10% and 12% WMCCs to the IRRs for the three economic conditions. The question becomes, How should the firm finance the investment levels?

Under the best economic conditions, the firm would need to retain all $30,000 of internal funds, borrow $30,000, and sell $10,000 in new common stock to invest $70,000. The firm would not pay dividends. In addition, the firm changes its optimal capital structure because the debt-asset ratio of the new investment is 43% ($30,000/$70,000), not 50%. If economic conditions were good, the firm should invest $50,000—$25,000 from internal funds and $25,000 from issuing new debt. Thus $5,000 is available to pay dividends, and a 50% debt-asset ratio is maintained. Under fair investment opportunities, again the financing should be done to stay in line with the target capital structure. Consequently, $15,000 of internal funds and $15,000 in new debt should be used to finance investments. This policy results in $15,000 from internal funds being used for dividends.

These decisions seem to present two contradictions: dividends fluctuate, depending on economic conditions, instead of remaining stable, and the target capital structure is not adhered to under the best economic condition. From both the practical and conceptual viewpoints, stability of dividends seems to be more important than a strict adherence to the target capital structure. In Chapter 12 it was argued that the cost of the capital structure changes by fairly small amounts when the debt-asset ratio is changed. Thus when very favorable economic conditions exist, larger amounts of debt can be raised to pay dividends; during very unfavorable economic conditions, debt can be repaid while maintaining dividends.

Consequently, under the best economic conditions, an additional $15,000 might be borrowed so that a $5,000 dividend could be paid and no common stock sold. The dividend would be the same as that paid under good economic conditions. The firm's debt-asset ratio would increase to 64% ($45,000/$70,000). However, in fair economic conditions, when $15,000 of internal funds is available, the $5,000 dividend could be maintained while $10,000 could be used to repay some of the debt borrowed in the extremely good years. Thus the debt-asset ratio would be brought back in line with the target capital structure.

A few firms use the residual theory of dividends, but the apparent contradictions and attempts to reconcile them suggest that alternative dividend policies may be used more frequently. Another alternative dividend policy is to have a constant payout ratio.

Constant Payout Ratio

The Penn-Central Railroad, prior to its bankruptcy, followed a practice of paying a constant percentage of earnings (50%) as a dividend. A few firms follow this policy as a means of determining dividends, perhaps because of its simplicity. A dividend policy based on a constant payout ratio is straightforward and easily implemented.

As noted previously, available internal funds may be used to pay dividends or to reinvest. The payout ratio is the percentage paid out, and the retention rate is the percentage of funds retained; together these two percentages must equal 100%. For example, a firm has $100,000 to divide between dividends and reinvestment. If the firm has a 40% payout ratio and a 60% retention rate, then $40,000 (.4 × $100,000) is available for dividends and $60,000 (.6 × $100,000) is available for reinvestment. Note that the entire pool, $100,000, must be used for one or the other purpose (i.e., the sum of the two must equal the whole). In general, for any values of p, the payout ratio, and r, the retention rate, Equation 14-2 must be true:

$$p + r = 1 \tag{14-2}$$

The value of p (or r) is determined by management after an evaluation of all the influences on dividend policy discussed earlier in this chapter.

However, firms that use this approach to determine dividends usually treat p as a constant value, never (or at least seldom) changing it. For example, the Penn-Central Railroad used 50% as the value of p. Once p is determined, the dividend per share for time period D_t is found by multiplying the EPS in that time period by p as shown by Equation 14-3:

$$D_t = p\text{EPS}_t \quad \text{or} \quad D_t = (1 - r)\text{EPS}_t \tag{14-3}$$

For example, if $\text{EPS}_t = \$1.00$ and $p = .5$, then Equation 14-3 produces a dividend of (.5)($1.00), or $.50.

Frequently, p is not a payout ratio that the firm would use under ideal conditions (a target payout ratio), but rather it is the payout ratio for all conditions. With a constant payout ratio, however, dividends can be unstable because of the tendency for EPS to fluctuate widely from period to period. As previously mentioned, fluctuating dividends may cause the price of common stock to be lower than it would be if dividends were stable.

The effects of a constant payout ratio (50%) and fluctuating EPS on dividends are shown in Table 14-7. Dividends were computed using Equation 14-3. As earnings fluctuate, the constant payout ratio causes dividends to fluctuate. Thus the price of a firm's common stock is likely to be lower than it would be for stable dividends, for reasons discussed earlier.

Because a fluctuating dividend can influence the price of common stock, other alternative dividend policies have been formulated. The stable dollar dividend per share is an alternative to the constant payout ratio dividend policy.

Stable Dollar Dividend Per Share

A stable dollar dividend per share is the most widely used dividend policy. The objective of this policy is to provide a stable but growing dividend. Under this alternative, the current dividend (D_t) is related to the previous dividend (D_{t-1}), current earnings per share (E_t), a target dividend (D_t^*), and an adjustment factor (a).

The target dividend (D_t^*) is the dividend the firm would pay under ideal conditions (i.e., stable but growing earnings per share). A problem arises, however, because fluctuating earnings per share are the rule rather than the exception. To reconcile this with the goal of providing a stable but growing dividend, an adjustment factor (a) is used. To illustrate the application of this policy, a dividend change (ΔD) can be found by solving Equation 14-4:

$$\Delta D = D_t - D_{t-1} \tag{14-4}$$

Table 14-7 The Effects of a Constant Payout Ratio and Fluctuating EPS on Dividends

Period	p	EPS	D
1	.5	$1.00	$ .50
2	.5	1.50	.75
3	.5	1.00	.50
4	.5	2.00	1.00
5	.5	1.80	.90

For example, the dividend change is $.12 if the planned current dividend is $.48 and the previous dividend was $.36. The factors that give rise to the dividend change are of prime importance and may be examined using Equation 14-5:

$$\Delta D = a(D_t^* - D_{t-1}) \tag{14-5}$$

This equation states that the change in dividend is caused by the difference between the target and the previous period's dividend multiplied by an adjustment factor. The value of the adjustment factor depends on management's assessment of the stability of any increase in EPS, the need to retain funds, the firm's liquidity position, and so on. For example, if the target dividend is $.75, the previous dividend was $.36, and the adjustment factor is 30%, the dividend change is .3($.39), or approximately $.12. Table 14-8 illustrates the application of the stable dollar dividend policy. All entries in column 7 for D_t were calculated using Equation 14-5.

Column 7 shows that dividends are stable and growing over time, even when EPS (column 5) decrease in periods 2 and 5. This is possible due to the calculation of the dividend change using the adjustment factor times the difference between the target and previous dividend. The actual payout ratio ($p = D_t/E_t$) shown in column 8 tends to vary as a consequence but approaches the target payout ratio (column 4) in periods when EPS fall.

Perhaps the unusual phenomenon of the actual payout ratio approaching the target payout ratio only in periods of low EPS is why some firms prefer still another alternative dividend policy. It would be more logical for the actual payment ratio to approach the targeted payout ratio during periods of higher than normal levels of EPS instead of the reverse. An alternative dividend policy that recognizes this behavior is the low regular dividend plus an extra dividend.

Table 14-8   Dividend Computations under a Stable Dollar Dividend Policy

(1) Period	(2) D_{t-1}	(3) a	(4) p^*	(5) E_t	(6) $a(p^*E_t - D_{t-1})$	(7) D_t	(8) p
1	$.30	.3	.5	$1.00	$.06	$.36	.36
2	.36	.3	.5	.75	.00	.36	.48
3	.36	.3	.5	1.50	.12	.48	.32
4	.48	.3	.5	2.00	.16	.64	.32
5	.64	.3	.5	1.50	.03	.67	.45
6	.67	.3	.5	2.00	.10	.77	.39

A Low Regular Plus An Extra Dividend

The low regular plus an extra dividend is a dividend policy that combines a constant payout ratio with a stable dollar dividend. Under this policy, the actual payout ratio is set very low. When this low payout ratio is multiplied by EPS for the period, a low regular dividend is declared for the period. The extra dividend is added to the low regular dividend only when EPS exceed some minimum amount. In periods when EPS do not meet the minimum, no extra dividend is declared.

Table 14-9 illustrates this dividend policy. A constant payout ratio (p) of 30% is assumed. When this is multiplied by the minimum EPS of $1.00, a low regular dividend (d_t^*) of $.30 is produced in any period. A variable payout ratio (p^*) of .1 is used to calculate the extra dividend (X) when EPS exceed $1.00. Thus, the value of p^* is either zero or 10%, depending on the actual EPS (E_t) relative to the minimum EPS of $1.00 ($E_t^*$). This policy is summarized by Equation 14-6:

$$d_t = pE_t^* + p^*(E_t - \$1.00) \tag{14-6}$$

where d_t = the dividend paid in the period t
$p^* = 0$ when $(E_t - \$1.00) \le 0$,
$p^* = .1$ when $(E_t - \$1.00) > 0$

For example, the period 1 dividend paid is .30($1.00) + 0($1.00 − $1.00) or $1.00.

This dividend alternative provides this firm with the flexibility to maintain a stable dividend when EPS fall, yet to increase the dividend when the level of EPS rises. For investors, however, there is some uncertainty about their dividend income from one period to the next. Nevertheless, this policy may be one of the best choices for a firm whose earnings are very volatile.

Summary

Dividend policy helps to determine the extent of internal financing, the capital structure, liquidity, and the market price of the firm's common stock. This chapter first developed the analytical model to determine the firm's dividend policy. The model shows that the dividend policy followed should be the one that maximizes the price of a share of common stock. However, there are many influences on dividend policy. The second part of the chapter discussed these influences: legal, liquidity, return on assets, growth rate on assets, access to financial markets, and stability of earnings.

Because these influences vary from one firm to another, several alternative dividend policies were discussed. In theory, the residual theory of dividends would produce the highest market price for the common stock. Under this policy, dividends are determined once the firm's debt policy and cost of capital are known.

Table 14-9 Dividend Computations under a Policy of a Low Regular Plus an Extra Dividend

(1) Period	(2) d_t^*	(3) E_t	(4) $E_t - \$1.00$	(5) X	(6) d_t
1	$.30	$1.00	$.00	$.00	$.30
2	.30	1.15	.15	.02	.32
3	.30	.80	(.20)	.00	.30
4	.30	1.20	.20	.02	.32
5	.30	1.30	.30	.03	.33

Since management does not have perfect information about these and other influences, however, alternative dividend policies are frequently followed. These alternative policies are constant payout ratio, stable dollars per share, and low regular plus an extra dividend. All these alternative dividend policies were illustrated, discussed, and analyzed. There is, however, no unique dividend policy applicable to all firms.

Questions

1. What is the primary objective in formulating a dividend policy?
2. How is it possible for a low dividend policy to produce the higher share price in future periods?
3. How do income taxes affect the dividend policy of a firm?
4. What legal influences affect a firm's dividend policy?
5. How does a firm's liquidity position affect its dividend policy?
6. Of what importance is a cash budget to the dividend payment decision?
7. What sources of cash are available to a firm if sufficient internally generated cash is unavailable to meet operating needs as well as dividend payments? Are these sources always available to all firms?
8. Why may it be true that stable dividends lead to higher common stock prices?
9. What is the residual theory of dividends? What contradictions are embedded in this particular dividend policy?
10. What are the advantages and disadvantages of the constant payout ratio dividend policy?
11. What is the objective of the stable dollar dividend per share dividend policy and how is this objective met?

Problems

1. The Pump and Centrifuge Company has a policy of maintaining a 25% dividend payout ratio. Estimate the firm's share price for this and the succeeding 5 years if the required return is 12%, the dividend growth rate is 5%, and the next year's expected dividend is $1.50.

2. The Pomp and Circumstance Company maintains a constant 60% dividend payout ratio. If this firm's required rate of return is 8%, the dividend growth rate is 2%, and the next year's expected dividend is $3.60, determine the firm's share price for the current and five succeeding years.

3. Using the information on the Pump and Centrifuge Company from Problem 1, determine the present value of a shareholder's share of a common stock if he has a 3-year holding period, a 45% tax rate on ordinary income, and a 15% capital gains tax rate.

4. Using the information from Problem 2 on the Pomp and Circumstance Company, determine the present value of 1 share of stock if the shareholder has a 3-year holding period, a 25% tax rate on ordinary income, and a capital gains tax rate of 7.5%.

5. Given no other information than the following balance sheet, what alternative dividends could be paid by the Swing Gear Company?

SWING GEAR COMPANY
Balance Sheet
as of December 31, 1981

Cash	75,000	Accounts payable	$300,000
Marketable securities	125,000	Mortgages payable	200,000
Accounts receivable	200,000	Bonds payable	200,000
Investments	150,000	Total liabilities	$700,000
Plants and equipment	700,000	Capital stock	250,000
Total assets	$1,250,000	Retained earnings	300,000
		Total equity	$550,000

6. The Vienna Bread Company has $200,000 available for investment and/or dividend payments. If the firm has $175,000 in profitable investment projects available, what range of possible dividend payments could the firm consider?

7. The Plastic Band Company has the following investment opportunities available, ranked by their IRRs under four possible economic conditions:

	IRR			
Investment	Poor	Fair	Good	Excellent
$20,000	12	14	16	20
30,000	10	13	15	17
15,000	10	12	13	14
25,000	8	10	12	13
30,000	6	7	8	9

The firm's WMCC is constant at 12% up to $50,000 but increases to 14% if new common stock must be purchased. If the firm's optimal debt-asset ratio is .4, and if it can borrow $20,000 and has $30,000 of internally generated funds available, determine (a) the level of investment for each economic condition, (b) how the firm should finance the level of investment, and (c) the dividend paid under the residual theory of dividends.

8. The Coffer Coffin Company follows a dividend policy of a constant payout ratio of .45. If current earnings are $240,000, how much will be paid out in dividends and how much will be retained by the firm for reinvestment?

9. The Rinky Dink Rink Roller Skate Company has as its ideal a payout ratio of .4 of EPS. Their earnings, however, have been relatively unstable in the past and are not expected to stabilize for a number of years. As a result, they use the stable dollar dividend per share dividend policy and have developed an adjustment factor of .25. Determine their dividend payment schedule and actual payout ratios for the years 1978 through 1983 if their 1977 dividend was $.45 per share and their EPS for the years 1978 through 1983 are as follows:

Year	EPS
1978	$2.25
1979	1.90
1980	1.60
1981	2.00
1982	2.40
1983	2.55

10. The Choko-Chip Cookie Company has been paying dividends rather haphazardly over the past five years. Given the following dividend history, EPS and ideal payout ratio, estimate the dividend adjustment factor that can be used for future dividend payments under the stable dollar dividend per share policy.

Year	EPS	p^*	Dividend
0	$3.00	.3	$1.00
1	4.50	.3	1.10
2	2.10	.3	1.10
3	2.95	.4	1.15
4	5.20	.4	1.25
5	3.90	.4	1.30
6	4.20	.4	1.50

11. The F & E Tanning Company has had the following EPS over the past 5 years:

Year	EPS
1975	$2.00
1976	2.75
1977	1.90
1978	2.90
1979	2.10

If it used the low regular plus an extra dividend policy with a constant payout ratio of .25 and a variable payout ratio of .2, and paid the extra dividend only when EPS exceeded $2.00, determine the dividend payments for years 1975 through 1979.

12. The Canada Dry Cleaning Company has developed an economic forecasting model that is capable of projecting earnings up to 3 years in advance. Their model has forecast earnings of $750,000, $475,000, and $910,000 for the next 3 years. The firm has 350,000 shares of stock outstanding and pays the extra dividend only when EPS exceeds

$1.50. If the variable payout ratio is .15, what dividends per share will be paid in the next 3 years?

BIBLIOGRAPHY

Barker, C. A. "Evaluation of Stock Dividends." *Harvard Business Review,* July–August 1958, pp. 99–114.

Business Week. "When a Company is Better Dead," March 26, 1979, p. 88.

Millar, James A., and Bruce D. Fielitz. "Stock-Split and Stock-Dividend Decisions." *Financial Management,* Winter 1973, pp. 35–45.

Norgaard, Richard, and Corine Norgaard. "A Critical Examination of Share Repurchase." *Financial Management,* Spring 1974, pp. 44–50.

Scott, David F., Jr., and J. William Petty. "A Note on the Relevance of Dividend Policy." *The Financial Review,* Winter 1979, pp. 59–65.

APPENDIX

INTEREST FACTOR TABLES

INTEREST FACTOR EQUATIONS

$$\text{caf} = (1 + i)^n$$

$$\text{cafA} = \frac{(1 + i)^n - 1}{i}$$

$$\text{pvf} = \frac{1}{(1 + i)^n}$$

$$\text{pvfA} = \frac{(1 + i)^n - 1}{i(1 + i)^n}$$

$$\text{sff} = \frac{i}{(1 + i)^n - 1}$$

$$\text{crf} = \frac{i(1 + i)^n}{(1 + i)^n - 1}$$

Periods	caf	cafA	pvf	pvfA	sff	crf
			1 PERCENT			
1	1.0100	1.0000	0.99010	0.99010	1.00000	1.01000
2	1.0201	2.0100	0.98030	1.97039	0.49751	0.50751
3	1.0303	3.0301	0.97059	2.94098	0.33002	0.34002
4	1.0406	4.0604	0.96098	3.90197	0.24628	0.25628
5	1.0510	5.1010	0.95147	4.85343	0.19604	0.20604
6	1.0615	6.1520	0.94205	5.79548	0.16255	0.17255
7	1.0721	7.2135	0.93272	6.72819	0.13863	0.14863
8	1.0829	8.2857	0.92348	7.65168	0.12069	0.13069
9	1.0937	9.3685	0.91434	8.56602	0.10674	0.11674
10	1.1046	10.4622	0.90529	9.47130	0.09558	0.10558
11	1.1157	11.5668	0.89632	10.36763	0.08645	0.09645
12	1.1268	12.6825	0.88745	11.25508	0.07885	0.08885
13	1.1381	13.8093	0.87866	12.13374	0.07241	0.08241
14	1.1495	14.9474	0.86996	13.00370	0.06690	0.07690
15	1.1610	16.0969	0.86135	13.86505	0.06212	0.07212
16	1.1726	17.2579	0.85282	14.71787	0.05794	0.06794
17	1.1843	18.4304	0.84438	15.56225	0.05426	0.06426
18	1.1961	19.6147	0.83602	16.39825	0.05098	0.06098
19	1.2081	20.8109	0.82774	17.22600	0.04805	0.05805
20	1.2202	22.0190	0.81954	18.04555	0.04542	0.05542
21	1.2324	23.2392	0.81143	18.85698	0.04303	0.05303
22	1.2447	24.4716	0.80340	19.66037	0.04086	0.05086
23	1.2572	25.7163	0.79544	20.45581	0.03889	0.04889
24	1.2697	26.9734	0.78757	21.24338	0.03707	0.04707
25	1.2824	28.2432	0.77977	22.02315	0.03541	0.04541
26	1.2953	29.5256	0.77205	22.79520	0.03387	0.04387
27	1.3082	30.8209	0.76440	23.55960	0.03245	0.04245
28	1.3213	32.1291	0.75684	24.31644	0.03112	0.04112
29	1.3345	33.4504	0.74934	25.06578	0.02990	0.03990
30	1.3478	34.7849	0.74192	25.80769	0.02875	0.03875
31	1.3613	36.1327	0.73458	26.54228	0.02768	0.03768
32	1.3749	37.4941	0.72730	27.26958	0.02667	0.03667
33	1.3887	38.8690	0.72010	27.98969	0.02573	0.03573
34	1.4026	40.2577	0.71297	28.70265	0.02484	0.03484
35	1.4166	41.6603	0.70591	29.40857	0.02400	0.03400

Periods	caf	cafA	pvf	pvfA	sff	crf
		2 PERCENT				
1	1.0200	1.0000	0.98039	0.98039	1.00000	1.02000
2	1.0404	2.0200	0.96117	1.94156	0.49505	0.51505
3	1.0612	3.0604	0.94232	2.88388	0.32675	0.34675
4	1.0824	4.1216	0.92385	3.80773	0.24262	0.26262
5	1.1041	5.2040	0.90573	4.71346	0.19216	0.21216
6	1.1262	6.3081	0.88797	5.60143	0.15853	0.17853
7	1.1487	7.4343	0.87056	6.47199	0.13451	0.15451
8	1.1717	8.5830	0.85349	7.32548	0.11651	0.13651
9	1.1951	9.7546	0.83676	8.16224	0.10252	0.12252
10	1.2190	10.9497	0.82035	8.98258	0.09133	0.11133
11	1.2434	12.1687	0.80426	9.78685	0.08218	0.10218
12	1.2682	13.4121	0.78849	10.57534	0.07456	0.09456
13	1.2936	14.6803	0.77303	11.34837	0.06812	0.08812
14	1.3195	15.9739	0.75787	12.10625	0.06260	0.08260
15	1.3459	17.2934	0.74301	12.84926	0.05783	0.07783
16	1.3728	18.6393	0.72845	13.57771	0.05365	0.07365
17	1.4002	20.0121	0.71416	14.29187	0.04997	0.06997
18	1.4282	21.4123	0.70016	14.99203	0.04670	0.06670
19	1.4568	22.8405	0.68643	15.67846	0.04378	0.06378
20	1.4859	24.2974	0.67297	16.35143	0.04116	0.06116
21	1.5157	25.7833	0.65978	17.01120	0.03878	0.05878
22	1.5460	27.2990	0.64684	17.65804	0.03663	0.05663
23	1.5769	28.8450	0.63416	18.29219	0.03467	0.05467
24	1.6084	30.4219	0.62172	18.91393	0.03287	0.05287
25	1.6406	32.0303	0.60953	19.52345	0.03122	0.05122
26	1.6734	33.6709	0.59758	20.12103	0.02970	0.04970
27	1.7069	35.3443	0.58586	20.70689	0.02829	0.04829
28	1.7410	37.0512	0.57437	21.28127	0.02699	0.04699
29	1.7758	38.7922	0.56311	21.84438	0.02578	0.04578
30	1.8114	40.5681	0.55207	22.39645	0.02465	0.04465
31	1.8476	42.3794	0.54125	22.93770	0.02360	0.04360
32	1.8845	44.2270	0.53063	23.46832	0.02261	0.04261
33	1.9222	46.1116	0.52023	23.98856	0.02169	0.04169
34	1.9607	48.0338	0.51003	24.49858	0.02082	0.04082
35	1.9999	49.9945	0.50003	24.99861	0.02000	0.04000

Periods	caf	cafA	pvf	pvfA	sff	crf
			3 PERCENT			
1	1.0300	1.0000	0.97087	0.97087	1.00000	1.03000
2	1.0609	2.0300	0.94260	1.91347	0.49261	0.52261
3	1.0927	3.0909	0.91514	2.82861	0.32353	0.35353
4	1.1255	4.1836	0.88849	3.71710	0.23903	0.26903
5	1.1593	5.3091	0.86261	4.57971	0.18835	0.21835
6	1.1941	6.4684	0.83748	5.41719	0.15460	0.18460
7	1.2299	7.6625	0.81309	6.23028	0.13051	0.16051
8	1.2668	8.8923	0.78941	7.01969	0.11246	0.14246
9	1.3048	10.1591	0.76642	7.78611	0.09843	0.12843
10	1.3439	11.4639	0.74409	8.53020	0.08723	0.11723
11	1.3842	12.8078	0.72242	9.25262	0.07808	0.10808
12	1.4258	14.1920	0.70138	9.95400	0.07046	0.10046
13	1.4685	15.6178	0.68095	10.63495	0.06403	0.09403
14	1.5126	17.0863	0.66112	11.29607	0.05853	0.08853
15	1.5580	18.5989	0.64186	11.93793	0.05377	0.08377
16	1.6047	20.1569	0.62317	12.56110	0.04961	0.07961
17	1.6528	21.7616	0.60502	13.16612	0.04595	0.07595
18	1.7024	23.4144	0.58739	13.75351	0.04271	0.07271
19	1.7535	25.1169	0.57029	14.32380	0.03981	0.06981
20	1.8061	26.8704	0.55368	14.87747	0.03722	0.06722
21	1.8603	28.6765	0.53755	15.41502	0.03487	0.06487
22	1.9161	30.5368	0.52189	15.93692	0.03275	0.06275
23	1.9736	32.4529	0.50669	16.44360	0.03081	0.06081
24	2.0328	34.4265	0.49193	16.93553	0.02905	0.05905
25	2.0938	36.4593	0.47761	17.41315	0.02743	0.05743
26	2.1566	38.5530	0.46369	17.87683	0.02594	0.05594
27	2.2213	40.7096	0.45019	18.32703	0.02456	0.05456
28	2.2879	42.9309	0.43708	18.76410	0.02329	0.05329
29	2.3566	45.2188	0.42435	19.18845	0.02211	0.05211
30	2.4273	47.5754	0.41199	19.60043	0.02102	0.05102
31	2.5001	50.0027	0.39999	20.00043	0.02000	0.05000
32	2.5751	52.5027	0.38834	20.38876	0.01905	0.04905
33	2.6523	55.0778	0.37703	20.76578	0.01816	0.04816
34	2.7319	57.7302	0.36604	21.13184	0.01732	0.04732
35	2.8139	60.4621	0.35538	21.48721	0.01654	0.04654

Periods	caf	cafA	pvf	pvfA	sff	crf
			4 PERCENT			
1	1.0400	1.0000	0.96154	0.96154	1.00000	1.04000
2	1.0816	2.0400	0.92456	1.88609	0.49020	0.53020
3	1.1249	3.1216	0.88900	2.77509	0.32035	0.36035
4	1.1699	4.2465	0.85480	3.62990	0.23549	0.27549
5	1.2167	5.4163	0.82193	4.45182	0.18463	0.22463
6	1.2653	6.6330	0.79031	5.24214	0.15076	0.19076
7	1.3159	7.8983	0.75992	6.00205	0.12661	0.16661
8	1.3686	9.2142	0.73069	6.73274	0.10853	0.14853
9	1.4233	10.5828	0.70259	7.43533	0.09449	0.13449
10	1.4802	12.0061	0.67556	8.11090	0.08329	0.12329
11	1.5395	13.4864	0.64958	8.76048	0.07415	0.11415
12	1.6010	15.0258	0.62460	9.38507	0.06655	0.10655
13	1.6651	16.6268	0.60057	9.98565	0.06014	0.10014
14	1.7317	18.2919	0.57748	10.56312	0.05467	0.09467
15	1.8009	20.0236	0.55526	11.11839	0.04994	0.08994
16	1.8730	21.8245	0.53391	11.65230	0.04582	0.08582
17	1.9479	23.6675	0.51337	12.16567	0.04220	0.08220
18	2.0258	25.6454	0.49363	12.65930	0.03899	0.07899
19	2.1068	27.6712	0.47464	13.13394	0.03614	0.07614
20	2.1911	29.7781	0.45639	13.59033	0.03358	0.07358
21	2.2788	31.9692	0.43883	14.02916	0.03128	0.07128
22	2.3699	34.2480	0.42196	14.45111	0.02920	0.06920
23	2.4647	36.6179	0.40573	14.85684	0.02731	0.06731
24	2.5633	39.0826	0.39012	15.24696	0.02559	0.06559
25	2.6658	41.6459	0.37512	15.62208	0.02401	0.06401
26	2.7725	44.3117	0.36069	15.98277	0.02257	0.06257
27	2.8834	47.0842	0.34682	16.32957	0.02124	0.06124
28	2.9987	49.9676	0.33348	16.66306	0.02001	0.06001
29	3.1187	52.9663	0.32065	16.98370	0.01888	0.05888
30	3.2434	56.0849	0.30832	17.29202	0.01783	0.05783
31	3.3731	59.3283	0.29646	17.58849	0.01686	0.05686
32	3.5081	62.7015	0.28506	17.87355	0.01595	0.05595
33	3.6484	66.2095	0.27409	18.14764	0.01510	0.05510
34	3.7943	69.8579	0.26355	18.41119	0.01431	0.05431
35	3.9461	73.6522	0.25342	18.66461	0.01358	0.05358

Periods	caf	cafA	pvf	pvfA	sff	crf
			5 PERCENT			
1	1.0500	1.0000	0.95238	0.95238	1.00000	1.05000
2	1.1025	2.0500	0.90703	1.85941	0.48780	0.53780
3	1.1576	3.1525	0.86384	2.72325	0.31721	0.36721
4	1.2155	4.3101	0.82270	3.54595	0.23201	0.28201
5	1.2763	5.5256	0.78353	4.32948	0.18097	0.23097
6	1.3401	6.8019	0.74622	5.07569	0.14702	0.19702
7	1.4071	8.1420	0.71068	5.78637	0.12282	0.17282
8	1.4775	9.5491	0.67684	6.46321	0.10472	0.15472
9	1.5513	11.0266	0.64461	7.10782	0.09069	0.14069
10	1.6289	12.5779	0.61391	7.72173	0.07950	0.12950
11	1.7103	14.2068	0.58468	8.30641	0.07039	0.12039
12	1.7959	15.9171	0.55684	8.86325	0.06283	0.11283
13	1.8856	17.7130	0.53032	9.39357	0.05646	0.10646
14	1.9799	19.5986	0.50507	9.89864	0.05102	0.10102
15	2.0789	21.5786	0.48102	10.37966	0.04634	0.09634
16	2.1829	23.6575	0.45811	10.83777	0.04227	0.09227
17	2.2920	25.8404	0.43630	11.27407	0.03870	0.08870
18	2.4066	28.1324	0.41552	11.68959	0.03555	0.08555
19	2.5269	30.5390	0.39573	12.08532	0.03275	0.08274
20	2.6533	33.0659	0.37689	12.46221	0.03024	0.08024
21	2.7860	35.7192	0.35894	12.82115	0.02800	0.07800
22	2.9253	38.5052	0.34185	13.16300	0.02597	0.07597
23	3.0715	41.4305	0.32557	13.48857	0.02414	0.07414
24	3.2251	44.5020	0.31007	13.79864	0.02247	0.07247
25	3.3864	47.7271	0.29530	14.09394	0.02095	0.07095
26	3.5557	51.1134	0.28124	14.37519	0.01956	0.06956
27	3.7335	54.6691	0.26785	14.64303	0.01829	0.06829
28	3.9201	58.4026	0.25509	14.89813	0.01712	0.06712
29	4.1161	62.3227	0.24295	15.14107	0.01605	0.06605
30	4.3219	66.4388	0.23138	15.37245	0.01505	0.06505
31	4.5380	70.7608	0.22036	15.59281	0.01413	0.06413
32	4.7649	75.2988	0.20987	15.80268	0.01328	0.06328
33	5.0032	80.0638	0.19987	16.00255	0.01249	0.06249
34	5.2533	85.0670	0.19035	16.19290	0.01176	0.06176
35	5.5160	90.3203	0.18129	16.37419	0.01107	0.06107

Periods	caf	cafA	pvf	pvfA	sff	crf
			6 PERCENT			
1	1.0600	1.0000	0.94340	0.94340	1.00000	1.06000
2	1.1236	2.0600	0.89000	1.83339	0.48544	0.54544
3	1.1910	3.1836	0.83962	2.67301	0.31411	0.37411
4	1.2625	4.3746	0.79209	3.46511	0.22859	0.28859
5	1.3382	5.6371	0.74726	4.21236	0.17740	0.23740
6	1.4185	6.9753	0.70496	4.91732	0.14336	0.20336
7	1.5036	8.3938	0.66506	5.58238	0.11913	0.17913
8	1.5938	9.8975	0.62741	6.20979	0.10104	0.16104
9	1.6895	11.4913	0.59190	6.80169	0.08702	0.14702
10	1.7908	13.1808	0.55839	7.36009	0.07587	0.13587
11	1.8983	14.9716	0.52679	7.88687	0.06679	0.12679
12	2.0122	16.8699	0.49697	8.38384	0.05928	0.11928
13	2.1329	18.8821	0.46884	8.85268	0.05296	0.11296
14	2.2609	21.0151	0.44230	9.29498	0.04758	0.10758
15	2.3966	23.2760	0.41727	9.71225	0.04296	0.10296
16	2.5404	25.6725	0.39365	10.10590	0.03895	0.09895
17	2.6928	28.2129	0.37136	10.47726	0.03544	0.09544
18	2.8543	30.9056	0.35034	10.82760	0.03236	0.09236
19	3.0256	33.7600	0.33051	11.15812	0.02962	0.08962
20	3.2071	36.7856	0.31180	11.46992	0.02718	0.08718
21	3.3996	39.9927	0.29416	11.76408	0.02500	0.08500
22	3.6035	43.3923	0.27751	12.04158	0.02305	0.08305
23	3.8197	46.9958	0.26180	12.30338	0.02128	0.08128
24	4.0489	50.8156	0.24698	12.55036	0.01968	0.07968
25	4.2919	54.8645	0.23300	12.78336	0.01823	0.07823
26	4.5494	59.1564	0.21981	13.00317	0.01690	0.07690
27	4.8223	63.7058	0.20737	13.21053	0.01570	0.07570
28	5.1117	68.5281	0.19563	13.40616	0.01459	0.07459
29	5.4184	73.6398	0.18456	13.59072	0.01358	0.07358
30	5.7435	79.0582	0.17411	13.76483	0.01265	0.07265
31	6.0881	84.8017	0.16425	13.92909	0.01179	0.07179
32	6.4534	90.8898	0.15496	14.08404	0.01100	0.07100
33	6.8406	97.3432	0.14619	14.23023	0.01027	0.07027
34	7.2510	104.1837	0.13791	14.36814	0.00960	0.06960
35	7.6861	111.4348	0.13011	14.49825	0.00897	0.06897

Periods	caf	cafA	pvf	pvfA	sff	crf

7 PERCENT

Periods	caf	cafA	pvf	pvfA	sff	crf
1	1.0700	1.0000	0.93458	0.93458	1.00000	1.07000
2	1.1449	2.0700	0.87344	1.80802	0.48309	0.55309
3	1.2250	3.2149	0.81630	2.62432	0.31105	0.38105
4	1.3108	4.4399	0.76290	3.38721	0.22523	0.29523
5	1.4026	5.7507	0.71299	4.10020	0.17389	0.24389
6	1.5007	7.1533	0.66634	4.76654	0.13980	0.20980
7	1.6058	8.6540	0.62275	5.38929	0.11555	0.18555
8	1.7182	10.2598	0.58201	5.97130	0.09747	0.16747
9	1.8385	11.9780	0.54393	6.51523	0.08349	0.15349
10	1.9672	13.8164	0.50835	7.02358	0.07238	0.14238
11	2.1049	15.7836	0.47509	7.49867	0.06336	0.13336
12	2.2522	17.8884	0.44401	7.94269	0.05590	0.12590
13	2.4098	20.1406	0.41496	8.35765	0.04965	0.11965
14	2.5785	22.5505	0.38782	8.74547	0.04434	0.11434
15	2.7590	25.1290	0.36245	9.10791	0.03979	0.10979
16	2.9522	27.8880	0.33873	9.44665	0.03586	0.10586
17	3.1588	30.8402	0.31657	9.76322	0.03243	0.10243
18	3.3799	33.9990	0.29586	10.05909	0.02941	0.09941
19	3.6165	37.3790	0.27651	10.33560	0.02675	0.09675
20	3.8697	40.9955	0.25842	10.59401	0.02439	0.09439
21	4.1406	44.8652	0.24151	10.83553	0.02229	0.09229
22	4.4304	49.0057	0.22571	11.06124	0.02041	0.09041
23	4.7405	53.4361	0.21095	11.27219	0.01871	0.08871
24	5.0724	58.1767	0.19715	11.46933	0.01719	0.08719
25	5.4274	63.2490	0.18425	11.65358	0.01581	0.08581
26	5.8074	68.6765	0.17220	11.82578	0.01456	0.08456
27	6.2139	74.4838	0.16093	11.98671	0.01343	0.08343
28	6.6488	80.6977	0.15040	12.13711	0.01239	0.08239
29	7.1143	87.3465	0.14056	12.27767	0.01145	0.08145
30	7.6123	94.4608	0.13137	12.40904	0.01059	0.08059
31	8.1451	102.0730	0.12277	12.53181	0.00980	0.07980
32	8.7153	110.2181	0.11474	12.64655	0.00907	0.07907
33	9.3253	118.9334	0.10723	12.75379	0.00841	0.07841
34	9.9781	128.2588	0.10022	12.85401	0.00780	0.07780
35	10.6766	138.2369	0.09366	12.94767	0.00723	0.07723

Periods	caf	cafA	pvf	pvfA	sff	crf
			8 PERCENT			
1	1.0800	1.0000	0.92593	0.92593	1.00000	1.08000
2	1.1664	2.0800	0.85734	1.78326	0.48077	0.56077
3	1.2597	3.2464	0.79383	2.57710	0.30803	0.38803
4	1.3605	4.5061	0.73503	3.31213	0.22192	0.30192
5	1.4693	5.8666	0.68058	3.99271	0.17046	0.25046
6	1.5869	7.3359	0.63017	4.62288	0.13632	0.21632
7	1.7138	8.9228	0.58349	5.20637	0.11207	0.19207
8	1.8509	10.6366	0.54027	5.74664	0.09401	0.17401
9	1.9990	12.4876	0.50025	6.24689	0.08008	0.16008
10	2.1589	14.4866	0.46319	6.71008	0.06903	0.14903
11	2.3316	16.6455	0.42888	7.13896	0.06008	0.14008
12	2.5182	18.9771	0.39711	7.53608	0.05270	0.13269
13	2.7196	21.4953	0.36770	7.90378	0.04652	0.12652
14	2.9372	24.2149	0.34046	8.24424	0.04130	0.12130
15	3.1722	27.1521	0.31524	8.55948	0.03683	0.11683
16	3.4259	30.3243	0.29189	8.85137	0.03298	0.11298
17	3.7000	33.7502	0.27027	9.12164	0.02963	0.10963
18	3.9960	37.4502	0.25025	9.37189	0.02670	0.10670
19	4.3157	41.4463	0.23171	9.60360	0.02413	0.10413
20	4.6610	45.7620	0.21455	9.81815	0.02185	0.10185
21	5.0338	50.4229	0.19866	10.01680	0.01983	0.09983
22	5.4365	55.4567	0.18394	10.20074	0.01803	0.09803
23	5.8715	60.8933	0.17032	10.37106	0.01642	0.09642
24	6.3412	66.7648	0.15770	10.52876	0.01498	0.09498
25	6.8485	73.1059	0.14602	10.67478	0.01368	0.09368
26	7.3964	79.9544	0.13520	10.80998	0.01251	0.09251
27	7.9881	87.3508	0.12519	10.93516	0.01145	0.09145
28	8.6271	95.3388	0.11591	11.05108	0.01049	0.09049
29	9.3173	103.9659	0.10733	11.15841	0.00962	0.08962
30	10.0627	113.2832	0.09938	11.25778	0.00883	0.08883
31	10.8677	123.3459	0.09202	11.34980	0.00811	0.08811
32	11.7371	134.2135	0.08520	11.43500	0.00745	0.08745
33	12.6760	145.9506	0.07889	11.51389	0.00685	0.08685
34	13.6901	158.6267	0.07305	11.58693	0.00630	0.08630
35	14.7853	172.3168	0.06763	11.65457	0.00580	0.08580

Periods	caf	cafA	pvf	pvfA	sff	crf
			9 PERCENT			
1	1.0900	1.0000	0.91743	0.91743	1.00000	1.09000
2	1.1881	2.0900	0.84168	1.75911	0.47847	0.56847
3	1.2950	3.2781	0.77218	2.53129	0.30505	0.39505
4	1.4116	4.5731	0.70843	3.23972	0.21867	0.30867
5	1.5386	5.9847	0.64993	3.88965	0.16709	0.25709
6	1.6771	7.5233	0.59627	4.48592	0.13292	0.22292
7	1.8280	9.2004	0.54703	5.03295	0.10869	0.19869
8	1.9926	11.0285	0.50187	5.53482	0.09067	0.18067
9	2.1719	13.0210	0.46043	5.99525	0.07680	0.16680
10	2.3674	15.1929	0.42241	6.41766	0.06582	0.15582
11	2.5804	17.5603	0.38753	6.80519	0.05695	0.14695
12	2.8127	20.1407	0.35553	7.16072	0.04965	0.13965
13	3.0658	22.9534	0.32618	7.48690	0.04357	0.13357
14	3.3417	26.0192	0.29925	7.78615	0.03843	0.12843
15	3.6425	29.3609	0.27454	8.06069	0.03406	0.12406
16	3.9703	33.0034	0.25187	8.31256	0.03030	0.12030
17	4.3276	36.9737	0.23107	8.54363	0.02705	0.11705
18	4.7171	41.3013	0.21199	8.75562	0.02421	0.11421
19	5.1417	46.0184	0.19449	8.95011	0.02173	0.11173
20	5.6044	51.1601	0.17843	9.12854	0.01955	0.10955
21	6.1088	56.7645	0.16370	9.29224	0.01762	0.10762
22	6.6586	62.8733	0.15018	9.44242	0.01590	0.10590
23	7.2579	69.5319	0.13778	9.58021	0.01438	0.10438
24	7.9111	76.7898	0.12640	9.70661	0.01302	0.10302
25	8.6231	84.7009	0.11597	9.82258	0.01181	0.10181
26	9.3992	93.3240	0.10639	9.92897	0.01072	0.10072
27	10.2451	102.7231	0.09761	10.02658	0.00973	0.09973
28	11.1671	112.9682	0.08955	10.11613	0.00885	0.09885
29	12.1722	124.1353	0.08215	10.19828	0.00806	0.09806
30	13.2677	136.3075	0.07537	10.27365	0.00734	0.09734
31	14.4618	149.5752	0.06915	10.34280	0.00669	0.09669
32	15.7633	164.0370	0.06344	10.40624	0.00610	0.09610
33	17.1820	179.8003	0.05820	10.46444	0.00556	0.09556
34	18.7284	196.9823	0.05339	10.51783	0.00508	0.09508
35	20.4140	215.7108	0.04899	10.56682	0.00464	0.09464

Periods	caf	cafA	pvf	pvfA	sff	crf
			10 PERCENT			
1	1.1000	1.0000	0.90909	0.90909	1.00000	1.10000
2	1.2100	2.1000	0.82645	1.73554	0.47619	0.57619
3	1.3310	3.3100	0.75131	2.48865	0.30211	0.40211
4	1.4641	4.6410	0.68301	3.16986	0.21547	0.31547
5	1.6105	6.1051	0.62092	3.79079	0.16380	0.26380
6	1.7716	7.7156	0.56447	4.35526	0.12961	0.22961
7	1.9487	9.4872	0.51316	4.86842	0.10541	0.20541
8	2.1436	11.4359	0.46651	5.33493	0.08744	0.18744
9	2.3579	13.5795	0.42410	5.75902	0.07364	0.17364
10	2.5937	15.9374	0.38554	6.14457	0.06275	0.16275
11	2.8531	18.5312	0.35049	6.49506	0.05396	0.15396
12	3.1384	21.3843	0.31863	6.81369	0.04676	0.14676
13	3.4523	24.5227	0.28966	7.10336	0.04078	0.14078
14	3.7975	27.9750	0.26333	7.36669	0.03575	0.13575
15	4.1772	31.7725	0.23939	7.60608	0.03147	0.13147
16	4.5950	35.9497	0.21763	7.82371	0.02782	0.12782
17	5.0545	40.5447	0.19784	8.02155	0.02466	0.12466
18	5.5599	45.5992	0.17986	8.20141	0.02193	0.12193
19	6.1159	51.1591	0.16351	8.36492	0.01955	0.11955
20	6.7275	57.2750	0.14864	8.51356	0.01746	0.11746
21	7.4002	64.0025	0.13513	8.64869	0.01562	0.11562
22	8.1403	71.4027	0.12285	8.77154	0.01401	0.11401
23	8.9543	79.5430	0.11168	8.88322	0.01257	0.11257
24	9.8497	88.4973	0.10153	8.98474	0.01130	0.11130
25	10.8347	98.3470	0.09230	9.07704	0.01017	0.11017
26	11.9182	109.1818	0.08391	9.16094	0.00916	0.10916
27	13.1100	121.0999	0.07628	9.23722	0.00826	0.10826
28	14.4210	134.2099	0.06934	9.30657	0.00745	0.10745
29	15.8631	148.6309	0.06304	9.36961	0.00673	0.10673
30	17.4494	164.4940	0.05731	9.42691	0.00608	0.10608
31	19.1943	181.9434	0.05210	9.47901	0.00550	0.10550
32	21.1138	201.1378	0.04736	9.52637	0.00497	0.10497
33	23.2251	222.2515	0.04306	9.56943	0.00450	0.10450
34	25.5477	245.4767	0.03914	9.60857	0.00407	0.10407
35	28.1024	271.0242	0.03558	9.64416	0.00369	0.10369

Periods	caf	cafA	pvf	pvfA	sff	crf
			11 PERCENT			
1	1.1100	1.0000	0.90090	0.90090	1.00000	1.11000
2	1.2321	2.1100	0.81162	1.71252	0.47393	0.58393
3	1.3676	3.3421	0.73119	2.44371	0.29921	0.40921
4	1.5181	4.7097	0.65873	3.10245	0.21233	0.32233
5	1.6851	6.2278	0.59345	3.69590	0.16057	0.27057
6	1.8704	7.9129	0.53464	4.23054	0.12638	0.23638
7	2.0762	9.7833	0.48166	4.71220	0.10222	0.21222
8	2.3045	11.8594	0.43393	5.14612	0.08432	0.19432
9	2.5580	14.1640	0.39092	5.53705	0.07060	0.18060
10	2.8394	16.7220	0.35218	5.88923	0.05980	0.16980
11	3.1518	19.5614	0.31728	6.20652	0.05112	0.16112
12	3.4985	22.7132	0.28584	6.49236	0.04403	0.15403
13	3.8833	26.2116	0.25751	6.74987	0.03815	0.14815
14	4.3104	30.0949	0.23199	6.98186	0.03323	0.14323
15	4.7846	34.4053	0.20900	7.19087	0.02907	0.13907
16	5.3109	39.1899	0.18829	7.37916	0.02552	0.13552
17	5.8951	44.5008	0.16963	7.54879	0.02247	0.13247
18	6.5436	50.3959	0.15282	7.70162	0.01984	0.12984
19	7.2633	56.9395	0.13768	7.83929	0.01756	0.12756
20	8.0623	64.2028	0.12403	7.96333	0.01558	0.12558
21	8.9492	72.2651	0.11174	8.07507	0.01384	0.12384
22	9.9336	81.2143	0.10067	8.17574	0.01231	0.12231
23	11.0263	91.1479	0.09069	8.26643	0.01097	0.12097
24	12.2392	102.1741	0.08170	8.34814	0.00979	0.11979
25	13.5855	114.4133	0.07361	8.42174	0.00874	0.11874
26	15.0799	127.9988	0.06631	8.48806	0.00781	0.11781
27	16.7386	143.0786	0.05974	8.54780	0.00699	0.11699
28	18.5799	159.8173	0.05382	8.60162	0.00626	0.11626
29	20.6237	178.3972	0.04849	8.65011	0.00561	0.11561
30	22.8923	199.0209	0.04368	8.69379	0.00502	0.11502
31	25.4104	221.9132	0.03935	8.73315	0.00451	0.11451
32	28.2056	247.3236	0.03545	8.76860	0.00404	0.11404
33	31.3082	275.5291	0.03194	8.80054	0.00363	0.11363
34	34.7521	306.8374	0.02878	8.82932	0.00326	0.11326
35	38.5748	341.5894	0.02592	8.85524	0.00293	0.11293

Periods	caf	cafA	pvf	pvfA	sff	crf
			12 PERCENT			
1	1.1200	1.0000	0.89286	0.89286	1.00000	1.12000
2	1.2544	2.1200	0.79719	1.69005	0.47170	0.59170
3	1.4049	3.3744	0.71178	2.40183	0.29635	0.41635
4	1.5735	4.7793	0.63552	3.03735	0.20923	0.32923
5	1.7623	6.3528	0.56743	3.60478	0.15741	0.27741
6	1.9738	8.1152	0.50663	4.11141	0.12323	0.24323
7	2.2107	10.0890	0.45235	4.56376	0.09912	0.21912
8	2.4760	12.2997	0.40388	4.96764	0.08130	0.20130
9	2.7731	14.7757	0.36061	5.32825	0.06768	0.18768
10	3.1058	17.5487	0.32197	5.65022	0.05698	0.17698
11	3.4785	20.6546	0.28748	5.93770	0.04842	0.16842
12	3.8960	24.1331	0.25668	6.19437	0.04144	0.16144
13	4.3635	28.0291	0.22917	6.42355	0.03568	0.15568
14	4.8871	32.3926	0.20462	6.62817	0.03087	0.15087
15	5.4736	37.2797	0.18270	6.81086	0.02682	0.14682
16	6.1304	42.7533	0.16312	6.97399	0.02339	0.14339
17	6.8660	48.8837	0.14564	7.11963	0.02046	0.14046
18	7.6900	55.7497	0.13004	7.24967	0.01794	0.13794
19	8.6128	63.4397	0.11611	7.36578	0.01576	0.13576
20	9.6463	72.0524	0.10367	7.46944	0.01388	0.13388
21	10.8038	81.6987	0.09256	7.56200	0.01224	0.13224
22	12.1003	92.5026	0.08264	7.64485	0.01081	0.13081
23	13.5523	104.6029	0.07379	7.71843	0.00956	0.12956
24	15.1786	118.1552	0.06588	7.78432	0.00846	0.12846
25	17.0001	133.3339	0.05882	7.84314	0.00750	0.12750
26	19.0401	150.3339	0.05252	7.89566	0.00665	0.12665
27	21.3249	169.3740	0.04689	7.94255	0.00590	0.12590
28	23.8839	190.6989	0.04187	7.98442	0.00524	0.12524
29	26.7499	214.5827	0.03738	8.02181	0.00466	0.12466
30	29.9599	241.3327	0.03338	8.05518	0.00414	0.12414
31	33.5551	271.2925	0.02980	8.08498	0.00369	0.12369
32	37.5817	304.8477	0.02661	8.11159	0.00328	0.12328
33	42.0915	342.4294	0.02376	8.13535	0.00292	0.12292
34	47.1425	384.5208	0.02121	8.15656	0.00260	0.12260
35	52.7996	431.6633	0.01894	8.17550	0.00232	0.12232

Periods	caf	cafA	pvf	pvfA	sff	crf

13 PERCENT

Periods	caf	cafA	pvf	pvfA	sff	crf
1	1.1300	1.0000	0.88496	0.88496	1.00000	1.13000
2	1.2769	2.1300	0.78315	1.66810	0.46948	0.59948
3	1.4429	3.4069	0.69305	2.36115	0.29352	0.42352
4	1.6305	4.8498	0.61332	2.97447	0.20619	0.33619
5	1.8424	6.4803	0.54276	3.51723	0.15431	0.28431
6	2.0820	8.3227	0.48032	3.99755	0.12015	0.25015
7	2.3526	10.4047	0.42506	4.42261	0.09611	0.22611
8	2.6584	12.7573	0.37616	4.79877	0.07839	0.20839
9	3.0040	15.4157	0.33288	5.13165	0.06487	0.19487
10	3.3946	18.4197	0.29459	5.42624	0.05429	0.18429
11	3.8359	21.8143	0.26070	5.68694	0.04584	0.17584
12	4.3345	25.6502	0.23071	5.91765	0.03899	0.16899
13	4.8980	29.9847	0.20416	6.12181	0.03335	0.16335
14	5.5348	34.8827	0.18068	6.30249	0.02867	0.15867
15	6.2543	40.4174	0.15989	6.46238	0.02474	0.15474
16	7.0673	46.6717	0.14150	6.60387	0.02143	0.15143
17	7.9861	53.7391	0.12522	6.72909	0.01861	0.14861
18	9.0243	61.7251	0.11081	6.83990	0.01620	0.14620
19	10.1974	70.7494	0.09806	6.93797	0.01413	0.14413
20	11.5231	80.9468	0.08678	7.02475	0.01235	0.15235
21	13.0211	92.4699	0.07680	7.10155	0.01081	0.14081
22	14.7138	105.4910	0.06796	7.16951	0.00948	0.13948
23	16.6266	120.2048	0.06014	7.22966	0.00832	0.13832
24	18.7881	136.8315	0.05323	7.28288	0.00731	0.13731
25	21.2305	155.6196	0.04710	7.32998	0.00643	0.13643
26	23.9905	176.8501	0.04168	7.37167	0.00565	0.13565
27	27.1093	200.8406	0.03689	7.40856	0.00498	0.13498
28	30.6335	227.9499	0.03264	7.44120	0.00439	0.13439
29	34.6158	258.5833	0.02889	7.47009	0.00387	0.13387
30	39.1159	293.1990	0.02557	7.49585	0.00341	0.13341
31	44.2010	332.3149	0.02262	7.51828	0.00301	0.13301
32	49.9471	376.5159	0.02002	7.53830	0.00266	0.13266
33	56.4402	426.4631	0.01772	7.55602	0.00234	0.13234
34	63.7774	482.9033	0.01568	7.57170	0.00207	0.13207
35	72.0685	546.6807	0.01388	7.58557	0.00183	0.13183

Periods	caf	cafA	pvf	pvfA	sff	crf
			14 PERCENT			
1	1.1400	1.0000	0.87719	0.87719	1.00000	1.14000
2	1.2996	2.1400	0.76947	1.64666	0.46729	0.60729
3	1.4815	3.4396	0.67497	2.32163	0.29073	0.43073
4	1.6890	4.9211	0.59208	2.91371	0.20320	0.34320
5	1.9254	6.6101	0.51937	3.43308	0.15128	0.29128
6	2.1950	8.5355	0.45559	3.88867	0.11716	0.25716
7	2.5023	10.7305	0.39964	4.28830	0.09319	0.23319
8	2.8526	13.2328	0.35056	4.63886	0.07557	0.21557
9	3.2519	16.0853	0.30751	4.94637	0.06217	0.20217
10	3.7072	19.3373	0.26974	5.21611	0.05171	0.19171
11	4.2262	23.0445	0.23662	5.45273	0.04339	0.18339
12	4.8179	27.2707	0.20756	5.66029	0.03667	0.17667
13	5.4924	32.0886	0.18207	5.84236	0.03116	0.17116
14	6.2613	37.5811	0.15971	6.00207	0.02661	0.16661
15	7.1379	43.8424	0.14010	6.14217	0.02281	0.16281
16	8.1372	50.9803	0.12289	6.26506	0.01962	0.15962
17	9.2765	59.1176	0.10780	6.37286	0.01692	0.15692
18	10.5752	68.3941	0.09456	6.46742	0.01462	0.15462
19	12.0557	78.9692	0.08295	6.55037	0.01266	0.15266
20	13.7435	91.0249	0.07276	6.62313	0.01099	0.15099
21	15.6676	104.7684	0.06383	6.68696	0.00954	0.14954
22	17.8810	120.4360	0.05599	6.74294	0.00830	0.14830
23	20.3616	138.2970	0.04911	6.79206	0.00723	0.14723
24	23.2122	158.6586	0.04308	6.83514	0.00630	0.14630
25	26.4619	181.8708	0.03779	6.87293	0.00550	0.14550
26	30.1666	208.3327	0.03315	6.90608	0.00480	0.14480
27	34.3899	238.4993	0.02908	6.93515	0.00419	0.14419
28	39.2045	272.8892	0.02551	6.96066	0.00366	0.14366
29	44.6931	312.0935	0.02237	6.98304	0.00320	0.14320
30	50.9501	356.7866	0.01963	7.00266	0.00280	0.14280
31	58.0832	407.7368	0.01722	7.01988	0.00245	0.14245
32	66.2148	465.8201	0.01510	7.03498	0.00215	0.14215
33	75.4849	532.0349	0.01325	7.04823	0.00188	0.14188
34	86.0528	607.5198	0.01162	7.05985	0.00165	0.14165
35	98.1002	693.5725	0.01019	7.07004	0.00144	0.14144

Periods	caf	cafA	pvf	pvfA	sff	crf
			15 PERCENT			
1	1.1500	1.0000	0.86957	0.86957	1.00000	1.15000
2	1.3225	2.1500	0.75614	1.62571	0.46512	0.61512
3	1.5209	3.4725	0.65752	2.28323	0.28798	0.43798
4	1.7490	4.9934	0.57175	2.85498	0.20027	0.35027
5	2.0114	6.7424	0.49718	3.35215	0.14832	0.29832
6	2.3131	8.7537	0.43233	3.78448	0.11424	0.26424
7	2.6600	11.0668	0.37594	4.16042	0.09036	0.24036
8	3.0590	13.7268	0.32690	4.48732	0.07285	0.22285
9	3.5179	16.7858	0.28426	4.77158	0.05957	0.20957
10	4.0456	20.3037	0.24718	5.01877	0.04925	0.19925
11	4.6524	24.3493	0.21494	5.23371	0.04107	0.19107
12	5.3502	29.0017	0.18691	5.42062	0.03448	0.18448
13	6.1528	34.3519	0.16253	5.58315	0.02911	0.17911
14	7.0757	40.5047	0.14133	5.72447	0.02469	0.17469
15	8.1371	47.5804	0.12289	5.84737	0.02102	0.17102
16	9.3576	55.7175	0.10686	5.95423	0.01795	0.16795
17	10.7613	65.0751	0.09293	6.04716	0.01537	0.16537
18	12.3755	75.8363	0.08081	6.12796	0.01319	0.16319
19	14.2318	88.2118	0.07027	6.19823	0.01134	0.16134
20	16.3665	102.4436	0.06110	6.25933	0.00976	0.15976
21	18.8215	118.8101	0.05313	6.31246	0.00842	0.15842
22	21.6447	137.6316	0.04620	6.35866	0.00727	0.15727
23	24.8914	159.2764	0.04017	6.39884	0.00628	0.15628
24	28.6252	184.1678	0.03493	6.43377	0.00543	0.15543
25	32.9189	212.7930	0.03038	6.46415	0.00470	0.15470
26	37.8568	245.7120	0.02642	6.49056	0.00407	0.15407
27	43.5353	283.5686	0.02297	6.51353	0.00353	0.15353
28	50.0656	327.1040	0.01997	6.53351	0.00306	0.15306
29	57.5754	377.1697	0.01737	6.55088	0.00265	0.15265
30	66.2118	434.7451	0.01510	6.56598	0.00230	0.15230
31	76.1435	500.9568	0.01313	6.57911	0.00200	0.15200
32	87.5651	577.1003	0.01142	6.59053	0.00173	0.15173
33	100.6998	664.6653	0.00993	6.60046	0.00150	0.15150
34	115.8048	765.3652	0.00864	6.60910	0.00131	0.15131
35	133.1755	881.1699	0.00751	6.61661	0.00113	0.15113

Periods	caf	cafA	pvf	pvfA	sff	crf
			16 PERCENT			
1	1.1600	1.0000	0.86207	0.86207	1.00000	1.16000
2	1.3456	2.1600	0.74316	1.60523	0.46296	0.62296
3	1.5609	3.5056	0.64066	2.24589	0.28526	0.44526
4	1.8106	5.0665	0.55229	2.79818	0.19738	0.35738
5	2.1003	6.8771	0.47611	3.27429	0.14541	0.30541
6	2.4364	8.9775	0.41044	3.68474	0.11139	0.27139
7	2.8262	11.4139	0.35383	4.03856	0.08761	0.24761
8	3.2784	14.2401	0.30503	4.34359	0.07022	0.23022
9	3.8030	17.5185	0.26295	4.60654	0.05708	0.21708
10	4.4114	21.3215	0.22668	4.83323	0.04690	0.20690
11	5.1173	25.7329	0.19542	5.02864	0.03886	0.19886
12	5.9360	30.8502	0.16846	5.19711	0.03241	0.19241
13	6.8858	36.7862	0.14523	5.34233	0.02718	0.18718
14	7.9875	43.6720	0.12520	5.46753	0.02290	0.18290
15	9.2655	51.6595	0.10793	5.57546	0.01936	0.17936
16	10.7480	60.9250	0.09304	5.66850	0.01641	0.17641
17	12.4677	71.6730	0.08021	5.74870	0.01395	0.17395
18	14.4625	84.1407	0.06914	5.81785	0.01188	0.17188
19	16.7765	98.6032	0.05961	5.87745	0.01014	0.17014
20	19.4608	115.3797	0.05139	5.92884	0.00867	0.16867
21	22.5745	134.8405	0.04430	5.97314	0.00742	0.16742
22	26.1864	157.4150	0.03819	6.01133	0.00635	0.16635
23	30.3762	183.6014	0.03292	6.04425	0.00545	0.16545
24	35.2364	213.9776	0.02838	6.07263	0.00467	0.16467
25	40.8742	249.2140	0.02447	6.09709	0.00401	0.16401
26	47.4141	290.0881	0.02109	6.11818	0.00345	0.16345
27	55.0004	337.5022	0.01818	6.13636	0.00296	0.16296
28	63.8004	392.5027	0.01567	6.15204	0.00255	0.16255
29	74.0085	456.3030	0.01351	6.16555	0.00219	0.16219
30	85.8499	530.3115	0.01165	6.17720	0.00189	0.16189
31	99.5858	616.1614	0.01004	6.18724	0.00162	0.16162
32	115.5196	715.7473	0.00866	6.19590	0.00140	0.16140
33	134.0027	831.2668	0.00746	6.20336	0.00120	0.16120
34	155.4432	965.2698	0.00643	6.20979	0.00104	0.16104
35	180.3141	1120.7129	0.00555	6.21534	0.00089	0.16089

Periods	caf	cafA	pvf	pvfA	sff	crf
			17 PERCENT			
1	1.1700	1.0000	0.85470	0.85470	1.00000	1.17000
2	1.3689	2.1700	0.73051	1.58521	0.46083	0.63083
3	1.6016	3.5389	0.62437	2.20958	0.28257	0.45257
4	1.8739	5.1405	0.53365	2.74323	0.19453	0.36453
5	2.1924	7.0144	0.45611	3.19935	0.14256	0.31256
6	2.5652	9.2068	0.38984	3.58918	0.10861	0.27861
7	3.0012	11.7720	0.33320	3.92238	0.08495	0.25495
8	3.5115	14.7733	0.28478	4.20716	0.06769	0.23769
9	4.1084	18.2847	0.24340	4.45057	0.05469	0.22469
10	4.8068	22.3931	0.20804	4.65860	0.04466	0.21466
11	5.6240	27.1999	0.17781	4.83641	0.03676	0.20676
12	6.5801	32.8239	0.15197	4.98839	0.03047	0.20047
13	7.6987	39.4040	0.12989	5.11828	0.02538	0.19538
14	9.0075	47.1027	0.11102	5.22930	0.02123	0.19123
15	10.5387	56.1101	0.09489	5.32419	0.01782	0.18782
16	12.3303	66.6488	0.08110	5.40529	0.01500	0.18500
17	14.4265	78.9791	0.06932	5.47460	0.01266	0.18266
18	16.8790	93.4056	0.05925	5.53385	0.01071	0.18071
19	19.7484	110.2845	0.05064	5.58449	0.00907	0.17907
20	23.1056	130.0329	0.04328	5.62777	0.00769	0.17769
21	27.0335	153.1385	0.03699	5.66476	0.00653	0.17653
22	31.6292	180.1721	0.03162	5.69637	0.00555	0.17555
23	37.0062	211.8013	0.02702	5.72340	0.00472	0.17472
24	43.2973	248.8076	0.02310	5.74649	0.00402	0.17402
25	50.6578	292.1047	0.01974	5.76623	0.00342	0.17342
26	59.2697	342.7625	0.01687	5.78310	0.00292	0.17292
27	69.3455	402.0322	0.01442	5.79753	0.00249	0.17249
28	81.1342	471.3777	0.01233	5.80985	0.00212	0.17212
29	94.9270	552.5120	0.01053	5.82038	0.00181	0.17181
30	111.0646	647.4390	0.00900	5.82939	0.00154	0.17154
31	129.9456	758.5037	0.00770	5.83708	0.00132	0.17132
32	152.0364	888.4492	0.00658	5.84366	0.00113	0.17113
33	177.8826	1040.4856	0.00562	5.84928	0.00096	0.17096
34	208.1226	1218.3682	0.00480	5.85409	0.00082	0.17082
35	243.5035	1426.4910	0.00411	5.85820	0.00070	0.17070

Periods	caf	cafA	pvf	pvfA	sff	crf
			18 PERCENT			
1	1.1800	1.0000	0.84746	0.84746	1.00000	1.18000
2	1.3924	2.1800	0.71818	1.56564	0.45872	0.63872
3	1.6430	3.5724	0.60863	2.17427	0.27992	0.45992
4	1.9388	5.2154	0.51579	2.69006	0.19174	0.37174
5	2.2878	7.1542	0.43711	3.12717	0.13978	0.31978
6	2.6996	9.4420	0.37043	3.49760	0.10591	0.28591
7	3.1855	12.1415	0.31393	3.81153	0.08236	0.26236
8	3.7589	15.3270	0.26604	4.07757	0.06524	0.24524
9	4.4355	19.0858	0.22546	4.30302	0.05239	0.23239
10	5.2338	23.5213	0.19106	4.49409	0.04251	0.22251
11	6.1759	28.7551	0.16192	4.65600	0.03478	0.21478
12	7.2876	34.9311	0.13722	4.79322	0.02863	0.20863
13	8.5994	42.2187	0.11629	4.90951	0.02369	0.20369
14	10.1472	50.8180	0.09855	5.00806	0.01968	0.19968
15	11.9737	60.9653	0.08352	5.09158	0.01640	0.19640
16	14.1290	72.9390	0.07078	5.16235	0.01371	0.19371
17	16.6722	87.0680	0.05998	5.22233	0.01149	0.19149
18	19.6732	103.7403	0.05083	5.27316	0.00964	0.18964
19	23.2144	123.4135	0.04308	5.31624	0.00810	0.18810
20	27.3930	146.6280	0.03651	5.35275	0.00682	0.18682
21	32.3238	174.0210	0.03094	5.38368	0.00575	0.18575
22	38.1421	206.3448	0.02622	5.40990	0.00485	0.18485
23	45.0076	244.4868	0.02222	5.43212	0.00409	0.18409
24	53.1090	289.4944	0.01883	5.45095	0.00345	0.18345
25	62.6686	342.6033	0.01596	5.46691	0.00292	0.18292
26	73.9490	405.2720	0.01352	5.48043	0.00247	0.18247
27	87.2598	479.2209	0.01146	5.49189	0.00209	0.18209
28	102.9666	566.4807	0.00971	5.50160	0.00177	0.18177
29	121.5005	669.4473	0.00823	5.50983	0.00149	0.18149
30	143.3706	790.9478	0.00697	5.51681	0.00126	0.18126
31	169.1774	934.3186	0.00591	5.52272	0.00107	0.18107
32	199.6293	1103.4958	0.00501	5.52773	0.00091	0.18091
33	235.5625	1303.1252	0.00425	5.53197	0.00077	0.18077
34	277.9636	1538.6877	0.00360	5.53557	0.00065	0.18065
35	327.9971	1816.6516	0.00305	5.53862	0.00055	0.18055

Periods	caf	cafA	pvf	pvfA	sff	crf
			19 PERCENT			
1	1.1900	1.0000	0.84034	0.84034	1.00000	1.19000
2	1.4161	2.1900	0.70616	1.54650	0.45662	0.64662
3	1.6852	3.6061	0.59342	2.13992	0.27731	0.46731
4	2.0053	5.2913	0.49867	2.63859	0.18899	0.37899
5	2.3864	7.2966	0.41905	3.05763	0.13705	0.32705
6	2.8398	9.6830	0.35214	3.40978	0.10327	0.29327
7	3.3793	12.5227	0.29592	3.70569	0.07985	0.26985
8	4.0214	15.9020	0.24867	3.95436	0.06289	0.25289
9	4.7854	19.9234	0.20897	4.16333	0.05019	0.24019
10	5.6947	24.7088	0.17560	4.33893	0.04047	0.23047
11	6.7767	30.4035	0.14757	4.48650	0.03289	0.22289
12	8.0642	37.1802	0.12400	4.61050	0.02690	0.21690
13	9.5964	45.2445	0.10421	4.71471	0.02210	0.21210
14	11.4198	54.8409	0.08757	4.80228	0.01823	0.20823
15	13.5895	66.2607	0.07359	4.87586	0.01509	0.20509
16	16.1715	79.8502	0.06184	4.93770	0.01252	0.20252
17	19.2441	96.0217	0.05196	4.98966	0.01041	0.20041
18	22.9005	115.2659	0.04367	5.03333	0.00868	0.19868
19	27.2516	138.1664	0.03670	5.07003	0.00724	0.19724
20	32.4294	165.4180	0.03084	5.10086	0.00605	0.19605
21	38.5910	197.8474	0.02591	5.12677	0.00505	0.19505
22	45.9233	236.4384	0.02178	5.14855	0.00423	0.19423
23	54.6487	282.3616	0.01830	5.16685	0.00354	0.19354
24	65.0320	337.0103	0.01538	4.18223	0.00297	0.19297
25	77.3881	402.0425	0.01292	5.19515	0.00249	0.19249
26	92.0918	479.4304	0.01086	5.20601	0.00209	0.19209
27	109.5892	571.5222	0.00912	5.21513	0.00175	0.19175
28	130.4112	681.1116	0.00767	5.22280	0.00147	0.19147
29	155.1893	811.5227	0.00644	5.22924	0.00123	0.19123
30	184.6753	966.7122	0.00541	5.23466	0.00103	0.19103
31	219.7636	1151.3875	0.00455	5.23921	0.00087	0.19087
32	261.5186	1371.1509	0.00382	5.24303	0.00073	0.19073
33	311.2070	1632.6697	0.00321	5.24625	0.00061	0.19061
34	370.3364	1943.8770	0.00270	5.24895	0.00051	0.19051
35	440.7004	2314.2136	0.00227	5.25121	0.00043	0.19043

Periods	caf	cafA	pvf	pvfA	sff	crf
			20 PERCENT			
1	1.2000	1.0000	0.83333	0.83333	1.00000	1.20000
2	1.4400	2.2000	0.69444	1.52778	0.45455	0.65455
3	1.7280	3.6400	0.57870	2.10648	0.27473	0.47473
4	2.0736	5.3680	0.48225	2.58873	0.18629	0.38629
5	2.4883	7.4416	0.40188	2.99061	0.13438	0.33438
6	2.9860	9.9299	0.33490	3.32551	0.10071	0.30071
7	3.5832	12.9159	0.27908	3.60459	0.07742	0.27742
8	4.2998	16.4991	0.23257	3.83716	0.06061	0.26061
9	5.1598	20.7989	0.19381	4.03097	0.04808	0.24808
10	6.1917	25.9587	0.16151	4.19247	0.03852	0.23852
11	7.4301	32.1504	0.13459	4.32706	0.03110	0.23110
12	8.9161	39.5805	0.11216	4.43922	0.02526	0.22526
13	10.6993	48.4966	0.09346	4.53268	0.02062	0.22062
14	12.8392	59.1959	0.07789	4.61057	0.01689	0.21689
15	15.4070	72.0351	0.06491	4.67547	0.01388	0.21388
16	18.4884	87.4421	0.05409	4.72956	0.01144	0.21144
17	22.1861	105.9305	0.04507	4.77463	0.00944	0.20944
18	26.6233	128.1167	0.03756	4.81219	0.00781	0.20781
19	31.9480	154.7400	0.03130	4.84350	0.00646	0.20646
20	38.3376	186.6880	0.02608	4.86958	0.00536	0.20536
21	46.0051	225.0256	0.02174	4.89132	0.00444	0.20444
22	55.2061	271.0305	0.01811	4.90943	0.00369	0.20369
23	66.2474	326.2368	0.01509	4.92453	0.00307	0.20307
24	79.4968	392.4841	0.01258	4.93710	0.00255	0.20255
25	95.3962	471.9810	0.01048	4.94759	0.00212	0.20212
26	114.4754	567.3772	0.00874	4.95632	0.00176	0.20176
27	137.3705	681.8525	0.00728	4.96360	0.00147	0.20147
28	164.8447	819.2231	0.00607	4.96967	0.00122	0.20122
29	197.8136	984.0679	0.00506	4.97472	0.00102	0.20102
30	237.3763	1181.8813	0.00421	4.97894	0.00085	0.20085
31	284.8516	1419.2578	0.00351	4.98245	0.00070	0.20070
32	341.8218	1704.1094	0.00293	4.98537	0.00059	0.20059
33	410.1860	2045.9312	0.00244	4.98781	0.00049	0.20049
34	492.2234	2456.1174	0.00203	4.98984	0.00041	0.20041
35	590.6682	2948.3411	0.00169	4.99153	0.00034	0.20034

Periods	caf	cafA	pvf	pvfA	sff	crf
			21 PERCENT			
1	1.2100	1.0000	0.82645	0.82645	1.00000	1.21000
2	1.4641	2.2100	0.68301	1.50946	0.45249	0.66249
3	1.7716	3.6741	0.56447	2.07393	0.27218	0.48218
4	2.1436	5.4457	0.46651	2.54044	0.18363	0.39363
5	2.5937	7.5892	0.38554	2.92598	0.13177	0.34177
6	3.1384	10.1830	0.31863	3.24461	0.09820	0.30820
7	3.7975	13.3214	0.26333	3.50795	0.07507	0.28507
8	4.5950	17.1189	0.21763	3.72558	0.05841	0.26841
9	5.5599	21.7139	0.17986	3.90543	0.04605	0.25605
10	6.7275	27.2738	0.14864	4.05408	0.03667	0.24667
11	8.1403	34.0013	0.12285	4.17692	0.02941	0.23941
12	9.8497	42.1416	0.10153	4.27845	0.02373	0.23373
13	11.9182	51.9913	0.08391	4.36235	0.01923	0.22923
14	14.4210	63.9085	0.06934	4.43170	0.01565	0.22565
15	17.4494	78.3305	0.05731	4.48901	0.01277	0.22277
16	21.1138	95.7799	0.04736	4.53637	0.01044	0.22044
17	25.5477	116.8937	0.03914	4.57551	0.00855	0.21855
18	30.9127	142.4413	0.03235	4.60786	0.00702	0.21702
19	37.4043	173.3540	0.02673	4.63460	0.00577	0.21577
20	45.2592	210.7583	0.02209	4.65669	0.00474	0.21474
21	54.7637	256.0176	0.01826	4.67495	0.00391	0.21391
22	66.2641	310.7813	0.01509	4.69004	0.00322	0.21322
23	80.1795	377.0452	0.01247	4.70251	0.00265	0.21265
24	97.0172	457.2249	0.01031	4.71282	0.00219	0.21219
25	117.3908	554.2419	0.00852	4.72134	0.00180	0.21180
26	142.0429	671.6328	0.00704	4.72838	0.00149	0.21149
27	171.8719	813.6758	0.00582	4.73420	0.00123	0.21123
28	207.9650	985.5479	0.00481	4.73901	0.00101	0.21101
29	251.6377	1193.5129	0.00397	4.74298	0.00084	0.21084
30	304.4814	1445.1506	0.00328	4.74626	0.00069	0.21069
31	368.4226	1749.6321	0.00271	4.74898	0.00057	0.21057
32	445.7915	2118.0549	0.00224	4.75122	0.00047	0.21047
33	539.4077	2563.8464	0.00185	4.75308	0.00039	0.21039
34	652.6833	3103.2544	0.00153	4.75461	0.00032	0.21032
35	789.7468	3755.9377	0.00127	4.75587	0.00027	0.21027

Periods	caf	cafA	pvf	pvfA	sff	crf
			22 PERCENT			
1	1.2200	1.0000	0.81967	0.81967	1.00000	1.22000
2	1.4884	2.2200	0.67186	1.49153	0.45045	0.67045
3	1.8158	3.7084	0.55071	2.04224	0.26966	0.48966
4	2.2153	5.5242	0.45140	2.49364	0.18102	0.40102
5	2.7027	7.7396	0.37000	2.86364	0.12921	0.34921
6	3.2973	10.4423	0.30328	3.16692	0.09576	0.31576
7	4.0227	13.7396	0.24859	3.41551	0.07278	0.29278
8	4.9077	17.7623	0.20376	3.61927	0.05630	0.27630
9	5.9874	22.6700	0.16702	3.78628	0.04411	0.26411
10	7.3046	28.6574	0.13690	3.92318	0.03489	0.25489
11	8.9116	35.9620	0.11221	4.03540	0.02781	0.24781
12	10.8722	44.8737	0.09198	4.12737	0.02228	0.24228
13	13.2641	55.7459	0.07539	4.20277	0.01794	0.23794
14	16.1822	69.0100	0.06180	4.26456	0.01449	0.23449
15	19.7423	85.1922	0.05065	4.31521	0.01174	0.23174
16	24.0856	104.9345	0.04152	4.35673	0.00953	0.22953
17	29.3844	129.0201	0.03403	4.39077	0.00775	0.22775
18	35.8490	158.4045	0.02789	4.41866	0.00631	0.22631
19	43.7358	194.2535	0.02286	4.44152	0.00515	0.22515
20	53.3576	237.9893	0.01874	4.46027	0.00420	0.22420
21	65.0963	291.3467	0.01536	4.47563	0.00343	0.22343
22	79.4175	356.4431	0.01259	4.48822	0.00281	0.22281
23	96.8894	435.8606	0.01032	4.49854	0.00229	0.22229
24	118.2050	532.7500	0.00846	4.50700	0.00188	0.22188
25	144.2101	650.9551	0.00693	4.51393	0.00154	0.22154
26	175.9364	795.1650	0.00568	4.51962	0.00126	0.22126
27	214.6423	971.1016	0.00466	4.52428	0.00103	0.22103
28	261.8635	1185.7439	0.00382	4.52810	0.00084	0.22084
29	319.4736	1447.6074	0.00313	4.53123	0.00069	0.22069
30	389.7578	1767.0813	0.00257	4.53379	0.00057	0.22057
31	475.5044	2156.8391	0.00210	4.53589	0.00046	0.22046
32	580.1155	2632.3438	0.00172	4.53762	0.00038	0.22038
33	707.7410	3212.4595	0.00141	4.53903	0.00031	0.22031
34	863.4441	3920.2004	0.00116	4.54019	0.00026	0.22026
35	1053.4016	4783.6445	0.00095	4.54114	0.00021	0.22021

Periods	caf	cafA	pvf	pvfA	sff	crf
			23 PERCENT			
1	1.2300	1.0000	0.81301	0.81301	1.00000	1.23000
2	1.5129	2.2300	0.66098	1.47399	0.44843	0.67843
3	1.8609	3.7429	0.53738	2.01137	0.26717	0.49717
4	2.2889	5.6038	0.43690	2.44827	0.17845	0.40845
5	2.8153	7.8926	0.35520	2.80347	0.12670	0.35670
6	3.4628	10.7079	0.28878	3.09225	0.09339	0.32339
7	4.2593	14.1708	0.23478	3.32704	0.07057	0.30057
8	5.2389	18.4300	0.19088	3.51791	0.05426	0.28426
9	6.4439	23.6689	0.15519	3.67310	0.04225	0.27225
10	7.9259	30.1128	0.12617	3.79927	0.03321	0.26321
11	9.7489	38.0387	0.10258	3.90184	0.02629	0.25629
12	11.9912	47.7877	0.08339	3.98524	0.02093	0.25093
13	14.7491	59.7788	0.06780	4.05304	0.01673	0.24673
14	18.1414	74.5280	0.05512	4.10816	0.01342	0.24342
15	22.3139	92.6694	0.04481	4.15298	0.01079	0.24079
16	27.4462	114.9834	0.03643	4.18941	0.00870	0.23870
17	33.7588	142.4295	0.02962	4.21904	0.00702	0.23702
18	41.5233	176.1883	0.02408	4.24312	0.00568	0.23568
19	51.0737	217.7116	0.01958	4.26270	0.00459	0.23459
20	62.8206	268.7852	0.01592	4.27861	0.00372	0.23372
21	77.2694	331.6057	0.01294	4.29156	0.00302	0.23302
22	95.0413	408.8752	0.01052	4.30208	0.00245	0.23245
23	116.9008	503.9165	0.00855	4.31063	0.00198	0.23198
24	143.7880	620.8174	0.00695	4.31759	0.00161	0.23161
25	176.8592	764.6052	0.00565	4.32324	0.00131	0.23131
26	217.5369	941.4646	0.00460	4.32784	0.00106	0.23106
27	267.5703	1159.0015	0.00374	4.33158	0.00086	0.23086
28	329.1113	1426.5718	0.00304	4.33461	0.00070	0.23070
29	404.8071	1755.6833	0.00247	4.33708	0.00057	0.23057
30	497.9128	2160.4905	0.00201	4.33909	0.00046	0.23046
31	612.4326	2658.4033	0.00163	4.34073	0.00038	0.23038
32	753.2922	3270.8362	0.00133	4.34205	0.00031	0.23031
33	926.5496	4024.1287	0.00108	4.34313	0.00025	0.23025
34	1139.6560	4950.6758	0.00088	4.34401	0.00020	0.23020
35	1401.7769	6090.3320	0.00071	4.34472	0.00016	0.23016

Periods	caf	cafA	pvf	pvfA	sff	crf
			24 PERCENT			
1	1.2400	1.0000	0.80645	0.80645	1.00000	1.24000
2	1.5376	2.2400	0.65036	1.45682	0.44643	0.68643
3	1.9066	3.7776	0.52449	1.98130	0.26472	0.50472
4	2.3642	5.6842	0.42297	2.40428	0.17593	0.41593
5	2.9316	8.0484	0.34111	2.74538	0.12425	0.36425
6	3.6352	10.9801	0.27509	3.02047	0.09107	0.33107
7	4.5077	14.6153	0.22184	3.24232	0.06842	0.30842
8	5.5895	19.1229	0.17891	3.42122	0.05229	0.29229
9	6.9310	24.7124	0.14428	3.56550	0.04047	0.28047
10	8.5944	31.6434	0.11635	3.68186	0.03160	0.27160
11	10.6571	40.2379	0.09383	3.77569	0.02485	0.26485
12	13.2148	50.8949	0.07567	3.85136	0.01965	0.25965
13	16.3863	64.1097	0.06103	3.91239	0.01560	0.25560
14	20.3190	80.4961	0.04921	3.96160	0.01242	0.25242
15	25.1956	100.8151	0.03969	4.00129	0.00992	0.24992
16	31.2426	126.0108	0.03201	4.03330	0.00794	0.24794
17	38.7408	157.2533	0.02581	4.05911	0.00636	0.24636
18	48.0386	195.9942	0.02082	4.07993	0.00510	0.24510
19	59.5679	244.0328	0.01679	4.09672	0.00410	0.24410
20	73.8641	303.6006	0.01354	4.11026	0.00329	0.24329
21	91.5915	377.4646	0.01092	4.12117	0.00265	0.24265
22	113.5735	469.0562	0.00880	4.12998	0.00213	0.24213
23	140.8311	582.6296	0.00710	4.13708	0.00172	0.24172
24	174.6306	723.4609	0.00573	4.14281	0.00138	0.24138
25	216.5420	898.0916	0.00462	4.14742	0.00111	0.24111
26	268.5120	1114.6335	0.00372	4.15115	0.00090	0.24090
27	332.9548	1383.1455	0.00300	4.15415	0.00072	0.24072
28	412.8640	1716.1006	0.00242	4.15657	0.00058	0.24058
29	511.9514	2128.9646	0.00195	4.15853	0.00047	0.24047
30	634.8198	2640.9163	0.00158	4.16010	0.00038	0.24038
31	787.1765	3275.7361	0.00127	4.16137	0.00031	0.24031
32	976.0991	4062.9128	0.00102	4.16240	0.00025	0.24025
33	1210.3628	5039.0117	0.00083	4.16322	0.00020	0.24020
34	1500.8499	6249.3750	0.00067	4.16389	0.00016	0.24016
35	1861.0540	7750.2227	0.00054	4.16443	0.00013	0.24013

Periods	caf	cafA	pvf	pvfA	sff	crf
			25 PERCENT			
1	1.2500	1.0000	0.80000	0.80000	1.00000	1.25000
2	1.5625	2.2500	0.64000	1.44000	0.44444	0.69444
3	1.9531	3.8125	0.51200	1.95200	0.26230	0.51230
4	2.4414	5.7656	0.40960	2.36160	0.17344	0.42344
5	3.0518	8.2070	0.32768	2.68928	0.12185	0.37185
6	3.8147	11.2588	0.26214	2.95142	0.08882	0.33882
7	4.7684	15.0735	0.20972	3.16114	0.06634	0.31634
8	5.9605	19.8418	0.16777	3.32891	0.05040	0.30040
9	7.4506	25.8023	0.13422	3.46313	0.03876	0.28876
10	9.3132	33.2529	0.10737	3.57050	0.03007	0.28007
11	11.6415	42.5661	0.08590	3.65640	0.02349	0.27349
12	14.5519	54.2077	0.06872	3.72512	0.01845	0.26845
13	18.1899	68.7596	0.05498	3.78010	0.01454	0.26454
14	22.7374	86.9495	0.04398	3.82408	0.01150	0.26150
15	28.4217	109.6868	0.03518	3.85926	0.00912	0.25912
16	35.5271	138.1085	0.02815	3.88741	0.00724	0.25724
17	44.4089	173.6357	0.02252	3.90993	0.00576	0.25576
18	55.5111	218.0446	0.01801	3.92794	0.00459	0.25459
19	69.3889	273.5557	0.01441	3.94235	0.00366	0.25366
20	86.7362	342.9446	0.01153	3.95388	0.00292	0.25292
21	108.4202	429.6807	0.00922	3.96311	0.00233	0.25233
22	135.5253	538.1011	0.00738	3.97048	0.00186	0.25186
23	169.4066	673.6262	0.00590	3.97639	0.00148	0.25148
24	211.7582	843.0327	0.00472	3.98111	0.00119	0.25119
25	264.6978	1054.7910	0.00378	3.98489	0.00095	0.25095
26	330.8721	1319.4888	0.00302	3.98791	0.00076	0.25076
27	413.5901	1650.3611	0.00242	3.99033	0.00061	0.25061
28	516.9878	2063.9514	0.00193	3.99226	0.00048	0.25048
29	646.2346	2580.9392	0.00155	3.99381	0.00039	0.25039
30	807.7935	3227.1741	0.00124	3.99505	0.00031	0.25031
31	1009.7419	4034.9678	0.00099	3.99604	0.00025	0.25025
32	1262.1772	5044.7070	0.00079	3.99683	0.00020	0.25020
33	1577.7217	6306.8867	0.00063	3.99746	0.00016	0.25016
34	1972.1521	7884.6055	0.00051	3.99797	0.00013	0.25013
35	2465.1902	9856.7578	0.00041	3.99838	0.00010	0.25010

Periods	caf	cafA	pvf	pvfA	sff	crf
			26 PERCENT			
1	1.2600	1.0000	0.79365	0.79365	1.00000	1.26000
2	1.5876	2.2600	0.62988	1.42353	0.44248	0.70248
3	2.0004	3.8476	0.49991	1.92344	0.25990	0.51990
4	2.5205	5.8480	0.39675	2.32019	0.17100	0.43100
5	3.1758	8.3684	0.31488	2.63507	0.11950	0.37950
6	4.0015	11.5442	0.24991	2.88498	0.08662	0.34662
7	5.0419	15.5458	0.19834	3.08331	0.06433	0.32433
8	6.3528	20.5876	0.15741	3.24073	0.04857	0.30857
9	8.0045	26.9404	0.12493	3.36565	0.03712	0.29712
10	10.0857	34.9449	0.09915	3.46481	0.02862	0.28862
11	12.7080	45.0306	0.07869	3.54350	0.02221	0.28221
12	16.0120	57.7386	0.06245	3.60595	0.01732	0.27732
13	20.1752	73.7506	0.04957	3.65552	0.01356	0.27356
14	25.4207	93.9258	0.03934	3.69485	0.01065	0.27065
15	32.0301	119.3465	0.03122	3.72607	0.00838	0.26838
16 :	40.3579	151.3766	0.02478	3.75085	0.00661	0.26661
17	50.8510	191.7345	0.01967	3.77052	0.00522	0.26522
18	64.0722	242.5855	0.01561	3.78613	0.00412	0.26412
19	80.7310	306.6675	0.01239	3.79851	0.00326	0.26326
20	101.7211	387.3887	0.00983	3.80834	0.00258	0.26258
21	128.1685	489.1096	0.00780	3.81614	0.00204	0.26204
22	161.4924	617.2783	0.00619	3.82234	0.00162	0.26162
23	203.4804	778.7705	0.00491	3.82725	0.00128	0.26128
24	256.3853	982.2510	0.00390	3.83115	0.00102	0.26102
25	323.0454	1238.6362	0.00310	3.83425	0.00081	0.26081
26	407.0371	1561.6816	0.00246	3.83670	0.00064	0.26064
27	512.8669	1968.7190	0.00195	3.83865	0.00051	0.26051
28	646.2122	2481.5859	0.00155	3.84020	0.00040	0.26040
29	814.2275	3127.7983	0.00123	3.84143	0.00032	0.26032
30	1025.9265	3942.0259	0.00097	3.84240	0.00025	0.26025
31	1292.6675	4967.9492	0.00077	3.84318	0.00020	0.26020
32	1628.7612	6260.6172	0.00061	3.84379	0.00016	0.26016
33	2052.2390	7889.3789	0.00049	3.84428	0.00013	0.26013
34	2585.8213	9941.6172	0.00039	3.84467	0.00010	0.26010
35	3258.1350	12527.4414	0.00031	3.84497	0.00008	0.26008

Periods	caf	cafA	pvf	pvfA	sff	crf
			27 PERCENT			
1	1.2700	1.0000	0.78740	0.78740	1.00000	1.27000
2	1.6129	2.2700	0.62000	1.40740	0.44053	0.71053
3	2.0484	3.8829	0.48819	1.89559	0.25754	0.52754
4	2.6014	5.9313	0.38440	2.27999	0.16860	0.43860
5	3.3038	8.5327	0.30268	2.58267	0.11720	0.38720
6	4.1959	11.8366	0.23833	2.82100	0.08448	0.35448
7	5.3288	16.0324	0.18766	3.00866	0.06237	0.33237
8	6.7675	21.3612	0.14776	3.15643	0.04681	0.31681
9	8.5948	28.1287	0.11635	3.27278	0.03555	0.30555
10	10.9153	36.7235	0.09161	3.36439	0.02723	0.29723
11	13.8625	47.6388	0.07214	3.43653	0.02099	0.29099
12	17.6053	61.5013	0.05680	3.49333	0.01626	0.28626
13	22.3588	79.1066	0.04473	3.53805	0.01264	0.28264
14	28.3957	101.4654	0.03522	3.57327	0.00986	0.27986
15	36.0625	129.8611	0.02773	3.60100	0.00770	0.27770
16	45.7994	165.9236	0.02183	3.62284	0.00603	0.27603
17	58.1652	211.7230	0.01719	3.64003	0.00472	0.27472
18	73.8698	269.8879	0.01354	3.65357	0.00371	0.27371
19	93.8147	343.7578	0.01066	3.66422	0.00291	0.27291
20	119.1446	437.5725	0.00839	3.67262	0.00229	0.27229
21	151.3137	556.7170	0.00661	3.67923	0.00180	0.27180
22	192.1683	708.0308	0.00520	3.68443	0.00141	0.27141
23	244.0538	900.1992	0.00410	3.68853	0.00111	0.27111
24	309.9482	1144.2529	0.00323	3.69175	0.00087	0.27087
25	393.6343	1454.2012	0.00254	3.69429	0.00069	0.27069
26	499.9155	1847.8357	0.00200	3.69629	0.00054	0.27054
27	634.8928	2347.7512	0.00158	3.69787	0.00043	0.27043
28	806.3140	2982.6443	0.00124	3.69911	0.00034	0.27034
29	1024.0186	3788.9583	0.00098	3.70009	0.00026	0.27026
30	1300.5037	4812.9766	0.00077	3.70086	0.00021	0.27021
31	1651.6396	6113.4805	0.00061	3.70146	0.00016	0.27016
32	2097.5825	7765.1172	0.00048	3.70194	0.00013	0.27013
33	2663.9297	9862.7031	0.00038	3.70231	0.00010	0.27010
34	3393.1909	12526.6328	0.00030	3.70261	0.00008	0.27008
35	4296.6523	15909.8203	0.00023	3.70284	0.00006	0.27006

Periods	caf	cafA	pvf	pvfA	sff	crf

28 PERCENT

Periods	caf	cafA	pvf	pvfA	sff	crf
1	1.2800	1.0000	0.78125	0.78125	1.00000	1.28000
2	1.6384	2.2800	0.61035	1.39160	0.43860	0.71860
3	2.0972	3.9184	0.47684	1.86844	0.25521	0.53521
4	2.6844	6.0156	0.37253	2.24097	0.16624	0.44624
5	3.4360	8.6999	0.29104	2.53201	0.11494	0.39494
6	4.3980	12.1359	0.22737	2.75938	0.08240	0.36240
7	5.6295	16.5339	0.17764	2.93701	0.06048	0.34048
8	7.2058	22.1634	0.13878	3.07579	0.04512	0.32512
9	9.2234	29.3692	0.10842	3.18421	0.03405	0.31405
10	11.8059	38.5925	0.08470	3.26892	0.02591	0.30591
11	15.1116	50.3985	0.06617	3.33509	0.01984	0.29984
12	19.3428	65.5100	0.05170	3.38679	0.01526	0.29526
13	24.7588	84.8529	0.04039	3.42718	0.01179	0.29179
14	31.6913	109.6116	0.03155	3.45873	0.00912	0.28912
15	40.5648	141.3029	0.02465	3.48339	0.00708	0.28708
16	51.9230	181.8677	0.01926	3.50264	0.00550	0.28550
17	66.4614	233.7907	0.01505	3.51769	0.00428	0.28428
18	85.0706	300.2520	0.01175	3.52945	0.00333	0.28333
19	108.8904	385.3225	0.00918	3.53863	0.00260	0.28260
20	139.3797	494.2129	0.00717	3.54580	0.00202	0.28202
21	178.4060	633.5925	0.00561	3.55141	0.00158	0.28158
22	228.3596	811.9985	0.00438	3.55579	0.00123	0.28123
23	292.3003	1040.3582	0.00342	3.55921	0.00096	0.28096
24	374.1443	1332.6584	0.00267	3.56188	0.00075	0.28075
25	478.9048	1706.8030	0.00209	3.56397	0.00059	0.28059
26	612.9980	2185.7078	0.00163	3.56560	0.00046	0.28046
27	784.6377	2798.7061	0.00127	3.56688	0.00036	0.28036
28	1004.3362	3583.3438	0.00100	3.56787	0.00028	0.28028
29	1285.5503	4587.6797	0.00078	3.56865	0.00022	0.28022
30	1645.5044	5873.2305	0.00061	3.56926	0.00017	0.28017
31	2106.2456	7518.7344	0.00047	3.56973	0.00013	0.28013
32	2695.9946	9624.9805	0.00037	3.57010	0.00010	0.28010
33	3450.8730	12320.9727	0.00029	3.57039	0.00008	0.28008
34	4417.1172	15771.8477	0.00023	3.57062	0.00006	0.28006
35	5653.9102	20188.9648	0.00018	3.57080	0.00005	0.28005

Periods	caf	cafA	pvf	pvfA	sff	crf
			29 PERCENT			
1	1.2900	1.0000	0.77519	0.77519	1.00000	1.29000
2	1.6641	2.2900	0.60093	1.37612	0.43668	0.72668
3	2.1467	3.9541	0.46583	1.84195	0.25290	0.54290
4	2.7692	6.1008	0.36111	2.20306	0.16391	0.45391
5	3.5723	8.8700	0.27993	2.48300	0.11274	0.40274
6	4.6083	12.4423	0.21700	2.70000	0.08037	0.37037
7	5.9447	17.0506	0.16822	2.86821	0.05865	0.34865
8	7.6686	22.9953	0.13040	2.99862	0.04349	0.33349
9	9.8925	30.6639	0.10109	3.09970	0.03261	0.32261
10	12.7614	40.5564	0.07836	3.17806	0.02466	0.31466
11	16.4622	53.3178	0.06075	3.23881	0.01876	0.30876
12	21.2362	69.7799	0.04709	3.28590	0.01433	0.30433
13	27.3947	91.0161	0.03650	3.32240	0.01099	0.30099
14	35.3391	118.4108	0.02830	3.35070	0.00845	0.29845
15	45.5875	153.7500	0.02194	3.37263	0.00650	0.29650
16	58.8078	199.3374	0.01700	3.38964	0.00502	0.29502
17	75.8621	258.1453	0.01318	3.40282	0.00387	0.29387
18	97.8622	334.0073	0.01022	3.41304	0.00299	0.29299
19	126.2422	431.8694	0.00792	3.42096	0.00232	0.29232
20	162.8524	558.1116	0.00614	3.42710	0.00179	0.29179
21	210.0796	720.9641	0.00476	3.43186	0.00139	0.29139
22	271.0027	931.0437	0.00369	3.43555	0.00107	0.29107
23	349.5933	1202.0464	0.00286	3.43841	0.00083	0.29083
24	450.9756	1551.6399	0.00222	3.44063	0.00064	0.29064
25	581.7583	2002.6155	0.00172	3.44235	0.00050	0.29050
26	750.4683	2584.3740	0.00133	3.44368	0.00039	0.29039
27	968.1042	3334.8425	0.00103	3.44471	0.00030	0.29030
28	1248.8545	4302.9453	0.00080	3.44551	0.00023	0.29023
29	1611.0225	5551.8008	0.00062	3.44613	0.00018	0.29018
30	2078.2188	7162.8203	0.00048	3.44662	0.00014	0.29014
31	2680.9023	9241.0430	0.00037	3.44699	0.00011	0.29011
32	3458.3640	11921.9453	0.00029	3.44728	0.00008	0.29008
33	4461.2891	15380.3086	0.00022	3.44750	0.00007	0.29006
34	5755.0625	19841.5977	0.00017	3.44768	0.00005	0.29005
35	7424.0313	25596.6602	0.00013	3.44781	0.00004	0.29004

Periods	caf	cafA	pvf	pvfA	sff	crf
			30 PERCENT			
1	1.3000	1.0000	0.76923	0.76923	1.00000	1.30000
2	1.6900	2.3000	0.59172	1.36095	0.43478	0.73478
3	2.1970	3.9900	0.45517	1.81611	0.25063	0.55063
4	2.8561	6.1870	0.35013	2.16624	0.16163	0.46163
5	3.7129	9.0431	0.26933	2.43557	0.11058	0.41058
6	4.8268	12.7560	0.20718	2.64275	0.07839	0.37839
7	6.2749	17.5828	0.15937	2.80211	0.05687	0.35687
8	8.1573	23.8577	0.12259	2.92470	0.04192	0.34192
9	10.6045	32.0150	0.09430	3.01900	0.03124	0.33124
10	13.7858	42.6195	0.07254	3.09154	0.02346	0.32346
11	17.9216	56.4053	0.05580	3.14734	0.01773	0.31773
12	23.2981	74.3270	0.04292	3.19026	0.01345	0.31345
13	30.2875	97.6250	0.03302	3.22328	0.01024	0.31024
14	39.3737	127.9125	0.02540	3.24867	0.00782	0.30782
15	51.1859	167.2863	0.01954	3.26821	0.00598	0.30598
16	66.5417	218.4722	0.01503	3.28324	0.00458	0.30458
17	86.5042	285.0137	0.01156	3.29480	0.00351	0.30351
18	112.4554	371.5178	0.00889	3.30369	0.00269	0.30269
19	146.1920	483.9734	0.00684	3.31053	0.00207	0.30207
20	190.0496	630.1653	0.00526	3.31579	0.00159	0.30159
21	247.0645	820.2151	0.00405	3.31984	0.00122	0.30122
22	321.1838	1067.2795	0.00311	3.32295	0.00094	0.30094
23	417.5388	1388.4634	0.00239	3.32535	0.00072	0.30072
24	542.8005	1806.0024	0.00184	3.32719	0.00055	0.30055
25	705.6409	2348.8032	0.00142	3.32861	0.00043	0.30043
26	917.3333	3054.4443	0.00109	3.32970	0.00033	0.30033
27	1192.5332	3971.7776	0.00084	3.33054	0.00025	0.30025
28	1550.2932	5164.3086	0.00065	3.33118	0.00019	0.30019
29	2015.3811	6714.6016	0.00050	3.33168	0.00015	0.30015
30	2619.9956	8729.9844	0.00038	3.33206	0.00011	0.30011
31	3405.9941	11349.9805	0.00029	3.33235	0.00009	0.30009
32	4427.7891	14755.9727	0.00023	3.33258	0.00007	0.30007
33	5756.1289	19183.7656	0.00017	3.33275	0.00005	0.30005
34	7482.9688	24939.8984	0.00013	3.33289	0.00004	0.30004
35	9727.8594	32422.8672	0.00010	3.33299	0.00003	0.30003

INDEX